# VEGETARIAN COOKING

In joyous gratitude for Alex,
my firstborn grandchild

atHome with
THE CULINARY INSTITUTE OF AMERICA

# VEGETARIAN COOKING

**KATHERINE POLENZ**

PHOTOGRAPHS BY BEN FINK

THE CULINARY INSTITUTE OF AMERICA

WILEY

JOHN WILEY & SONS, INC.

**THE CULINARY INSTITUTE OF AMERICA**

| | |
|---|---|
| President | Dr. Tim Ryan '77 |
| Vice-President, Dean of Culinary Education, Provost | Mark Erickson '77 |
| Senior Director, Educational Enterprises | Susan Cussen |
| Director of Publishing | Nathalie Fischer |
| Editorial Project Manager | Lisa Lahey '00 |
| Editorial Assistant | Erin Jeanne McDowell '08 |

Published by John Wiley & Sons, Inc., Hoboken, New Jersey
Published simultaneously in Canada

For general information on our other products and services or for technical support, please contact our Customer Care Department within the United States at (800) 762-2974, outside the United States at (317) 572-3993 or fax (317) 572-4002.

Wiley also publishes its books in a variety of electronic formats. Some content that appears in print may not be available in electronic books. For more information about Wiley products, visit our web site at www.wiley.com.

**Library of Congress Cataloging-in-Publication Data**

Polenz, Katherine.
  Vegetarian cooking at home with the Culinary Institute of America / Katherine Polenz ; photographs by Ben Fink.
      p. cm.
  Includes index.
  ISBN 978-0-470-42137-6 (cloth : acid-free paper)
  1.  Vegetarian cooking. 2.  Lacto-ovo vegetarianism. 3.  Cookbooks.  I. Culinary Institute of America. II. Title.
  TX837.P653 2012
  641.5'636—dc22
                                    2011007538

Printed in China

10  9  8  7  6  5  4  3  2  1

# Contents

# ACKNOWLEDGMENTS

Creativity, like cooking, is a very personal endeavor. As a chef creates and envisions new dishes and concepts, she often feels as though the creation is hers alone. However, when it comes to cooking the new creation into being, it often takes a number of talented and skillful writers and cook-technicians to complete the task. This book is no exception to that creative rule.

My first thank-you goes to Nathalie Fischer and Lisa Lahey, for gifting me with and guiding me through this wonderfully fulfilling undertaking.

My next thank-you goes to Erin McDowell, who was my liaison throughout this entire process. In culinary terms, a liaison is a pairing of egg yolks and heavy cream that when properly tempered into a dish adds a quality of smoothness, color, richness, and finesse that could otherwise never be obtained. Thank you, Erin, for being my liaison.

I extend my deep appreciation to the CIA for giving *Vegetarian Cooking* the attention it so deserves and to the food

purchasers and storeroom staff for seeing to it that I had beautiful produce to work with every day.

I owe bowls upon bowls full of gratitude to Kyle Felt, who during his externship with our publishing department worked tirelessly to keep the recipe testing and photo shoot preparation organized and on schedule.

And of course there are my student kitchen assistants, Angela Diaz, Danika Meheux, James DeSilvestri, Lauren Salvesen, Kiersten Seufer, and Victoria Mulroy, to whom I extend a hearty "Job well done!" You will see their culinary skills and enthusiasm sparkle in every photo.

Ben Fink, you shed your magical lighting on every dish we prepared, and the colorful results are simply yummy.

Special thanks to my Delicious for being so understanding of all those days I stayed late after school.

This chapter will cover everything you need to know about cooking and eating vegetarian food, including tips on how to use this book and the recipes in it.

# INTRODUCTION

1

# VEGETARIAN EATING

You will begin to see, as you read and use these recipes, that you don't have to be a vegetarian to eat vegetarian. Following a vegetarian diet just a few days a week is a great way for nonvegetarians to increase their consumption of healthy foods. That being said, there are a variety of recipes in this book, recipes that all cooks—vegetarians or not—will enjoy. Each chapter and recipe will also try to stimulate your creativity, showing you how to make your own favorite dishes vegetarian or how to create new dishes that will be flavorful, healthy, and homemade. Look for charts or lists in each chapter that show ways to mix up a recipe and help you think outside the box.

There are many types of vegetarians. This book is molded around the basis of lacto-ovo vegetarianism, in which meat, fish, and seafood (and items containing those foods or their by-products) are not consumed, but other animal products such as dairy and eggs are. So recipes in this book may contain cheese, milk, cream, eggs, and other animal products such as honey. Other types of vegetarianism include lacto-vegetarianism, in which dairy is consumed, but no other animal products; and veganism, in which no animal products of any kind are consumed (including items processed with animal products, such as sugar).

## HEALTHY, BALANCED, NUTRITIOUS EATING

Following a vegetarian diet, when done correctly, is a very healthy lifestyle. It can be an excellent way for nonvegetarians to eat more vegetables, healthy fats, and fiber. A vegetarian diet promotes:

**CONSUMPTION OF THE HEALTHY FATS** Healthy fats serve many functions to keep our bodies working correctly, including regulating body cells, helping to digest vitamins and minerals, and providing energy that bodies need. Healthy fats can be found in olive oil, avocados, nuts, and seeds.

**CONTROLLED PROTEIN INTAKE** Contrary to popular belief, the recommended protein requirement for the average diet is met when 8 to 9 percent of daily calories consumed are derived from protein (with the maximum recommended amount being between 30 and 35 percent). Since the vegetarian diet is not based on animal protein, vegetarians are more likely to have a protein intake between 10 and 15 percent. (The main vegetarian protein sources are eggs, beans, and alternative sources such as tofu, tempeh, and seitan.)

**INCREASED FIBER INTAKE** Fiber cannot be found in animal products (dairy, meat, eggs, and so on), but it is prevalent in vegetables and whole grains.

**INCREASED INTAKE OF VITAMINS AND MINERALS** These are plentiful in fruits and vegetables.

## SEASONALITY

While seasonality is important in all cooking, it is especially important to the vegetarian cook. Using produce that is in season will ensure maximum nutritional value, better-quality products, and more flavorful food. Try shopping at your local health food store, community market, farmers' markets, or farmstands whenever possible. Purchasing from these markets supports your local economy and often means you are supporting the local farmers themselves.

Buying seasonally is also a great way to stay within a budget, as seasonally plentiful items are often less expensive. Take advantage of locally grown fruits and vegetables that are available seasonally in your area.

Canning, preserving, and freezing are a great way to capture the freshness of seasonal items for use year-round.

## TOOLS

The right tools are ideal for precise preparation. These basic tools will take you a long way:

**SOUP POTS** Large deep pots with straight sides and two loop handles. Best used for soups, broths, and for the simmering, boiling, and poaching cooking methods.

**SKILLETS AND SAUTÉ PANS** Wide shallow pans with one long handle. Ideal for a number of preparations, including sautéing, pan frying, and poaching.

**DUTCH OVEN** Large heavy pot with sides as high as the pot is wide. Has a tight-fitting lid and two loop handles and can be used on the stovetop or in the oven, making it great for braising and stewing.

**CASSEROLES** Sometimes called *baking dishes;* typically only for use in the oven.

**STEAMER** Large lidded pot with perforated inserts or stacking layers. As water boils in the pot, steam rises and circulates in the insert, gently cooking the food.

**BAKING PANS OR CAKE PANS** Usually square, rectangular or round in shape with 2-inch sides. For home use, these pans are typically 8, 9, or 10 inches across or 9 by 13 inch.

**BAKING SHEETS** Large rectangular pans with low sides that allow for free circulation of heat in the oven.

**WOK** Large bowl-shaped pan with either two loop handles or one long handle. Distributes heat evenly while allowing for rapid stirring. Perfect for stir-frying.

**CRÊPE AND OMELETTE PANS** Small shallow skillets with very short, slightly sloping sides.

**GRILL PAN AND GRIDDLE** Grill pans are cast-iron skillets or long rectangular pans with ridges that mimic the grate of a grill. Creates grilled flavor and appearance without having to fire up the real thing. Often, the other side of the long pan is a flat griddle, perfect for pancakes or cooking large amounts of eggs or vegetables.

**MEASURING CUPS AND SPOONS** Cups are available in two varieties, one a set of metal or plastic for measuring dry ingredients and the other, usually of clear glass or plastic, for measuring liquids. Spoons are calibrated in tablespoons, teaspoons, and half- and quarter-teaspoons; sometimes smaller spoons are also part of a set. Precise measurement is especially important in baking.

**THERMOMETERS** Handy to have on hand for accuracy. Different types are used to check oven temperature; the internal temperature of loaves, burgers, or alternative proteins (instant-read thermometers); oil temperature for deep-frying; and the temperature of caramel or preserves (candy thermometers).

**WHISKS** For aerating, mixing, and stirring. A few different sizes and shapes are ideal to have for different tasks.

**SPOONS** For mixing, stirring, placing, and serving. Have several different sizes on hand, solid and slotted, in wood and metal.

**RUBBER SPATULAS** Soft, flexible utensils for folding foams and batters and for scraping bowls clean. Be sure to have a few that are totally heat-safe, such as those made from silicone.

**MIXING BOWLS** Ideal to have in a variety of sizes and materials, such as glass, stainless steel, and plastic.

**TONGS** To allow quick turning of large pieces of food during cooking.

**METAL SPATULAS** Good for lifting and turning foods during cooking.

**SIEVES AND STRAINERS** Made from fine mesh; come in several shapes and sizes. Colanders have larger holes for draining food.

**SKIMMERS** A shallow bowl of perforated metal or mesh on a long handle. Useful for removing food from hot liquid or fat, and for removing foam from the surface of a soup.

**FOOD MILLS AND RICERS** Ideal for puréeing cooked or soft raw foods. Food mills have a curved blade that rests flat against a perforated disk. Turning the crank attached to the blade forces food through the disk's holes, puréeing it and straining out solids. A ricer is a cylindrical hopper with a perforated bottom; a pressure plate at the end of a lever pushes the cooked food through the perforated bottom, creating a purée.

**CUTTING BOARDS** It's a smart idea to have cutting boards for different types of foods, such as a specific board for cutting particularly aromatic vegetables like onions and garlic. Cutting boards made of wood or plastic are best for preserving the edge of your knives.

Knives are the most important tools in your kitchen. It is very important to keep your knives sharp and well honed (see Sharpening and Honing Knives, below). A basic set should include:

**CHEF'S KNIFE** Blades can range from 6 to 14 inches long. Used for a number of cutting tasks.

**PARING KNIFE** Blades range from 2 to 4 inches long. Designed for peeling and trimming fruits and vegetables.

**SLICER** Long, thin blade, often serrated. Good for cutting even slices of cooked foods or bread.

# INGREDIENTS

Having a well-stocked pantry is key to cooking. The following is a list of ingredients to always keep on hand. These are the items used in the basic preparation of many dishes, in their seasoning, or as their finishing components:

**HERBS** Available fresh and dried, herbs are important for seasoning and flavoring dishes. Store fresh herbs at room temperature in fresh water. Dried herbs can be stored with spices in a cool, dry place.

**SPICES** Most spices have intense flavors and are used in small amounts. Whole spices retain their aromatic oils longer than ground spices, so grinding your own leads to deeper flavor.

**SALT** Salt comes in a variety of grain sizes, colors, and flavors. It highlights the natural flavors of foods. In this book kosher salt is the common choice, but your favorite sea salt may be used as well.

**PEPPER** Also a classic, basic seasoning, it comes in many varieties. Black pepper is most commonly used; grind it fresh for the best flavor.

**GARLIC** Garlic is present in many of the recipes in this book; and adds great flavor both raw and cooked.

## SHARPENING AND HONING KNIVES

A sharp knife not only cuts better but is safer to use. Sharpening stones are used to establish or refresh a sharp edge on the blade. Sharpening stones are available at kitchen supply stores, many of which also provide sharpening services for a small fee. Keep a steel on hand to hone knives before use. Honing a knife refreshes the sharpness of the blade or removes fine burrs or metal fragments from the edge of the blade after sharpening it on a stone. Store your knives in racks or holders, not loose in a drawer where they could be damaged or lead to an injury.

**GINGER** Ginger is an excellent aromatic addition to many recipes, especially Asian dishes.

**AROMATIC VEGETABLES** Onions, carrots, celery, leeks, and parsnips are good to have on hand, because many dishes start out with these ingredients.

**FATS** Butter and oils transfer heat to foods during cooking and prevent them from sticking. They also hold heat in food, emulsify sauces, create crisp textures on the outside of cooked foods, and add flavor to dishes.

**NUTS** A great source of protein, nuts are perfect in burgers, salads, baked goods, or even as a snack.

**GRAINS AND LEGUMES** Having a variety of whole grains and legumes such as beans and lentils on hand will make preparing a well-balanced meal easier. (See Chapters 5 and 6 for more information.)

# COOKING BASICS

Below are basic definitions of various cooking methods, as well as suggestions for when to use them. The chapters in this book address the specific cooking techniques utilized in the recipes they contain.

## DRY HEAT METHODS

Dry heat cooking methods cook food either by direct radiant heat (such as a grill) or by indirect heat contained in a closed environment (such as an oven). No water, broth, or other liquids are added during cooking, though fats and oils can be used. Dry heat methods include: grilling, broiling, roasting, sautéing, stir-frying, pan frying, and deep-frying.

> **GRILLING AND BROILING** Similar methods that quickly cook food with direct heat (grilling from below, broiling from above).

# KNIFE SKILLS

There are a number of knife techniques that are important to know when preparing a meal.

CHOPPING Used for rustic dishes or for ingredients that will later be puréed or strained out of a finished dish. Pieces do not need to be perfectly even in shape, but they should all be roughly the same size.

MINCING This technique reduces food to a relatively fine, even cut—ideal for vegetables, herbs, garlic, or ginger. Roughly chop the food first, then gather it into a pile. Holding the knife tip against the cutting board, move the blade in a rocking motion to cut firmly and rapidly until you achieve the desired fineness.

DICING This cut produces neat cubes. Cubes vary in size based on guidelines specified in recipes but generally come in three categories: small, ¼ by ¼ inch; medium, ½ by ½ inch, and large dice, ¾ by ¾ inch. Cut food lengthwise into slices as thick as the size dice you want. Stack these slices and slice again lengthwise to make strips. Gather the strips and cut crosswise into the finished dice.

SHREDDING OR CHIFFONADE This technique cuts food into thin strips. Chiffonade is finer than shredding. Stack a few leaves of vegetables or herbs and roll them tightly lengthwise. Use your knife to make thin crosswise cuts.

**ROASTING AND BAKING** Surround food with indirect heat of the oven; the terms are often used interchangeably.

**SAUTÉING AND STIR-FRYING** Similar methods that cook food rapidly in a small amount of fat over high heat. In stir-frying, the food is kept in constant motion by stirring, while in sautéing, the food is stirred or tossed to make it "jump" from time to time.

**PAN FRYING** Cooks food quickly in a small amount of moderately heated fat. Dredging, breading, or battering can be utilized to create other textures on the outer crust.

**DEEP-FRYING** Submerges food completely in fat to create a crisp exterior and a tender interior.

## MOIST HEAT METHODS

Moist heat cooking methods cook food in liquid or vapor (steam). This often allows all of the components for a meal to be cooked in the same pot. Moist heat cooking methods include: steaming, poaching, boiling, simmering, braising, and stewing.

**STEAMING** Surrounds food with gentle, moist heat of vapor from water or a flavorful liquid.

**BOILING AND SIMMERING** Submerge food completely in large quantities of very hot liquid; can result in tender products.

**POACHING** Submerge food completely in liquid to just cover, and cooks at a constant moderate temperature.

**SHALLOW POACHING** Combines the speed of sautéing with the delicate heat of poaching.

**BRAISING AND STEWING** Gentle, slow cooking techniques in which the food is usually first browned using a dry heat method, then finished by simmering. (Braising refers to larger items, while stewing refers to bite-size pieces.)

This chapter is all about the perfect complements to a meal. Some of the recipes in this chapter fall into other categories as well—grains, legumes, vegetables, salads, and so on—but were placed in this chapter because they would go well before or with a variety of main dishes. Of course, many of these items make great snacks and party food as well.

2

# STARTERS AND SIDES

# STARTERS

Appetizers or starters can be based on almost anything: pasta, grains, vegetables, or protein. They can be warm or chilled, with or without sauces, served on a plate or eaten out of hand. What can generally be said about appetizers is that they are small servings of very flavorful foods. In some cases they are bite-size or can be eaten with one's hands, making them easy and fun.

# SIDE DISHES

Side dishes can have a variety of flavors, textures, colors, and be made using several different cooking techniques. They can be rich, to complement lean foods, or hearty when served with lighter dishes.

# GENERAL TIPS

The following tips are useful when preparing starters and sides:

**KEEP THE PORTION SIZE SMALL.** If a starter is too large, diners will be full before they make it to the main course. The same can be said of side dishes: if they are too large, they will overwhelm the entrée. Many items that are served as appetizers or side dishes can be entrées as well; the portion size is simply increased.

**CONSIDER THE QUALITIES OF THE ENTRÉE.** Use texture, flavor, and cooking technique as guidelines to find complements for an entrée. If the dish has a chewy texture, perhaps something smooth will make the perfect side. Or if the entrée is spicy, choose a mild appetizer or a side dish that will calm the level of spice. If the main dish is grilled, try another method, such as roasting, for the starter or sides.

**CONSIDER NUTRITIONAL CONTENT WHEN PAIRING DISHES.** Try using starters and side dishes to fill in any nutritional gaps in the meal. If an entrée is composed of a protein, it might be wise to serve it with something high in fiber, such as a whole grain or legume.

## MASHING AND PURÉEING VEGETABLES

Mashed potatoes are a classic side dish that pairs pretty well with most meals. But other vegetables, when prepared similarly, make an equally delicious side with different flavors and, sometimes, increased health benefits. Think beyond the classic potato and try other vegetables such as celeriac (celery root), turnips, rutabaga, carrot, cauliflower, or corn. Some vegetables don't "mash" quite like potatoes and therefore are called purées. The purées in this chapter aren't like the soupy kind similar to baby food but are substantial sides with a thick, creamy texture.

Different techniques and tools can be used for mashing and puréeing. There are, of course, potato mashers, handheld tools that are inexpensive and get the job done. For small batches, a large fork can be similarly effective. Two other excellent tools are a food mill or ricer; these are usually made of sturdy metal, can be a bit more expensive, but are handy and versatile tools that yield a smoother texture than a masher. They are easy to use and can make the sometimes arduous task of making a large batch of mashed or puréed vegetables seem like a breeze. But for some vegetable purées, it may be necessary to use a food processor or blender to achieve a smooth texture. You may need to add liquid to some vegetables (see specific recipes for more details). Instead of adding plain water, try using vegetable broth or juices, which will add flavor as well as improve texture.

Beans and other legumes can also be mashed or puréed. And because of their starchy texture, they make an equally smooth and satisfying side dish or sauce.

# Eggplant Caponata

This is an incredibly simple but versatile dish. Use it to top Crostini (page 15) for a simple appetizer or toss with pasta for a flavorful entrée.

2 tbsp olive oil

2¾ cups diced eggplant

1 red bell pepper, diced

2 cloves garlic, minced

4 canned plum (Roma) tomatoes, drained and diced

1 tbsp fresh basil, chopped

1 tsp fresh marjoram, chopped

2 tsp balsamic vinegar

¼ pound Parmesan, thinly sliced

1. In a large sauté pan, heat the oil over medium heat. Add the eggplant and sauté until it is lightly browned and tender, 4 to 5 minutes. Add the red pepper and sauté until tender, about 3 minutes more. Add the garlic and sauté until fragrant, about 1 minute. Add the tomatoes and cook for 1 minute more. Stir in the basil, marjoram, and vinegar.

2. Serve topped with thin strips of cheese.

**MAKES ABOUT 2 CUPS**

# Spicy White Bean and Avocado Dip

White beans and avocados make this dip incredibly creamy—without any guilt. Serve with toasted wedges of Pita Bread (page 274).

1 large ripe avocado, pitted and peeled

¾ cup cooked white beans (see chart, page 131)

2 cloves garlic, minced

½ jalapeño, seeded and minced

½ cup chopped cilantro

2 tbsp chopped mint

2 tsp fresh lime juice

2 tsp olive oil

Salt and freshly ground black pepper, as needed

1. Place the avocados, beans, garlic, and jalapeño in a mixing bowl. Mash with a fork until the mixture is combined but still chunky.

2. Fold in the cilantro, mint, lime juice, and oil. Season with salt and pepper. Serve at room temperature.

**MAKES ABOUT 1½ CUPS**

Eggplant Caponata

Hummus (front), Guacamole, (middle), and
Tapenade, page 14 (rear)

# Hummus

*Tahini is a flavorful sesame seed paste, available in the international section of most grocery stores.*

1 cup cooked chickpeas (see chart, page 131)

3 tbsp fresh lemon juice

2 cloves garlic

⅓ cup tahini

¾ cup extra-virgin olive oil

¼ cup water, or as needed to adjust consistency

Salt, as needed

GARNISH

Extra-virgin olive oil, as needed

Paprika, as needed

Chopped flat-leaf parsley, as needed

1. In a food processor or blender, pulse the chickpeas, lemon juice, and garlic to form a smooth paste.

2. Add the tahini and oil and blend until smooth, adding water as needed to adjust the consistency. Season with salt.

3. Serve garnished with a drizzle of oil and a sprinkling of paprika and parsley.

MAKES ABOUT 2 CUPS

# Guacamole

*Choose ripe avocados with no visible bruising, blisters, or wrinkles on the skin. Don't squeeze avocados too much when choosing one; it will bruise their flesh.*

2 avocados, diced

2 plum (Roma) tomatoes, seeded and chopped

½ small red onion, diced

1 jalapeño, seeded and minced

Juice of 2 limes

1 clove garlic, minced

2 tbsp chopped cilantro

Salt and freshly ground black pepper, as needed

In a large bowl, combine all ingredients. Mash lightly with a fork to obtain a chunky consistency. Season with salt and pepper. Serve immediately or cover the surface of the guacamole directly with plastic wrap and refrigerate until needed. To avoid blackening or oxidation, prepare guacamole as close to the time of use as possible.

MAKES ABOUT 3 CUPS

# Tapenade

*This flavorful combination of olives, capers, and herbs works perfectly as either a dip or a spread.*

1 cup pitted green olives

1 cup pitted black olives, oil cured or brined

⅓ cup capers, rinsed

2 cloves garlic, minced

3 tbsp fresh lemon juice

¼ cup extra-virgin olive oil

2 tbsp chopped oregano

2 tbsp chopped basil

Salt and freshly ground black pepper, as needed

1. In food processor, briefly pulse the olives, capers, and garlic. Slowly stream in the lemon juice and oil and blend until nearly smooth.

2. Transfer to a bowl and stir in the oregano and basil. Season with salt and pepper. Serve immediately or store refrigerated in a ceramic container or jar with a cover.

**MAKES ABOUT 2 CUPS**

# Radish, Poppy Seed, and Arugula Tea Sandwiches

*Radishes and arugula both have a delicious peppery flavor. Lots of salt and the smooth cream cheese make this an excellent sandwich for snacking.*

½ cup minced radish

½ tsp poppy seeds

¼ tsp kosher salt

½ cup cream cheese, softened

4 tbsp (½ stick) unsalted butter

6 slices rye bread

Freshly ground black pepper, as needed

½ bunch arugula, leaves only

1. Combine the radishes, poppy seeds, and salt.

2. In a food processor, combine cream cheese and butter; process to a smooth paste. Divide the cream cheese mixture evenly on 6 slices of bread; spread the cream cheese mixture to an even layer. Sprinkle lightly with salt and pepper. Divide the radish filling between 3 pieces of bread and top each with several leaves of arugula. Top with the remaining 3 bread slices, spread side down.

3. Remove the crusts, if desired, and cut each sandwich into 4 triangles. Serve immediately at room temperature.

**MAKES 12 SMALL SANDWICHES**

# Roasted Beet "Tartare" with Goat Cheese and Extra-Virgin Olive Oil Financiers

*This "tartare" has a wonderful beet flavor and is also fantastic served simply on crackers or Crostini (below).*

2 large red or golden beets, about 8 to 10 ounces

5 tbsp extra-virgin olive oil

Salt and freshly ground black pepper, as needed

2 tbsp sherry vinegar

1 clove garlic, minced

2 tbsp capers, rinsed, minced

1½ tsp honey

¼ cup crumbled fresh goat cheese

½ recipe Extra-Virgin Olive Oil Financiers, approximately 12 (page 269)

GARNISH

2 tbsp diced shallot

2 tbsp chopped chives

1. Preheat the oven to 375°F.

2. Wash and dry the beets well. Rub them with 2 tbsp of the oil. Sprinkle with salt and pepper. Place them on a baking sheet and roast until they are fork-tender, 45 minutes to 1 hour.

3. Allow the beets to cool until you can handle them. Peel off the skin and finely dice the beets. Place the beets in a medium bowl.

4. In a small bowl, whisk the vinegar, the remaining oil, the garlic, capers, and honey to combine. Pour the dressing over the beets and toss to coat. Taste the mixture and add more vinegar or honey if necessary to obtain a tart-sweet flavor.

5. Slice the financiers in half. Spread the goat cheese on the bases of the financiers. Spoon tartare on the top. Garnish with shallots and chives. Serve immediately.

**MAKES 4 TO 6 SERVINGS**

# Crostini

*The perfect vessel for any of your favorite spreads or toppings.*

1 18-inch baguette, cut on the diagonal into ½-inch-thick slices

¼ cup extra-virgin olive oil

2 cloves garlic, minced

Salt and freshly ground black pepper, as needed

1. Heat a grill or grill pan until hot. Grill the bread until lightly charred on both sides.

2. In a small bowl, combine the oil and garlic. Brush both sides of the bread with the oil mixture and season well with salt and pepper. Serve immediately.

**MAKES ABOUT 24 TO 30 CROSTINI**

# Steamed Vegetable Dumplings

*These dumplings make a wonderful snack or appetizer. Dip them in Peanut Dipping Sauce (page 301) or Sweet Chile Sauce (page 302).*

10 ounces firm tofu, diced

1 cup minced fresh white button or shiitake mushrooms, stems removed

¾ cup minced canned water chestnuts, drained

1 bunch green onions, minced (white and green parts)

3 cloves garlic, minced

2 tbsp minced fresh ginger

⅓ cup soy sauce

3 tbsp rice vinegar

1 tbsp chopped cilantro

Pinch cayenne

1 cup cooked brown rice (see chart, page 176)

1 package square dumpling wrappers, as needed (about 36 wrappers)

1. In a medium bowl, toss the tofu, mushrooms, water chestnuts, green onions, garlic, ginger, soy sauce, vinegar, cilantro, cayenne, and rice to combine. Cover and marinate, refrigerated, for 15 to 20 minutes.

2. Spread several dumpling wrappers out on a work surface. Brush two adjacent edges of the wrappers with water and place a tablespoon of filling into the center. Be careful not to overfill.

3. Fold the wrappers diagonally over the filling so that the dry edges meet the moistened edges. Press to seal, releasing any air trapped inside. Repeat with remaining filling and wrappers.

4. Place a steamer basket over simmering water. Place the dumplings in the basket and steam until the wrappers are translucent and the filling is heated through, 5 to 7 minutes. Serve hot.

**MAKES 4 TO 6 SERVINGS, ABOUT 36 DUMPLINGS**

VARIATION: **Pan-Fried Dumplings:** For super crisp dumplings, fry the dumplings in batches of 12 in 3 tbsp vegetable oil in a large sauté pan over medium heat until they are golden brown on one side, 2 minutes. Add approximately ⅓ cup of water to the pan and cover. Allow to steam over medium heat for 5 to 8 minutes, or until the dumplings appear plump and opaque.

Steamed Vegetable Dumplings

Barbecued Vegetable Empanadas, page 20 (right) and Corn Tortilla Cups with
Black Beans, Queso Chihuahua and Guacamole (left)

# Corn Tortilla Cups with Black Beans, Queso Chihuahua, and Guacamole

*This recipe makes the perfect appetizer—it's crunchy, chewy, cheesy, and creamy all in one. If you can't find queso Chihuahua, substitute Monterey Jack.*

4 Corn Tortillas (page 273 or store-bought)

Olive oil, as needed for brushing

Kosher salt, as needed

1 tbsp vegetable oil

¼ cup minced onion

1 clove garlic, minced

1 jalapeño, seeded and minced

1 tbsp tomato paste

½ cup cooked black beans
(see chart, page 131)

1 tsp ground cumin

1 tsp dried thyme

1 tsp dried oregano

Pinch cayenne

Freshly ground black pepper, as needed

¾ cup shredded *queso Chihuahua*

1 cup Guacamole (page 13)

1. Preheat the oven to 400°F. Using a 2½-inch round cookie cutter or the rim of a large glass, cut 3 circles from each tortilla.

2. Brush the circles with olive oil on both sides. Season with salt. Press the circles into the cups of a muffin pan and bake until crisp, approximately 5 minutes. Set aside to cool until needed.

3. In a large sauté pan, heat the vegetable oil over medium heat. Add the onions, cover, and sweat until they are translucent but not colored, 4 to 5 minutes. Add the garlic and jalapeño, and sauté until fragrant, about 1 minute more. Add the tomato paste, and cook 1 to 2 minutes more, until tomato paste is aromatic. Stir in the beans, cumin, thyme, oregano, and cayenne and season with salt and pepper. Let the filling simmer until it has good flavor, 5 to 7 minutes. Cool slightly.

4. Spoon the filling into the tortilla cups. Top with the cheese and guacamole and serve immediately.

**MAKES ABOUT 12 TORTILLA CUPS**

# Barbecued Vegetable Empanadas

*These empanadas also make a great entrée and taste wonderful with Jícama Slaw (page 51) and Stewed Black Bean and Ancho Chile Sauce (page 302).*

## EMPANADA DOUGH

1½ cups all-purpose flour, plus more as needed for rolling

1 tsp sugar

1 tsp kosher salt

¼ cup vegetable oil, plus more as needed for frying

## FILLING

1 green bell pepper, halved

1 red bell pepper, halved

1 yellow bell pepper, halved

1 large Spanish onion, halved

1 medium zucchini, halved lengthwise

3 medium ears corn, husked

2 tbsp olive oil, plus more as needed

Salt and freshly ground black pepper, as needed

2 tbsp chili powder

1 tbsp ground cumin

1 tbsp ground coriander

1 cup Barbecue Sauce (page 294)

2 tbsp chopped cilantro

½ cup shredded Monterey Jack cheese

1. For the empanada dough, combine the flour, sugar, and salt in a large bowl. Make a well in the center. Add ¼ cup vegetable oil and mix to combine. Add ⅓ to ½ cup water; mix until a dough forms. Knead the dough until it is smooth and even, about 5 minutes. Cover the dough in plastic wrap, and let it rest for at least 1 hour.

2. Meanwhile, heat a grill or grill pan until very hot. Brush the peppers, onion, zucchini, and corn with olive oil. Season with salt and pepper. In a small bowl, combine the chili powder, cumin, and coriander. Rub this mixture on the vegetables.

3. Grill the vegetables until they are tender and lightly charred, turning them frequently to ensure even cooking. The peppers, onion, and zucchini will take 2 to 3 minutes per side total. The corn will need 4 to 5 minutes with frequent turning.

4. Remove the vegetables from the grill and let cool enough to be handled. Thinly slice the peppers, onion, and zucchini. Cut the corn kernels from the cobs.

5. In a large saucepan, bring the barbecue sauce to a simmer over medium heat. Add the vegetables and stir to coat. Remove from the heat and stir in the cilantro. Keep the filling warm.

6. On a floured surface, roll out the empanada dough to about ¼ inch thick. Using a 4-inch round cookie cutter, cut circles out of the dough. Press the scraps of dough together, roll out again, and cut until you have 15 circles.

7. Spoon filling into the center of each circle and top with cheese. (Be careful not to overfill them, or they won't seal properly.) Brush half of the circle lightly with water or egg wash. Fold the dough over the filling and press with a fork to seal.

8. Fill a large broad heavy-bottomed pot with oil to a depth of 3 to 4 inches and heat until it registers 325°F on a deep-fry thermometer.

9. Fry the empanadas 2 or 3 at a time until they are golden brown and float to the surface, 3 to 5 minutes. Drain on paper towels and serve immediately.

**MAKES 15 EMPANADAS**

VARIATIONS: **Tempeh Empanadas:** Omit the zucchini and corn. Replace omitted vegetables with ½ pound cooked diced tempeh. Season with ½ tsp cayenne. Replace the barbeque sauce with ¾ cup ketchup and 3 tbsp hot sauce. **Baked Empanadas:** Eggwash (page 315) the empanadas and bake in a 350°F oven until golden brown.

# Vegetarian Refried Beans

*If you like your beans to have a little kick, toss in a pinch of cayenne when you fry them. Try these beans alongside the Seitan Fajitas on page 164.*

1¼ cups dried pinto beans, soaked overnight in enough water to cover by 1 inch (see chart, page 132)

3 cups Vegetable Broth (page 287), plus more as needed

2 tsp ground cumin

1 tsp oregano

3 cloves garlic, minced

Salt and freshly ground black pepper, as needed

3 tbsp grape seed or canola oil

¼ cup minced yellow onion

1. Drain the water from the soaked beans. In a medium saucepan, bring the beans and 3 cups broth to a simmer. Add 1 tsp of the cumin, the oregano, and two-thirds of the garlic. Season with salt and pepper.

2. Cover the pot and cook, stirring occasionally, until the beans are tender, 30 to 40 minutes. Add broth as needed to keep the beans moist.

3. Drain the beans but reserve the cooking liquid. Mash the beans with a potato masher or process in a blender or food processor until smooth. Add reserved cooking liquid as needed to achieve a moist, semi-coarse texture.

4. In a medium skillet, heat the oil over medium heat. Add the onion, the remaining cumin and garlic, and the mashed beans. Fry the mixture, stirring occasionally, until it reaches the consistency of mashed potatoes.

5. Taste and adjust seasoning with salt and pepper. Serve hot.

**MAKES 5 SIDE DISH SERVINGS**

# Whole Wheat Flatbread with Oven-Roasted Vegetables and Jack Cheese

*Crispy flatbread is loaded with vegetables for a delicious appetizer that also makes a great entrée when served with soup or a salad.*

1 tbsp extra-virgin olive oil, plus more as needed

4 medium plum (Roma) tomatoes, thinly sliced, about ¼ inch thick

2 tsp chopped thyme

1 tsp chopped oregano

1 tbsp chopped basil

Salt, as needed

1 medium eggplant, cut crosswise into 8 slices

1 cup Pesto (page 297)

4 Pita Breads (page 274 or store-bought)

2 cups roasted red peppers, sliced into ¼ inch strips

¾ cup grated mozzarella

¾ cup grated Monterey Jack cheese

Freshly ground black pepper, as needed

1. Preheat the oven to 225°F. Heat a grill or grill pan until hot. Lightly brush a baking sheet with oil.

2. Place the tomatoes on the oiled baking sheet. Sprinkle with the thyme, oregano, and basil, season with salt, and drizzle with 1 tbsp oil. Roast the tomatoes until they have dried slightly, about 45 minutes. Set aside to cool. Increase the oven heat to 400°F.

3. Meanwhile, sprinkle the eggplant slices with salt. Set them on paper towels to drain for about 15 minutes (this will remove excess liquid). Blot dry and lightly brush each eggplant round with oil. Grill the eggplant until nicely browned and tender, 3 to 4 minutes per side.

4. Spread an even layer of pesto on each pita bread and top evenly with tomatoes, eggplant, roasted peppers, and cheese.

5. Bake the flatbreads until the bread is crisp and the cheese is bubbly on the surface, about 12 to 15 minutes. Let cool slightly before sprinkling with a grind of black pepper and serving.

**MAKES 4 SIDE DISH SERVINGS**

Whole Wheat Flatbread with Oven Roasted Vegetables and Jack Cheese

Jícama Slaw, page 51 (front), Black Bean Mash (middle), and
Mexican-Style Rice, page 27 (rear)

# Black Bean Mash

*Mashing the beans gives them a creamy texture. Serve this with Seitan Fajitas (page 164) or the Aztec Vegetable Casserole (page 221).*

1 cup dried black beans, soaked overnight in enough water to cover by 1 inch (see chart, page 131)

2½ cups Vegetable Broth (page 287), plus more as needed

1 bay leaf

2 tbsp tomato paste

1 tsp fresh oregano, finely chopped

2 tbsp olive oil

1 medium yellow onion, minced

2 cloves garlic, minced

2 tsp ground cumin

Salt and freshly ground black pepper, as needed

1. Drain the water from the soaked beans. In a medium saucepan, combine the beans, 2½ cups broth, the bay leaf, tomato paste, and oregano. Add more broth as needed to ensure the beans are covered by 1 inch.

2. Bring the mixture to a simmer over medium heat, cover, and cook gently until the beans are tender, 45 to 60 minutes. Add more broth as needed to keep the beans moist. Remove and discard the bay leaf.

3. Meanwhile, in a small sauté pan, heat the oil over medium heat. Add the onion and garlic and sauté until the onions are translucent, 4 to 5 minutes. Add the cumin and cook until fragrant, about 30 seconds.

4. Drain the cooking liquid from the beans but reserve the liquid. Add the onion mixture to the beans and purée in a food processor or blender, adding reserved liquid to achieve the consistency of mashed potatoes. Season with salt and pepper. Serve immediately or cover and keep warm in a 200°F oven. Bean mash may also be cooled and refrigerated for up to 2 days. Save remaining cooking liquid to use when reheating the beans. Reheat beans in a sauté pan or double boiler to avoid scorching.

**MAKES 4 SIDE DISH SERVINGS**

# Black Bean Crêpes

*The crêpe batter can be made up to 12 hours ahead and stored covered in the refrigerator. If you can't find queso Chihuahua, substitute Monterey Jack cheese.*

## CRÊPES

2 large eggs

½ cup liquid from cooking black beans for filling

1 tbsp unsalted butter, melted

⅓ cup all-purpose flour, plus more as needed

⅓ cup corn flour or masa harina

1 tsp kosher salt

2 to 4 tbsp milk (optional)

Olive oil, as needed for cooking

## FILLING

1 tbsp olive oil

⅓ cup diced yellow or white onion

2 cloves garlic, minced

1 jalapeño, seeded and minced

½ cup drained cooked black beans (see chart, page 131; set aside ½ cup of the liquid for making the crêpes)

⅓ cup sun-dried tomatoes, ¼-inch dice

½ tsp ground cumin

½ tsp ground coriander

Salt and freshly ground black pepper, as needed

2 tbsp chopped cilantro

1 cup shredded *queso Chihuahua*

## GARNISH

¾ cup Salsa Verde (page 309) or Pico de Gallo (page 305)

¼ cup sour cream

3 tbsp minced green onion (white and green parts)

1. Combine the eggs, bean liquid, butter, flours, and salt for the crêpes in a food processor or blender. Blend for 30 seconds. Scrape down the sides and blend for 1 minute more. The batter should be very smooth and have the consistency of heavy cream. If necessary, adjust the consistency with milk or all-purpose flour. Rest the batter in the refrigerator for at least 30 minutes.

2. To make the filling, heat the olive oil in a medium sauté pan over medium heat. Add the onion, garlic, and jalapeño. Sauté until the onions are translucent, 3 to 4 minutes.

3. Add the beans and tomatoes. Stir to heat through. Stir in the cumin and coriander, and season with salt and pepper.

4. Heat a crêpe pan or small skillet over medium heat. Brush the pan with oil. Pour ¼ cup batter into the hot pan, swirling and tilting the pan to coat the bottom. Cook, reducing heat if necessary, until the first side is set and has a little color, about 2 minutes. Turn the crêpe over and cook for about 30 to 45 seconds on the second side. Remove the crêpe from the pan and place on a warm flat plate. Cover with a damp towel and keep warm in a 200°F oven. Continue making crêpes, stacking the finished crêpes on top of one another.

5. Once all of the crêpes have been made, spoon about 3 tbsp filling onto each crêpe. Sprinkle with cilantro and cheese. Fold the crêpes into quarters. Serve with salsa and sour cream, and garnish with the green onions.

**MAKES 4 SIDE DISH SERVINGS**

# Mexican-Style Rice

*Tomato purée gives this rice its reddish hue and great flavor that makes it the perfect complement to Aztec Vegetable Casserole (page 221) or Poblanos Rellenos (page 234).*

1 tbsp olive oil

¼ cup minced white or yellow onion

1 clove garlic, minced

½ cup long-grain white rice

3 tbsp tomato purée

1 cup water

½ serrano chile, seeded and minced

¼ cup diced carrot

¼ cup green peas (fresh or thawed frozen)

Salt and freshly ground black pepper, as needed

1. Preheat the oven to 325°F.

2. In a small ovenproof saucepan, heat the oil over medium heat. Add the onion and garlic and sauté until fragrant, about 2 minutes. Add the rice and sauté, stirring, until the onions are translucent and the grains separate, about 3 to 4 minutes.

3. Stir in the tomato purée and cook for about 1 minute more. Stir in 1 cup water, the chile, carrots, and peas. Season with salt and pepper and bring to a boil.

4. Cover the pot and place in the oven until the rice absorbs all the liquid and is tender, 10 to 12 minutes. Serve immediately.

**MAKES 4 SIDE DISH SERVINGS**

# Arroz Blanco

*This dish, called "white rice" in Spanish, is a perfect basic side dish for a variety of meals. It can also be an excellent addition to casseroles and the perfect base for a rice bowl.*

1½ tbsp vegetable oil

1 cup long-grain white rice

½ cup minced white onion

1 clove garlic, minced

1½ cup Vegetable Broth (page 287)

½ cup corn kernels (fresh or thawed frozen)

Salt and freshly ground black pepper, as needed

1. Preheat the oven to 350°F.

2. In a medium ovenproof saucepan, heat the oil over medium heat. Add the rice and stir to coat the grains with oil. Cook, stirring often, until it begins to toast and take on a golden color.

3. Add the onion and garlic and continue to cook until the onions turn golden, 4 to 5 minutes. Add the broth and corn, season with salt and pepper, and bring to a simmer.

4. Cover the pot and place in the oven until the rice absorbs all of the liquid and is tender, 10 to 12 minutes.

5. Let the rice rest for 15 minutes, then fluff with a fork and serve.

**MAKES 4 SIDE DISH SERVINGS**

NOTE: Long-grain brown rice may be substituted for the long-grain white rice. The quantity of vegetable broth should be increased to 2 cups.

# Coconut Rice

*This rice has great flavor and is incredibly creamy. It is the perfect way to complement spicy food, such as the Ragada on page 236.*

2 tsp vegetable oil

¼ cup minced white onion

2 cloves garlic, minced

½ cup unsweetened coconut milk

1 tsp minced fresh ginger

1 cup long-grain white rice

1 bay leaf

Salt and freshly ground black pepper, as needed

**GARNISH**

2 to 3 tbsp toasted coconut, as needed

Chopped cilantro, as needed

1. Preheat the oven to 350°F.

2. In a small sauté pan, heat the oil over medium heat. Add the onion and garlic and sauté until the onion is translucent, 4 to 5 minutes.

3. In a medium ovenproof saucepan, bring 1½ cups water and the coconut milk to a boil. Add the onion mixture, ginger, rice, and bay leaf and season with salt and pepper. Bring to a simmer.

4. Cover the pot and place in the oven until the rice absorbs all of the liquid and is tender, 10 to 12 minutes. The rice will appear to have a creamy layer on top when it has absorbed all of the liquid. Check below this layer of "cream" to be sure all liquid has been absorbed. Fluff the rice with a fork.

5. Let the rice rest for 15 minutes. Remove and discard the bay leaf. Adjust the seasoning and fluff the rice once more before serving. Serve garnished with toasted coconut and cilantro.

**MAKES 4 SIDE DISH SERVINGS**

NOTE: Long-grain brown rice may be substituted for long-grain white rice, and water should be increased to 2 cups.

# Wild Rice Cakes

*These cakes would be a perfect appetizer paired with Sweet Potato Coulis (page 311) but would also make an excellent sandwich or side dish topped with Tahini-Soy Dressing (page 292).*

1 tbsp unsalted butter

2 stalks celery, minced

¾ cup minced red bell pepper

⅓ cup thinly sliced green onion (white and green parts)

2 cloves garlic, minced

1 tbsp minced fresh ginger

1 tbsp hot sauce

3 large eggs

⅓ cup mayonnaise

⅔ cup sour cream

3 tbsp chopped chives

3 cups cooked hominy (see chart, page 175)

3 cups cooked wild rice (see chart, page 176)

Salt and freshly ground black pepper, as needed

All-purpose flour, as needed

1 cup panko bread crumbs, plus more as needed for dredging

Grape seed or olive oil, as needed for pan frying

1. In a large sauté pan, melt the butter over medium heat. Add the celery and red pepper and sauté until tender, 4 to 5 minutes. Remove from heat and let cool.

2. In a large bowl, combine the green onions, garlic, ginger, hot sauce, 1 egg, the mayonnaise, sour cream, chives, and hominy. Purée one-third of the mixture in a blender or food processor to create a binder.

3. Return the puréed mixture to the bowl and stir in the wild rice and the celery mixture. Season with salt and pepper.

4. Lightly beat the remaining eggs. Set up a breading station with the flour, eggs, and panko in separate shallow dishes. Form the rice mixture into 4 large or 8 to 12 small cakes. Dredge the cakes in flour, then eggs, and lastly panko to coat.

5. In a large skillet, heat about ¼ inch oil over medium-high heat. Fry the cakes until golden brown and crisp, 3 to 5 minutes per side. Drain briefly on paper towels and serve hot.

**MAKES 4 SIDE DISH SERVINGS**

# Fontina Risotto Fritters
## Arancini

*This recipe transforms leftover risotto into a crowd-pleasing appetizer. Try stuffing the fritters with different kinds of cheeses, such as fresh mozzarella, Gouda, or even Cheddar.*

3 cups leftover risotto, plain, or Sweet Corn Risotto chilled (page 30)

⅓ cup plus ¼ cup grated Parmesan

¼ tsp red pepper flakes

Salt and freshly ground black pepper, as needed

1 large egg

16 small cubes Fontina (about ½ cup)

All-purpose flour, as needed for coating

Egg Wash (page 315), as needed for coating

¾ cup bread crumbs

Grape seed or canola oil, as needed for frying

**OPTIONAL GARNISH**

1 cup Tomato Sauce (page 303), warm

Grated Parmesan

1. In a medium bowl, mix the risotto with ⅓ cup Parmesan and pepper flakes. Season with salt and pepper to taste before adding the egg. Add the egg and mix thoroughly to incorporate.

2. With your hands, mold some of the risotto mixture around a cube of Fontina and roll into a small ball. Repeat with remaining risotto and cheese cubes to make 16 balls. Place the balls onto a baking sheet, cover, and refrigerate. Hint: Lightly oiling your hands first makes rolling the risotto balls a bit easier.

3. Meanwhile, prepare a breading station: Place the flour in one shallow bowl and the egg wash in another. Combine the bread crumbs and the remaining Parmesan in a third bowl. Roll the risotto balls in flour to coat, then egg wash, then the bread crumb mixture. Set back on the baking sheet. Repeat with the remaining balls. Refrigerate or freeze the breaded risotto balls before frying; this assures they will be crisp and the cheese will not leak out.

4. Pour the oil to a depth of 4 inches in a medium pot that is taller than it is wide. Heat the oil to 350°F, as registered on a deep-fry thermometer. Fry the fritters until they are golden brown and rise to the surface, 5 to 7 minutes. Remove with a skimmer and drain briefly on paper towels.

5. Serve warm as is or optionally with tomato sauce and more Parmesan, if desired.

**MAKES 16 FRITTERS**

# Grits Cakes with Tomato Butter Sauce

*Grits take on a new form in these crisp cakes. Paired with a slightly spicy tomato sauce, this dish makes an excellent appetizer or an entrée served with a Chopped Salad (page 101).*

**GRITS CAKES**

1½ cups milk

2 cups Vegetable Broth (page 287)

1⅓ cup quick-cooking grits

4 tbsp (½ stick) unsalted butter

1 tbsp grape seed or olive oil

½ cup corn kernels (fresh or thawed frozen)

½ cup diced red bell pepper

¼ cup thinly sliced green onion (white and green parts)

½ cup shredded Cheddar

Salt and freshly ground black pepper, as needed

**TOMATO BUTTER SAUCE**

1 tbsp olive oil

1 shallot, minced

2 cloves garlic, minced

1 jalapeño, seeded and minced

2 tbsp white wine

⅓ cup canned crushed tomatoes

2 tbsp unsalted butter

Salt and freshly ground black pepper, as needed

1. For the grits cakes, in a medium saucepan, bring the milk and broth to a simmer over medium heat. Add the grits and stir continuously for 10 minutes. Add 1 tbsp of the butter and stir to combine. Continue to simmer until the grits are tender, 5 to 6 minutes.

2. Meanwhile, heat the oil in a medium sauté pan over medium heat. Add the corn and red pepper and sauté until tender, 4 to 5 minutes. Add the green onions, and stir until fragrant, about 1 minute more.

3. Stir the corn mixture and the cheese into the grits. Season with salt and pepper. Pour the mixture onto a baking sheet lined with parchment paper. If necessary, use a rolling pin to create an even layer of grits about ½ inch thick. Let cool until firm.

4. To prepare the sauce, heat the olive oil in a small saucepan over medium heat. Add the shallots, garlic, and jalapeño. Sauté until the shallots are translucent, 2 to 3 minutes. Add the wine, and stir until the mixture is almost entirely dry.

5. Add the tomatoes and bring to a simmer, stirring occasionally. Simmer until the sauce has reduced slightly and developed good flavor, about 5 minutes. Stir in 2 tbsp butter and season with salt and pepper. Keep warm.

6. Using a 2- or 3-inch round cookie cutter or the rim of a large glass, cut cakes out of the grits mixture.

7. In a large sauté pan, melt the remaining 3 tbsp butter over medium heat. Add the cakes and sauté until golden brown, 3 to 5 minutes per side. Serve the cakes warm with sauce.

**MAKES 4 SIDE DISH SERVINGS, ABOUT 8 MEDIUM CAKES OR 12 SMALL CAKES**

Grits with Corn and Hominy

# Grits with Corn and Hominy

*This dish combines three types of corn for a hearty side. Try it for breakfast with a fried egg on top.*

1 tbsp olive oil

1½ cups yellow or Spanish minced onion

1 tbsp minced garlic

1 cup seeded and minced poblano chiles

½ cup minced red bell pepper

1½ tsp kosher salt

6 cups Vegetable Broth (page 287)

2 cups coarse whole-grain old-fashioned grits

3 cups corn kernels (fresh or thawed frozen)

2⅔ cups cooked hominy (see chart, page 175)

Freshly ground black pepper, as needed

GARNISH

Shredded cheddar or Monterey
Jack cheese, as needed

½ cup diced plum (Roma) tomatoes

1. Heat the oil in a large skillet over medium heat. Add the onion and sauté over medium heat until translucent, 4 to 5 minutes. Add the garlic, chiles, and red pepper. Cover and cook over low heat until the peppers are soft, about 10 minutes. Season with the salt.

2. Pour in the broth and bring to a boil. Slowly sprinkle in the grits, stirring constantly. Continue cooking over very low heat until the grits are tender, 40 to 45 minutes. Stir frequently. More stirring results in creamier grits.

3. Gently fold in the corn and hominy. Cover, remove from the heat, and let stand for 5 minutes. Season with pepper, garnish with cheese and tomatoes, and serve warm.

**MAKES 6 SIDE DISH SERVINGS**

# Mashed Sweet Potatoes with Ginger

*Ginger is the perfect complement to the natural sweetness of sweet potatoes, and it makes this side dish anything but ordinary.*

6 medium sweet potatoes, about 2½ to 3 pounds

2 russet potatoes, about 1 pound

4 tbsp (½ stick) unsalted butter

¾ to 1 cup heavy cream

1 tbsp minced fresh ginger

Salt and freshly ground black pepper, as needed

1. Preheat the oven to 400°F.

2. Puncture the skin of each potato with the tip of a knife or sharp fork to create a vent for the steam. Bake them directly on the rack in the oven until they are fork-tender, 20 to 25 minutes for the sweet potatoes and 45 to 50 minutes for russet potatoes.

3. Let the potatoes cool enough to handle, then peel them. Mash them in a large bowl using a fork or potato masher, or use a food mill. Keep warm.

4. In a small saucepan, combine the butter and heavy cream and bring to a simmer. Add the ginger and let steep for 15 minutes before stirring into the potatoes. Season with salt and pepper and serve immediately.

**MAKES 8 SIDE DISH SERVINGS**

# Potato Pancakes

*Serve these pancakes alongside Matzo Brei (page 170) for a delicious and hearty breakfast.*

2 to 2½ pounds russet potatoes

1 tbsp fresh lemon juice

1 cup thinly sliced medium yellow onion

1 large egg, lightly beaten

¾ cup all-purpose flour

¾ cup matzo meal

1 tbsp chopped flat-leaf parsley

3 tbsp chopped chives

Salt and freshly ground black pepper, as needed

Grape seed or peanut oil, as needed for pan frying

GARNISH

½ cup sour cream

1. Peel the potatoes. Store in water after peeling to prevent browning. Using a box grater, shred the potatoes into a large bowl. (You should have about 4 cups.) Stir in the lemon juice and sliced onions; toss to coat evenly with lemon juice. Let the potatoes and onions sit for 10 minutes. Drain the potatoes and squeeze out the excess liquid.

2. In a large bowl, combine the potatoes, egg, flour, matzo meal, parsley, and 1 tbsp of the chives, and season with salt and pepper.

3. Heat about ½ inch of oil in a medium sauté pan over medium heat. Form the potato mixture into small patties, and pan fry until golden, 5 to 7 minutes per side. Drain on paper towels. Serve with sour cream and the remaining chives.

**MAKES 4 SIDE DISH SERVINGS**

# Yuca Tots with Buttermilk Sauce

*These creamy, crispy bites are a childhood favorite, all grown up. The tots can be frozen and will be even crispier when fried frozen.*

Salt, as needed

2½ to 3 pounds yuca, peeled and diced, woody core removed (about 6 cups)

¼ cup grated dry Jack cheese

2 tbsp unsalted butter, cubed

¼ cup buttermilk powder

2 tsp onion powder

2 tsp garlic powder

½ tsp sugar

Freshly ground black pepper, as needed

Peanut oil, as needed for frying

**BUTTERMILK DIPPING SAUCE**

2 tbsp sour cream

2 tbsp buttermilk

½ cup mayonnaise

⅓ cup chopped chives

¼ cup thinly sliced green onion (white and green parts)

¼ cup chopped flat-leaf parsley

1. Cook the yuca in a large pot of salted boiling water until tender, 15 to 20 minutes. Drain very well and allow steam to dissipate; the yuca will cool slightly. Use a food mill with a coarse screen to mash the yuca into a large bowl.

2. Mix the cheese, butter, buttermilk powder, onion and garlic powders, and sugar into the warm yuca. Season with salt and pepper.

3. Form into balls approximately 1 inch in diameter. Cover and refrigerate until well chilled, at least 3 hours or up to overnight.

4. Combine all the sauce ingredients in a small bowl. Cover and refrigerate until needed.

5. Pour oil to a depth of 4 inches into a medium pot that is taller than it is wide. Heat the oil to 350°F.

6. Working in batches if necessary, fry the tots until they are golden brown on all sides and have risen to the surface, 4 to 6 minutes. Drain on paper towels. Serve immediately with the sauce.

**MAKES 4 SIDE DISH SERVINGS**

*Yuca Tots with Buttermilk Sauce*

# Hush Puppies

*These hush puppies are made even more delicious with Monterey Jack cheese and a hint of spicy cayenne. Try using other herbs and spices as well.*

1¾ cups white cornmeal

⅔ cup all-purpose flour

2 tsp baking powder

⅓ cup grated Monterey Jack cheese

⅓ cup minced yellow onion

3 cloves garlic, minced

¾ tsp sugar

¼ tsp cayenne

2 large eggs

⅓ cup heavy cream

1½ tbsp unsalted butter, melted

1 tsp kosher salt and ¼ tsp freshly ground black pepper, as needed

Grape seed or peanut oil, as needed for frying

1. In a large bowl, combine the cornmeal, flour, baking powder, cheese, onion, garlic, sugar, and cayenne. In a small bowl, combine the eggs, cream, and melted butter. Then add the liquids to the dry ingredients, and stir until a smooth batter forms. Season with salt and pepper. Let the mixture rest until it stiffens slightly, about 15 minutes.

2. Pour oil to a depth of 4 inches into a medium pot that is taller than it is wide. Heat the oil to 350°F.

3. Working in batches if necessary, scoop the batter using a small cookie scoop (number 50 or 60 size scoop) into the hot oil. Fry until the hush puppies are golden on all sides, 5 to 6 minutes.

4. Drain on paper towels and serve immediately.

**MAKES 4 TO 6 SIDE DISH SERVINGS**

# Blue Corn Stuffing

*Classic herb stuffing with a twist: blue cornbread. Of course, this recipe also works well with the traditional Cornbread on page 257.*

2 tbsp unsalted butter, plus more for greasing

½ cup diced yellow onion

2 tbsp diced celery

1 clove garlic, minced

2 tsp chopped thyme

1½ tsp chopped sage

2 tbsp half-and-half

1 large egg, lightly beaten

½ cup Vegetable Broth (page 287)

2½ cups coarsely crumbled Blue Cornbread (page 257)

Salt and freshly ground black pepper, as needed

1. Preheat the oven to 375°F. Grease a 9-inch square baking pan.

2. Melt the butter in a small sauté pan over medium heat. Add the onion, celery, and garlic and sauté until the onions are translucent.

3. Transfer the mixture to a bowl and add the thyme, sage, half-and-half, egg, and broth. Mix well. Add the cornbread and toss to coat. Season with salt and pepper.

4. Pour the mixture into the prepared dish. Bake, uncovered, until the top is evenly browned, 25 to 35 minutes. Serve immediately.

**MAKES 4 SIDE DISH SERVINGS**

# Mushrooms with Guajillo Chiles and Garlic

*Cremini (brown) mushrooms have much more flavor than white button mushrooms. If you can't find guajillo chiles, ancho chiles can be substituted. This dish can be served as a side or as a taco filling. If it is used as a filling, the mushrooms should be chopped before roasting.*

2 tbsp olive oil, plus more as needed for greasing

3½ cups cremini mushrooms

2 cloves garlic, minced

½ cup minced yellow onion

2 guajillo chiles, stemmed, seeded, toasted, and coarsely crumbled

Salt and freshly ground black pepper, as needed

1. Preheat the oven to 350°F. Lightly grease a roasting pan with olive oil.

2. In a medium bowl, toss the mushrooms, oil, garlic, onion, and chiles to combine. Season with salt and pepper.

3. Pour the mixture into the prepared pan and roast until the mushrooms are tender and fragrant, 15 to 20 minutes.

4. Serve immediately hot, or cool to room temperature.

MAKES 5 SIDE DISH SERVINGS

# Millet and Cauliflower Purée

*Puréed cauliflower has a texture similar to mashed potatoes. Millet adds a unique texture. And plenty of garlic gives this purée great flavor.*

2 tbsp vegetable oil

1 cup millet

Salt and freshly ground black pepper, as needed

1½ cups coarsely chopped cauliflower

2½ cups Vegetable Broth (page 287), plus more as needed

4 cloves Roasted Garlic (page 315), peeled

1. In a large saucepan, heat the oil over medium heat. Add the millet and stir constantly until it turns golden, about 3 minutes.

2. Season with salt and pepper. Add the cauliflower and broth. Bring to a boil over medium-high heat. Lower the heat to medium-low, and simmer, stirring occasionally, until the millet bursts, about 30 minutes. Add additional broth if the mixture seems to be drying out too much.

3. Remove from the heat and add the garlic. In a food processor or blender, purée the mixture. If it is too thick, add more broth as needed. Return to the pan and reheat gently. Serve warm.

MAKES 4 SIDE DISH SERVINGS

# Scalloped Sunchokes and Fingerling Potatoes

*Sunchokes (also known as Jerusalem artichokes) are a tuberous root vegetable. In this recipe, they are cooked much like a gratin, with added flavors from shallots and smoked Gouda cheese.*

Unsalted butter, as needed for greasing the casserole

1½ pounds fingerling potatoes (about 16), peeled

1 medium sunchoke, peeled, about 4 ounces

1 cup whole milk

1 cup heavy cream

2 small shallots, minced

4 cloves garlic, minced

Salt and freshly ground black pepper, as needed

2 cups grated smoked Gouda cheese (½ pound)

1. Preheat the oven to 325°F. Butter a 2-quart casserole.

2. With a mandoline, slice the potatoes and sunchoke lengthwise into ¹⁄₁₆-inch-thick slices, letting the slices fall into a medium bowl. Add the milk, cream, shallots, and garlic and season with salt and pepper.

3. Transfer the mixture to a large saucepan. Bring to a simmer over medium-low heat and cook 3 minutes.

4. Remove from the heat and gently stir in 1½ cups of the cheese. Transfer the mixture to the prepared casserole and sprinkle the top with the remaining cheese.

5. Bake, uncovered, until the vegetables are tender and golden brown, about 45 minutes. Let rest 15 minutes before cutting.

**MAKES 4 SIDE DISH SERVINGS**

# Baked Acorn Squash

*Slowly cooking squash in the oven caramelizes it and brings out its natural sweetness. In this recipe, butter and brown sugar amplify those flavors.*

1 acorn squash, cut into wedges, seeded, and peeled

4 tbsp (½ stick) unsalted butter, melted

¼ cup light brown sugar

Salt and freshly ground black pepper, as needed

1. Preheat the oven to 350°F.

2. On a baking sheet, brush the squash with the butter to coat. Sprinkle generously with the sugar and season with salt and pepper.

3. Roast the squash until tender, 25 to 35 minutes. Serve immediately.

**MAKES 4 SIDE DISH SERVINGS**

NOTES: Maple syrup or honey can be substituted for the brown sugar. | Different varieties of squash may be substituted for the acorn squash, such as butternut, carnival, buttercup, or pumpkin. Butternut squash would be peeled, seeded, and cut into ¾-inch-thick slices or wedges approximately 3 inches long and ¾ inch wide. The bulbous end would be cut into wedges similar to the acorn squash. | If you use delicata squash, you may omit the sugar. Delicata should be cut lengthwise into wedges. Spaghetti squash would not really be appropriate for this type of method. | You may omit the sugar and add herbs such as fresh or dried thyme, oregano, or rosemary.

# White Beans with Lemon, Fennel, and Avocado

*This dish has a variety of flavors and textures and is reminiscent of a ceviche gone vegetarian. It's good all by itself or served on Crostini (page 15).*

3 cups cooked cannellini beans
(see chart, page 131)

1 medium bulb fennel, trimmed and shredded

1 cup halved grape tomatoes

¼ cup minced red onion

¼ cup chopped flat-leaf parsley

¼ cup sliced pitted Kalamata olives

¼ cup olive oil

2 tbsp fresh lemon juice

1 tbsp chopped basil

Salt and freshly ground black pepper, as needed

2 avocados, diced

1. In a large bowl, combine the beans, fennel, tomatoes, onion, parsley, and olives.

2. In a small bowl, mix the oil, lemon juice, and basil to combine. Season with salt and pepper. Add the dressing to the bean mixture, and toss to coat. Fold in the avocado and serve immediately.

**MAKES 4 SIDE DISH SERVINGS**

White Beans with Lemon, Fennel, and Avocado

Tostones

# Tostones

*Tostones are crispy plantains that get their signature crunch from being fried twice.*

Peanut or grape seed oil, as needed for frying

3 medium green plantains, peeled and sliced 1½ inches thick on the bias

1 tbsp kosher salt, plus more as needed

2 cloves garlic, minced

1. Fill a large pot or deep skillet half full with oil and place over medium-high heat until the oil registers 350°F on a deep-fry thermometer. Working in batches if necessary, fry the plantains until they are just beginning to turn golden, 3 to 5 minutes.

2. Remove the plantain slices with a skimmer or slotted spoon and drain on paper towels. While the plantains are still warm, smash them lightly between 2 sheets of plastic wrap, using the base of a small sauté pan, to about ¼ inch thick.

3. In a small bowl, combine ½ cup water, 1 tbsp salt, and the garlic. Mix until the salt dissolves.

4. Bring the oil back to 350°F. A few slices at a time, dip the plantains in the water, shake off the excess, and fry a second time until they are fully golden on all sides, 3 to 4 minutes.

5. Drain on clean paper towels, and season lightly with salt. Serve immediately.

**MAKES 4 SIDE DISH SERVINGS**

# Sherry-Braised Baby Bok Choy

*Sherry is a fortified wine from Spain. Its sweet-and-sour flavors are perfect with vegetables, especially with tender baby bok choy.*

3 tbsp olive oil

3 cloves garlic, minced

1 tbsp minced fresh ginger

4 medium heads baby bok choy, approximately ¾ pound

½ cup dry sherry

3 tbsp soy sauce

⅓ cup Vegetable Broth (page 287)

Salt and freshly ground black pepper, as needed

1. In a large sauté pan, heat the oil over medium heat. Add the garlic and ginger and cook until fragrant, about 1 minute.

2. Add the bok choy in a single layer. Pour in the sherry, soy sauce, and broth. Cover the pan and simmer over medium-low heat until the bok choy is tender, 8 to 12 minutes. Turn the bok choy halfway through cooking to assure even doneness. Season generously with salt and pepper.

3. Serve immediately hot or at room temperature.

**MAKES 4 SIDE DISH SERVINGS**

# Succotash

*A quick, easy, and always satisfying side dish that makes the best of fresh summer produce. If you're a succotash fan, try the "Succotash" Risotto with Lima Beans, Corn, Butternut Squash, and Dry Jack Cheese on page 193.*

1 tbsp unsalted butter

½ cup minced shallots

⅓ cup Vegetable Broth (page 287)

1 cup corn kernels (fresh or thawed frozen)

1 cup trimmed and diced green beans

1 cup lima beans (cooked fresh or thawed frozen)

Salt and freshly ground black pepper, as needed

1. In a medium sauté pan, melt the butter over medium heat. Add the shallots and cook until they are translucent, about 2 minutes.

2. Add the broth and bring to a simmer. Add the corn, green beans, and lima beans and cook until most of the liquid has evaporated, 5 to 6 minutes. Season generously with salt and pepper. Serve immediately.

**MAKES 4 SIDE DISH SERVINGS**

Smoked Tofu and Celery Salad, page 49 (front) and
Sherry-Braised Baby Bok Choy (rear)

# Indonesian-Style Potato Salad

*This potato salad is anything but ordinary. Unlike traditional mayonnaise-laden salads, this flavorful salad gets its creaminess from peanut butter and coconut milk.*

1½ pounds small white potatoes, unpeeled

Salt, as needed

1 cup halved snap peas

½ cup shredded carrots

1 bunch green onions, thinly sliced (white and green parts)

1 tbsp peanut oil

1 clove garlic, minced

⅓ cup creamy peanut butter

1 tbsp light brown sugar

½ tsp red chili paste

2 tbsp soy sauce

1 tbsp rice vinegar

¾ cup unsweetened coconut milk

¼ cup chopped cilantro

¼ cup chopped toasted peanuts

1. Place the potatoes in a large pot with enough cold salted water to cover. Cook until they are fork-tender, 20 to 25 minutes.

2. Drain the potatoes and let them cool slightly. Cut the potatoes into large dice and put them in a large bowl. Add the snap peas, carrots, and green onions and toss to combine.

3. In a small sauté pan, heat the oil over medium heat. Add the garlic and cook until fragrant, about 1 minute.

4. Stir in the peanut butter, sugar, chili paste, soy sauce, vinegar, and coconut milk. Bring the mixture to a simmer and cook, stirring occasionally, until the mixture forms a thick, smooth sauce, about 5 minutes.

5. Pour the dressing over the vegetables, and toss to coat. Add the cilantro and peanuts, and toss to combine. Finished salad may be served warm or at room temperature.

**MAKES 4 TO 6 SIDE DISH SERVINGS**

# Smoked Tofu and Celery Salad

*Sesame oil has a very strong flavor, so be sure to taste the dressing before adding any additional oil. It is available in the international section of most grocery stores or at Asian specialty markets.*

2½ cups very thinly sliced celery

¼ pound smoked tofu, very thinly sliced

¼ cup soy sauce

1 tbsp sugar

1 tbsp toasted sesame oil

1 tsp minced fresh ginger

1 clove garlic, minced

2 green onions, minced (white and green parts)

1. In a steamer, steam the celery until tender, about 1 minute. Let cool to room temperature.

2. In a medium bowl, toss the celery and tofu to combine.

3. In a small bowl, combine the remaining ingredients. Pour the dressing over the celery and tofu, and toss to coat. Serve at room temperature.

**MAKES 4 SIDE DISH SERVINGS**

# Couscous with Spinach, Zucchini, and Citrus Poppy Seed Vinaigrette

*Israeli couscous is larger than regular couscous. Combined with spinach, zucchini, and a zesty dressing, this is a hearty side dish.*

1 tbsp olive oil

1 cup Israeli couscous

1½ cups Vegetable Broth (page 287)

3 cups baby spinach, stems removed, lightly packed

1½ cups ½-inch dice zucchini

**DRESSING**

2 oz drained silken tofu

2 tbsp fresh orange juice

1 tbsp grated lemon zest

1 tbsp Dijon mustard

1 tsp honey

3 tbsp apple cider vinegar

1 tbsp poppy seeds

2 tbsp olive oil

Salt and freshly ground black pepper, as needed

1. In a small saucepan, heat the oil over medium heat. Add the couscous and toast, stirring, for about 1 minute. Add the broth and bring the mixture to a boil.

2. Cover the pot, reduce the heat to low, and simmer until the couscous has absorbed the liquid, 5 to 6 minutes. Fluff the finished couscous with a fork. Let cool to room temperature.

3. In a large bowl, toss the spinach and zucchini to combine. Add the cooled couscous and toss to combine.

4. In a blender or food processor, combine the tofu, orange juice, lemon zest, mustard, honey, vinegar, and poppy seeds. With the machine running, slowly add the olive oil. Season with salt and pepper.

5. Pour the dressing over the couscous mixture and toss to coat. Serve at room temperature or chilled.

**MAKES 4 SIDE DISH SERVINGS**

# Jícama Slaw

*The addition of beans makes this a hearty slaw, and its flavorful dressing makes it perfect to go with a variety of dishes. Try it alongside a Black Bean Burger (page 121).*

1 cup cooked black beans
(see chart, page 131)

3 cups thinly sliced jícama, cut into julienne

1 cup thinly sliced red onion

1 small red bell pepper, thinly sliced

1 small yellow bell pepper, thinly sliced

1 small green bell pepper, thinly sliced

1 cup corn kernels (fresh or thawed frozen)

DRESSING

¼ cup sherry vinegar

1 clove garlic, minced

1 serrano chile, seeded and minced

¾ cup olive oil

Grated zest and juice of 1 lime

¼ cup chopped cilantro

Pinch cayenne

Salt and freshly ground black
pepper, as needed

1. In a large bowl, toss the beans, jícama, onion, peppers, and corn to combine.

2. In a small bowl, combine the vinegar, garlic, chile, oil, lime zest and juice, cilantro, and cayenne. Season with salt and pepper.

3. Pour the dressing over the vegetables and toss to coat. Cover and refrigerate until well chilled.

4. Serve chilled.

**MAKES 6 TO 8 SIDE DISH SERVINGS**

# Soba Noodle Salad

*Soba noodles are made from buckwheat flour and are available in the international section of most grocery stores. Try pairing this salad with the Tempeh-Cashew Noodles on page 156.*

Salt, as needed

12 ounces soba noodles

1 tbsp toasted sesame oil

2 tbsp peanut oil

2 cups shiitake mushrooms, stems removed, caps thinly sliced

1 tbsp tamari

2 cups bean sprouts

2 cups thinly sliced snow peas

1 cup thinly sliced daikon radish, peeled and cut into julienne

1 bunch green onions, thinly sliced (white and green parts)

1 cup Tahini-Soy Dressing (page 292)

GARNISH

¼ cup toasted sesame seeds

1. In a large pot of boiling salted water, cook the noodles until tender (this will only take 1 to 2 minutes). Drain in a colander and rinse under cold running water to stop the cooking. Drain completely. Toss the noodles with the sesame oil to prevent them from sticking.

2. In a medium sauté pan, heat the peanut oil over medium heat. Add the mushrooms and sauté until they are tender, 3 to 5 minutes. Add the tamari.

3. Place the noodles, mushrooms, bean sprouts, snow peas, daikon, green onions, and dressing in a large bowl. Toss to combine. Sprinkle with toasted sesame seeds. Serve chilled or at room temperature.

**MAKES 4 SIDE DISH SERVINGS**

# Yellow Squash Noodles

*Squash can have a remarkably pasta-like texture, which makes a perfect, healthy side dish.*

3¼ cups thinly sliced yellow squash, cut into long julienne using a mandoline

¾ cup thinly sliced carrots, cut into long julienne using a mandoline

2 cups thinly sliced leeks (white and light green parts), cut lengthwise into long julienne

2 tbsp minced shallots

½ cup thinly sliced green onions (white and green parts)

1 tbsp unsalted butter

½ cup Vegetable Broth (page 287)

Salt and freshly ground black pepper, as needed

1. In a large bowl, toss the squash, carrots, leeks, shallots, and green onions to combine.

2. In a large sauté pan, melt the butter into the broth over medium heat. Bring to a boil; add the vegetables and toss to coat with the butter broth mixture. Season with salt and pepper. Cook the vegetables until they are tender and have absorbed most of the liquid, 4 to 5 minutes.

3. Serve hot.

**MAKES 4 SIDE DISH SERVINGS**

# Green Bean Bake with Crispy Leeks

*This tasty side dish may remind you of Thanksgiving dinner—but the addition of mushrooms, white wine, and fresh herbs takes it up a notch.*

1 pound green beans, trimmed

2 tbsp olive oil

2 medium shallots, minced

2 cloves garlic, minced

3 cups thinly sliced cremini mushrooms, stems removed

2 tsp chopped thyme

1 tbsp chopped rosemary

Salt and freshly ground black pepper, as needed

¼ cup white wine

½ cup plus 3 tbsp all-purpose flour

1 cup Vegetable Broth (page 287)

1 cup whole milk

1 cup grape seed oil for frying

1 medium leek (white and light green parts), cut into long julienne

1. Preheat the oven to 350°F. Grease a 10-inch square baking pan.

2. Bring a large pot of salted water to a boil. Cook the green beans until tender yet still crisp, about 5 minutes. Drain and cool under cold running water.

3. In a large skillet, heat the olive oil over medium heat. Add the shallots and garlic and cook until the shallots are translucent, 2 to 3 minutes. Add the mushrooms, thyme, and rosemary, season with salt and pepper, and cook until the mushrooms are tender, about 4 minutes.

4. Add the wine and simmer until it is almost completely evaporated, 2 to 3 minutes.

5. Stir in 3 tbsp of the flour. Stir in the broth until smooth and simmer to heat through. Reduce the heat slightly and stir in the milk. Cook until the mixture thickens enough to coat the back of a spoon, 6 to 8 minutes.

6. Remove from the heat and stir in the green beans. Transfer the mixture to the prepared baking pan. Bake until the green beans are tender and the sauce is bubbly, 15 to 20 minutes.

7. Meanwhile, make the crispy leeks: In a small saucepan, heat the grape seed oil over medium heat until it registers 350°F on a deep-fry thermometer.

8. In a medium bowl, combine the remaining flour, ¼ tsp salt, and pinch of pepper. Dredge the leek strips in the flour mixture, shaking off any excess. Gently lower the leek into the oil. Fry until the strips are crisp and golden, 1 to 2 minutes. Remove with a skimmer or slotted spoon and drain on paper towels.

9. When the green beans are finished, top with the crispy leeks and serve.

**MAKES 4 SERVINGS**

Soups are wonderful for so many reasons: They are easy to make—especially in advance—and can be made with an incredibly wide variety of ingredients. They are an excellent way to showcase seasonal ingredients and can be served warm in the winter and chilled in the summer. This chapter has soups that are perfect to serve at the beginning of a meal and soups that are hearty enough to be a meal on their own.

3

# SOUPS

# GENERAL GUIDELINES FOR SOUPS

Soups are known for their ease of cooking, and they truly are one-pot meals. However, be aware of cooking time for each ingredient being added to the soup. Ingredients that take a while to cook or are often being used as aromatics to flavor the soup need to be added early in the simmering time, while vegetables that cook quickly should be added near the end. Soups gain flavor as they simmer (though no vegetarian soup benefits from hours on the stove), and the best way to tell when a soup is ready is by tasting and seasoning along the way. When the soup has developed lots of flavor, it is ready to serve.

Thick soups, such as those made with legumes or starchy vegetables, may continue to thicken during cooking, storage, and reheating. It may be necessary to thin a soup with some warm broth to bring it back to the correct consistency. Cream soups should be about the same texture as heavy cream, and puréed soups are usually a bit thicker than that.

Store leftover soup in an airtight container in the refrigerator for no more than 5 days or in the freezer for up to 2 months (see specific recipes for more detailed storage instructions). When reheating soup, heat only the amount you'll need—the soup will stay fresher longer.

# BROTHY SOUPS

Broth-based soups are often called "hearty broths" because they have more flavor and substance than broths alone. Vegetables are cooked in the soup until tender, infusing the broth with their flavor. Grains, legumes, and pasta are often added for body and texture. These soups can be made with a single type of vegetable or multiple varieties. Vegetable juices can also be added to these soups for more flavor. Most soups in this category are cooked in one pot from beginning to end. Use a large pot that is taller than it is wide, which will allow the soup to cook evenly at a constant simmer.

## Brothy Soup Method

1. Sweat or sauté the vegetables.

2. Add the liquid. Bring the soup to a boil, skimming as needed.

3. Add the herbs or other seasonings and bring to a simmer.

4. Add the remaining ingredients at proper intervals to ensure proper doneness.

5. Season, garnish, and serve.

## CLEAR SOUPS VERSUS CLOUDY SOUPS

Hearty broths lack the clarity of broths or consommés because vegetables are cooked directly in the broth, giving it a cloudier appearance. The inclusion of beans, grains, or pasta will also affect the color and cloudiness of soups. If cooked directly in the soup, they will release their starches into the soup as they become tender. If you're hoping for a clearer soup, cook those ingredients separately and add toward the end of simmering time.

## THICKENING A THIN SOUP

If a soup becomes too thin, it can easily be thickened. One easy method is to thicken with a slurry of starch (such as cornstarch) that has been diluted with a few tablespoons of broth. Add the slurry while the soup simmers and stir constantly as the soup thickens, 2 to 3 minutes.

MAKING BROTHY SOUPS: *Caramelize onions until deep golden brown before adding broth to the soup.*

*The onions contribute to the golden color of the finished soup.*

## SKIMMING A SOUP

As soups simmer, impurities from the ingredients can float to the top, creating a sort of foam on the surface. Removing the impurities will make a clearer soup and will also keep the soup fresh for a longer period of time, as the impurities can promote spoilage. Use a skimmer, a tool with a large, flat head punctured with holes, to gently lift any impurities from the surface.

MAKING CREAM SOUPS: Add flour, the thickening agent, to the aromatics and cook briefly before adding the liquid.

After the soup has thickened, stir in warm cream to give the soup its silky texture.

# CREAM SOUPS

Cream soups can be made in a variety of different ways. Traditionally, cream soups were made with a thickened milk sauce (béchamel) and finished with heavy cream, or with a thickened stock-based sauce (velouté) and finished with a liaison of cream and egg yolks. Today, a cream soup can simply be a soup that is finished with heavy cream. No matter the method, these soups have a decadent flavor and a silky-smooth texture. Generally they are made with a single type of vegetable. Be sure to cut the vegetables uniformly so they cook evenly, and use a large pot with a heavy bottom to avoid scorching.

## Cream Soup Method

1. Sweat the aromatic vegetables. Add the flour and cook until the floury taste is gone.

2. Add the liquid and bring to a boil.

3. Add the herbs or other seasonings and the main ingredient. Bring to a simmer, skimming as needed.

4. Cook until the main ingredient is very tender.

5. Strain the soup, purée the solids, and reincorporate the purée into the liquid.

6. Add the cream, season, and serve.

# PURÉE SOUPS

Purée soups are thicker than cream soups. Purée soups are usually made with legumes or vegetables, and depending on the main ingredient the texture can be smooth or on the coarser side. The soup can be puréed totally, but often some of the main ingredient is left whole for added texture and flavor.

If the soup is legume-based, first sort through the legumes and remove any rotten pieces, stones, or other debris. Rinse the legumes under running water. Soak the legumes as directed in the chart on pages 131–32. If the soup is vegetable-based, cut the vegetables uniformly to ensure even cooking. Use a large pot with a heavy bottom to avoid scorching and hot spots.

## Purée Soup Method

1. Sweat the aromatic vegetables.

2. Add the liquid. Bring to a boil.

3. Add the herbs or other seasonings and the main ingredient. Cook until the main ingredient is tender.

4. Strain the soup, purée all or part of the solids, and reincorporate the purée and any solids into the liquid.

5. Season, garnish, and serve.

MAKING PURÉE SOUPS: An immersion blender is the best way to purée a soup. It simplifies the process, allowing the soup to stay in the same pot, and helps prevent potential burns from steam or splashes.

The finished texture of a purée soup should be thick enough to coat a spoon.

# Butternut Squash Soup with Coconut Milk and Ginger

*This soup combines the subtle flavors of ginger and lemongrass with creamy butternut squash.*

1 very large butternut squash (about 3 pounds), halved lengthwise and seeded

Salt and freshly ground black pepper, as needed

2 tbsp unsalted butter

½ cup sliced leek (white and light green parts)

½ cup sliced yellow onion

2 cloves garlic, minced

1 quart Vegetable Broth (page 287)

2 sprigs thyme

1 bay leaf

1 stalk lemongrass, split lengthwise

⅓ cup unsweetened coconut milk

⅓ cup minced fresh ginger

**GARNISH**

¼ cup crème fraîche, as needed

Chopped chives, as needed

1. Preheat the oven to 300°F.

2. Season the cut side of the squash with salt and pepper. Roast the squash until the flesh is tender and lightly browned, 40 to 45 minutes. When it is cool enough to handle, remove the flesh and discard the skin. Set aside.

3. In a large soup pot, heat the butter over medium heat. Add the leeks and onions and sweat until translucent, 4 to 5 minutes. Add the garlic and sauté until translucent, about 1 minute more.

4. Add the broth, thyme, bay leaf, and lemongrass. Reduce heat to medium low, and simmer until the vegetables are completely tender and broth has become rich and flavorful, 20 to 25 minutes.

5. Remove and discard the thyme, bay leaf, and lemongrass. Add the roasted squash and use an immersion blender to blend until smooth, or working in batches, combine the squash and liquid in a blender or food processor and process until smooth.

6. If necessary, return the soup to the pot. Bring to a simmer. Stir in the coconut milk and ginger, and simmer for 4 to 5 minutes, until heated through.

7. Ladle into warm bowls and garnish with a dollop of crème fraîche and a sprinkling of chives.

**MAKES ABOUT 2 QUARTS**

*Butternut Squash Soup with Coconut Milk and Ginger*

# Tomatillo, Poblano, and Chickpea Soup

*Use a good-quality white wine in this soup to bring out the flavors of the tomatillos and poblano chiles. Something slightly sweet and fruity is recommended, such as Riesling or Gewürztraminer.*

1 tbsp olive oil

1 cup thinly sliced onions

2 poblano chiles, seeded and thinly sliced

2 cloves garlic, minced

1½ cups chopped tomatillos

¼ tsp fennel seeds

¼ tsp ground cumin

¼ tsp ground coriander

1 tsp dried oregano

Pinch ground cinnamon

1 cup diced tomatoes, fresh or canned

2 quarts Vegetable Broth (page 287)

¾ cup white wine

1 cup cooked chickpeas (see chart, page 131)

Salt and freshly ground black pepper, as needed

GARNISH

Chopped cilantro, as needed

Diced avocado, as needed

Lime wedges, as needed

1. In a large soup pot, heat the olive oil over medium heat. Add the onions, poblanos, and garlic. Sauté until the onions are translucent, 4 to 5 minutes.

2. Add the tomatillos, fennel seeds, cumin, coriander, oregano, cinnamon, tomatoes, broth, and wine. Simmer gently until everything is tender and combined, 10 to 15 minutes.

3. Add the chickpeas and season generously with salt and pepper. Heat through.

4. Serve garnished with cilantro, avocado, and a wedge of lime.

**MAKES ABOUT 2 QUARTS**

# Black Bean, Quinoa, and Corn Chili

*Adding a grain such as quinoa makes chili even heartier. It cooks quickly, which makes this a great chili to make with short notice.*

2 tbsp canola oil

2 medium red onions, diced

2 red bell peppers, diced

2 cloves garlic, minced

3 cups canned crushed tomatoes

¾ tsp ground cumin

¾ tsp chili powder

1 tsp dried oregano

1 tsp dried thyme

2⅔ cups cooked black beans
(see chart, page 131)

2 cups corn kernels (fresh or thawed frozen)

2⅔ cups cooked quinoa (see chart, page 175)

Salt and freshly ground black pepper, as needed

½ cup chopped cilantro

GARNISH

Shredded Monterey Jack cheese, as needed

Thinly sliced green onions, as needed

Sour cream, as needed

1. In a large pot, heat the oil over medium heat. Add the onions and sauté until translucent, 4 to 5 minutes.

2. Add the red peppers and sauté until tender, 3 to 5 minutes more. Add the garlic and sauté until aromatic, about 1 minute more.

3. Add the tomatoes, cumin, chili powder, oregano, and thyme. Bring to a boil, reduce the heat to low, and simmer to develop flavor, about 15 minutes.

4. Add the beans, corn, and cooked quinoa. Simmer until the quinoa is tender, about 5 minutes. Season with salt and pepper.

5. Just before serving, stir in the cilantro. Serve warm, garnished with cheese, green onions, and sour cream.

**MAKES ABOUT 2 QUARTS**

VARIATION: **Red Bean and Chickpea Chili:** Replace the red peppers with poblano chiles. After the onions, chiles, and garlic have been sautéed, add 2 cups beer. Simmer to reduce the mixture until almost dry. Replace the black beans with an equal amount of red beans and the quinoa with an equal amount of cooked chickpeas. Finish as above. Garnish with salsa and guacamole.

Red Bean and Chickpea Chili page 63
(front), and Vegetable Chili (rear)

# Vegetable Chili

*Chili is all about layering flavors. Taste this dish along the way to see if it needs more spices.*

½ cup sun-dried tomatoes, medium dice

2 dried Anaheim chiles, toasted, seeded, and chopped

1½ cups tomato purée

3 cups Vegetable Broth (page 287)

½ bunch cilantro, coarsely chopped

2 tbsp honey

3 tbsp red wine vinegar

1 tsp ground cumin

1 tsp chili powder

2 cloves garlic, minced

2 tbsp grapeseed or canola oil

1¼ cups diced onions

⅔ cup cooked black beans (see chart, page 131)

⅔ cup cooked pinto beans (see chart, page 132)

⅔ cup cooked hominy (see chart, page 175)

Salt and freshly ground black pepper, as needed

GARNISH

Shredded Monterey Jack cheese, *queso Chihuahua,* or *queso fresco,* as needed

Sour cream, as needed

Chopped cilantro, as needed

Minced raw jalapeño or serrano chiles, as needed

1. In a large soup pot, combine the sun-dried tomatoes, chiles, tomato purée, broth, cilantro, honey, vinegar, cumin, chili powder, and garlic. Bring to a simmer and cook until good flavor develops, about 45 minutes.

2. Let the mixture cool slightly and purée in a food processor or blender until smooth. Set aside.

3. In a large soup pot, heat the oil over medium heat. Add the onions and sauté until transparent, 4 to 5 minutes. Add the black beans, pinto beans, and hominy. Stir in the puréed tomato mixture, and bring the chili to a simmer. Season with salt and pepper.

4. Garnish with cheese, sour cream, and cilantro. For added spiciness, top with chiles. Serve immediately.

**MAKES ABOUT 2 QUARTS**

# Roasted Eggplant and Garlic Soup with Aged Jack Cheese

*This soup tastes almost like baba ghanoush (a Mediterranean eggplant spread) in soup form. Get creative with the garnishes to create a truly special soup.*

2½ pounds eggplant (2 medium)

Kosher salt, as needed

2 tbsp extra-virgin olive oil

1 medium yellow onion, coarsely chopped

2 stalks celery, coarsely chopped

1 medium carrot, coarsely chopped

2 medium leeks, coarsely chopped (green and light green parts)

¼ cup all-purpose flour

2 quarts Vegetable Broth (page 287)

1 sprig thyme

1 sprig rosemary

1 sprig oregano

1 bay leaf

Peeled cloves from 2 heads Roasted Garlic (page 315)

1 large russet potato, peeled and diced

½ cup tahini

¾ cup heavy cream

Salt and freshly ground black pepper, as needed

## GARNISH

Toasted pine nuts, as needed

Thinly sliced roasted red peppers, as needed

Grated dry Jack cheese, as needed

Chopped fresh flat-leaf parsley, as needed

1. Preheat the oven to 350°F.

2. Cut the eggplant in half lengthwise. Sprinkle each half with salt. Roast the eggplant, cut side up, until soft in the middle, 15 to 20 minutes.

3. When cool enough to handle, use a spoon to scrape the flesh away from the skin. Set aside the flesh and discard the skin.

4. In a large soup pot, heat the oil over medium heat. Add the onions, celery, carrot, and leeks, and sweat, covered, until the onions are translucent, 4 to 5 minutes.

5. Sprinkle the flour over the vegetables, and cook, about 3 minutes.

6. Add the broth, thyme, rosemary, oregano, and bay leaf. Whisk to a smooth consistency. Add the garlic, potatoes, and roasted eggplant flesh. Simmer until the potatoes are tender, 15 to 20 minutes.

7. Remove from the heat and let cool slightly. Remove and discard the herb sprigs and bay leaf. Working in batches if necessary, process the mixture with the tahini in a food processor or blender until smooth. Or add the tahini and blend in the pot with an immersion blender until smooth.

8. Transfer the mixture back to the soup pot, if necessary. Stir in the cream and bring the soup back to a simmer. Season with salt and pepper.

9. Serve the soup in warm bowls, garnished with pine nuts, roasted peppers, cheese, and parsley.

**MAKES ABOUT 2 QUARTS**

# Sweet Potato and Peanut Soup

*This soup has the perfect balance of sweet and savory, combining the delicious natural flavor of sweet potatoes with salty peanuts.*

2 tbsp unsalted butter

1 cup diced celery

1 cup diced onion

1 cup thinly sliced leeks (white and light green parts)

2 cloves garlic, minced

6 cups Vegetable Broth (page 287)

3 medium sweet potatoes, peeled and thinly sliced

1 cinnamon stick

3 tbsp peanut butter

⅓ cup heavy cream

Salt and freshly ground black pepper, as needed

GARNISH (ENOUGH FOR 8 SERVINGS)

½ cup heavy cream

2 tbsp molasses

Pinch freshly grated nutmeg

Salt, as needed

½ cup chopped toasted peanuts

1. In a large soup pot, melt the butter over medium heat. Add the celery, onions, leeks, and garlic and cook until the onions are translucent, 4 to 5 minutes.

2. Add the broth, sweet potatoes, cinnamon stick, and peanut butter, and simmer until the sweet potatoes are very tender, 15 to 20 minutes.

3. Remove from the heat and let cool slightly. Remove and discard the cinnamon.

4. Working in batches if necessary, process the soup in a food processor or blender until smooth. Or blend in the pot with an immersion blender until smooth.

5. Transfer the mixture back to the pot, if necessary. Stir in the cream and season with salt and pepper. Keep warm over low heat.

6. To make the garnish, in a medium bowl, combine the cream, molasses, and nutmeg and whisk to form medium peaks. Season with salt.

7. Serve the soup in warm bowls, with a dollop of molasses cream and a sprinkling of peanuts.

**MAKES ABOUT 2 QUARTS**

*Pea and Mint Soup with Lemon Cream*

# Pea and Mint Soup with Lemon Cream

*This soup is smooth, delicate, and decadent, and it can be eaten warm or chilled—perfect for an early spring lunch.*

2 tbsp unsalted butter

½ cup minced shallots

2 cloves garlic, minced

4 cups green peas, fresh blanched or thawed frozen

1 quart Vegetable Broth (page 287)

¼ cup chopped mint

Salt and freshly ground black pepper, as needed

½ cup heavy cream

Grated zest and juice of 1 lemon

1. In a large pot, melt the butter over medium heat. Add the shallots and garlic and sauté until tender, 2 to 3 minutes.

2. Add the peas, broth, and mint. Season with salt and pepper.

3. Bring the soup to a boil, reduce the heat to low, cover the pot, and simmer until the peas are tender, 10 to 15 minutes.

4. Working in batches if necessary, process the soup in a food processor or blender until smooth. Or blend in the pot with an immersion blender until smooth.

5. Transfer the mixture back to the pot, if necessary. Season once more with salt and pepper. Keep warm over low heat.

6. In a medium bowl, whip the cream to soft peaks. Fold in the lemon juice and half of the zest. Season with salt and pepper. Serve the soup in warm bowls topped with a dollop of lemon cream and a sprinkling of the remaining zest.

**MAKES ABOUT 2 QUARTS**

# Mediterranean Vegetable "Bouillabaisse"

Bouillabaisse is traditionally a Provençal fish stew flavored with a variety of aromatic vegetables and herbs. In this recipe, vegetables play the starring role, stewing together to create the same Mediterranean flavors.

## BROTH

2 tbsp olive oil

1 cup diced yellow onions

⅔ cup diced carrots

5 cloves garlic, crushed

¾ cup diced celery

1 cup diced fennel

2 cups diced mushroom stems from caps used later in recipe

½ cup white wine

6 cups Vegetable Broth (page 287)

1½ tsp fennel seeds

3 sprigs basil

3 sprigs flat-leaf parsley

2 sprigs thyme

1 bay leaf

Salt and freshly ground black pepper, as needed

## BOUILLABAISSE

5 medium plum (Roma) tomatoes, halved lengthwise

1 medium waxy potato

Olive oil, as needed

1 cup peeled cipollini onions

1 bell pepper (any color), finely diced

1 cup finely diced fennel

3 tbsp minced garlic

1 cup diced mushroom caps

1 cup diced zucchini

1½ cups halved cherry tomatoes

3 tbsp chopped flat-leaf parsley

3 tbsp chopped basil

## GARNISH

Pesto (page 297), as needed

1. To make the broth, in a large pot, heat the oil over medium heat. Add the onions, carrots, and garlic, and sauté until lightly browned, 4 to 5 minutes. Add the celery, fennel, and mushroom stems, and cook until softened, 5 to 6 minutes more.

2. Add the wine. Simmer over medium heat until only about half the liquid remains.

3. Add the vegetable broth, fennel seeds, basil, parsley, thyme, and bay leaf and season with salt and pepper. Simmer over low heat until good, full flavor has developed, about 1 hour.

4. To make the bouillabaisse, heat the broiler to high. Place the tomatoes cut side up on a baking sheet and broil until lightly browned. Coarsely chop and set aside.

5. In a small saucepan, cover the potato with cold water. Bring to a boil and simmer until tender, about 12 minutes. Drain, cool briefly, peel, dice ½-inch cubes, and set aside.

6. In a large sauté pan, heat the oil over medium heat. Add the cipollini onions, bell pepper, fennel, and 2 tbsp of the garlic. Sauté until onions and bell pepper are tender, 5 to 7 minutes. Add the mushroom caps and zucchini and sauté until mushrooms are tender, 3 to 5 minutes more.

7. Add the potato, broiled tomatoes, cherry tomatoes, and the remaining 1 tbsp of garlic. Sauté until the mixture is fragrant and heated through, about 2 minutes. Season well with salt and pepper. Stir in the chopped parsley and basil and keep warm.

8. When the broth has finished simmering, add the vegetable mixture. Simmer briefly to heat through, stirring to combine. Remove and discard the herb sprigs, and bay leaves. Serve immediately with a dollop of pesto.

**MAKES ABOUT 2 QUARTS**

# Potato, Leek, and Mushroom Soup

*Basic potato soup gets body and earthy flavor from the addition of mushrooms. Try this soup with a variety of root vegetables such as carrots and parsnips instead of potatoes.*

1 tbsp unsalted butter

2 medium leeks, thinly sliced (white and light green parts)

2 large russet potatoes, thinly sliced

2 quarts Mushroom Broth (page 287)

¼ cup heavy cream

¼ cup whole milk

1 to 2 tsp chopped rosemary, to taste

Salt and freshly ground black pepper, as needed

**GARNISH (ENOUGH FOR 4 TO 8 SERVINGS)**

1 tbsp unsalted butter

1 cup thinly sliced mushrooms

1 medium leek, thinly sliced (white and light green parts)

Salt and freshly ground black pepper, as needed

1. In a large soup pot, melt the butter over medium heat. Add the leeks and sauté until tender, 3 to 4 minutes.

2. Add the potatoes and broth and bring to a simmer. Cook until the potatoes are tender and the soup is flavorful, 15 to 20 minutes.

3. Stir in the cream and milk.

4. Working in batches if necessary, process the soup in a food processor or blender until smooth. Or blend in the pot with an immersion blender until smooth.

5. Transfer the mixture back to the pot, if necessary. Stir in the rosemary and season with salt and pepper. Bring the soup back to a simmer.

6. To make the garnish, in a small sauté pan, melt the butter over medium heat. Add the mushrooms and leeks and sauté until very tender, 5 to 6 minutes. Season with salt and pepper.

7. Serve the soup in warm bowls, topped with the sautéed mushroom mixture.

**MAKES ABOUT 2 QUARTS**

Summer Vegetable Stew with Tomatoes, Olives, and Roasted Garlic Broth

# Summer Vegetable Stew with Tomatoes, Olives, and Roasted Garlic Broth

*For the best results, cut all of the vegetables to equal sizes that will fit in your spoon. After preparing the baby artichokes, place them in a medium bowl with water and add 1 tbsp lemon juice to keep them from turning brown.*

¼ cup olive oil

⅓ cup thinly sliced yellow onion

1 head Roasted Garlic (page 315)

3 tbsp tomato purée

⅔ cup white wine

6 cups Vegetable Broth (page 287)

2 fresh flat-leaf parsley stems

1 bay leaf

Salt and freshly ground black pepper, as needed

1¾ cups diced red-skin potatoes

4 baby artichokes, trimmed and diced

11 baby carrots, diced

¾ cup diced zucchini

3 small bulbs fennel, thinly sliced (about 4 cups)

10 ounces green beans, trimmed and diced (about 3 cups)

⅔ cup diced plum (Roma) tomatoes

3 tbsp basil chiffonade

2 tbsp chopped rosemary

GARNISH (ENOUGH FOR 8 SERVINGS)

¼ cup medium dice sun-dried tomatoes

¼ cup pitted Kalamata olives

2 tbsp extra-virgin olive oil

1. In a medium pot, heat 1 tbsp of the olive oil over medium heat. Add the onions, cover, and sweat until tender, 6 to 7 minutes.

2. Add the garlic, tomato purée, and wine and lower heat to a simmer. Simmer until the mixture has reduced by half, about 10 minutes.

3. Add the broth, parsley stems, and bay leaf and simmer until it has developed good flavor, about 1 hour. Strain and discard the solids. Season with salt and pepper and keep warm.

4. Meanwhile, preheat the oven to 350°F. In a large bowl, combine the potatoes, artichokes, carrots, zucchini, fennel, green beans, and tomatoes. Add the remaining olive oil, the basil, and rosemary, season with salt and pepper, and toss to combine.

5. Roast the vegetables until lightly browned and tender, about 30 minutes.

6. Add the roasted vegetables to the broth and keep warm.

7. To make the garnish, combine all the ingredients in a food processor or blender and process to a finely chopped mixture.

8. Serve the stew in warm bowls with a dollop of the tomato-olive purée on top.

**MAKES ABOUT 2 QUARTS**

# Matzo Ball Soup

*Using tofu to make matzo balls makes this soup filling and perfect as a main course. Make sure to plan ahead; the batter for the matzoh needs to be refrigerated overnight.*

**MATZO BALLS**

¼ cup olive oil

5 tbsp minced yellow onion

1 cup matzo meal

½ tsp kosher salt

¼ tsp freshly ground black pepper

¾ cup crumbled drained firm tofu

⅓ cup Vegetable Broth (page 287)

3 tbsp chopped fresh flat-leaf parsley

**SOUP**

1 tbsp olive oil

1 medium yellow onion, diced

1 **medium** carrot, diced

1 stalk celery, diced

1 bunch green onions, chopped (white and green parts)

6 cups Vegetable Broth (page 287)

2 tbsp chopped fresh flat-leaf parsley

1 tsp chopped dill

Salt and freshly ground black pepper, as needed

1. To make the matzo balls, in a small sauté pan, heat 2 tbsp of the oil over medium heat. Add 3 tbsp of the onion and cook until translucent, 4 to 5 minutes.

2. In a medium bowl, mix the matzo meal, sautéed and raw onion, salt, and pepper to combine.

3. In a food processor or blender, combine the tofu, broth, parsley, and remaining oil until smooth.

4. Add the tofu mixture to the matzo meal mixture and mix to combine. Cover the bowl and refrigerate the batter overnight.

5. To make the soup, in a large soup pot, heat the oil over medium heat. Add the onion, carrot, and celery, and cook until the vegetables are tender, 4 to 5 minutes.

6. Add the green onions and cook until they are softened, 2 to 3 minutes more.

7. Add the broth, parsley, and dill. Season with salt and pepper. Bring to a boil, reduce the heat, and simmer until the vegetables are very tender, about 30 minutes.

8. Meanwhile, use a scoop or your hands to form the batter into approximately 8 to 12 balls. Add the matzo balls to the soup and simmer until they float to the surface and are cooked through, 15 to 20 minutes. Serve immediately.

**MAKES ABOUT 2 QUARTS**

# Vegetable "Cioppino"

*Cioppino is a flavorful tomato-based brothy soup. This vegetarian version has the same incredible flavors as the traditional version typically made with seafood.*

3 tbsp olive oil

1 cup minced yellow onion

½ cup thinly sliced green onions (white and green parts)

1 cup diced green bell pepper

½ cup diced fennel

Salt and freshly ground black pepper, as needed

1 clove garlic, minced

4½ cups diced tomatoes

1½ cups Vegetable Broth (page 287)

⅓ cup dry white wine

1 cup tomato purée

1 bay leaf

½ tsp chopped thyme

1 tsp red pepper flakes

8 baby carrots

2 cups corn kernels (fresh or thawed frozen)

½ cup cooked chickpeas (see chart, page 131)

½ pound drained firm tofu, cubed

GARNISH

3 tbsp chopped basil

8 Crostini (page 15)

1. In a large soup pot, heat the olive oil over medium heat. Add the onion, green onions, green pepper, and fennel and season with salt and pepper. Sauté until the onions are translucent, 7 to 8 minutes.

2. Add the garlic and sauté until aromatic, about 1 minute more.

3. Add the tomatoes, broth, wine, tomato purée, bay leaf, thyme, and pepper flakes. Cover the pot and simmer until flavorful, about 20 minutes. Remove and discard the bay leaf.

4. Meanwhile, cook the carrots in lightly salted water until barely tender. Drain.

5. Add the corn, chickpeas, carrots, and tofu to the soup. Simmer until everything is tender, 8 to 10 minutes.

6. Ladle into warm bowls. Garnish each portion with basil and a crostino.

**MAKES ABOUT 2 QUARTS**

NOTE: To add a little taste of the sea and some extra nutrition to this stew, add a few tablespoons, minced, of your favorite dried seaweed variety in Step 3.

# White Bean and Tomato Soup with Herb-Tomato Gougères

*White beans have an incredible creamy texture that makes them seem decadent, and their role in this soup is no exception.*

2 tbsp olive oil

1 cup diced onions

¾ cup diced carrots

½ cup diced celery

3 cloves garlic, minced

⅔ cup white wine

7 cups Vegetable Broth (page 287)

1 cup tomato juice

1½ cups diced tomatoes

1 bay leaf

2 sprigs thyme

2 cups cooked white beans
(see chart, page 131)

⅓ cup chopped fresh flat-leaf parsley

¼ cup chopped basil

GARNISH

Good-quality olive oil, as needed

Herb-Tomato Gougères (page 259), as needed

1. In a large pot, heat the oil over medium heat. Add the onions, carrots, and celery and sauté until all are lightly browned and tender, 5 to 7 minutes.

2. Add the garlic and sauté until aromatic, about 1 minute more.

3. Add the wine. Simmer over medium heat until only about half the liquid remains.

4. Add the broth, tomato juice, tomatoes, bay leaf, and thyme. Bring to a boil, reduce heat to low, and simmer until good flavor has developed, 15 to 20 minutes.

5. Remove and discard the bay leaf and thyme. Add the beans. Simmer to heat through.

6. Just before serving, stir in the parsley and basil, and simmer 1 to 2 minutes more.

7. Serve in warm bowls, drizzled with olive oil and topped with 2 to 3 gougères per serving.

**MAKES ABOUT 2 QUARTS**

White Bean and Tomato Soup with Herb-Tomato Gougères

# Green and Yellow Split Pea Soup

*Split peas make a very hearty, filling soup. Feel free to use just one kind of split pea if you don't have access to both colors, or try substituting your favorite kind of lentils.*

2 tbsp olive oil

1¼ cups diced yellow onion

1 cup diced carrot

1 stalk celery, diced

3 cloves garlic, minced

1 potato, peeled and diced

1¼ cups green split peas, rinsed

1 cup yellow split peas, rinsed

2 quarts Vegetable Broth (page 287)

1 bay leaf

1 sprig thyme

1 sprig rosemary

Salt and freshly ground black pepper, as needed

1. In a large soup pot, heat the oil over medium heat. Add the onion, carrot, celery, and garlic and cook until the vegetables are tender, about 5 minutes.

2. Add the potato, split peas, broth, bay leaf, thyme, and rosemary and season with salt and pepper. Bring the soup to a boil over medium heat. Reduce the heat to a simmer and cook, stirring occasionally, until the soup is very thick and the split peas are very soft, 20 to 30 minutes.

3. Remove and discard the bay leaf, thyme, and rosemary. Soup may be left as a coarse-textured purée or blended to your favorite texture using an immersion blender. Serve hot.

**MAKES ABOUT 2 QUARTS**

# Hearty Black Bean Soup

*This soup is called "hearty" for a reason—it's a thick, chunky soup that gets lots of extra flavor from a variety of vegetables. Try puréeing the soup for a silkier texture.*

2 tbsp olive oil

1 cup diced yellow onions

2 cups thinly sliced leeks (white and light green parts)

1 red bell pepper, diced

1 green bell pepper, diced

1 jalapeño, seeded, minced

¾ cup diced celery

3 cloves garlic, minced

2⅓ cups cooked black beans (see chart, page 131)

5 cups Vegetable Broth (page 287)

1 poblano chile, roasted, peeled and seeded, diced

2 sprigs thyme

1 sprig oregano

1 bay leaf

1 tbsp sherry vinegar

Salt and freshly ground black pepper, as needed

GARNISH

¼ cup diced fresh tomatoes

Sour cream, as needed

Chopped cilantro, as needed

1. In a large pot, heat the oil over medium heat. Add the onions, leeks, red and green peppers, jalapeño, celery, and garlic. Sauté until lightly softened, 3 to 4 minutes.

2. Stir in the black beans and broth. Add the poblano chile, thyme, oregano, and bay leaf. Reduce the heat to low and simmer the mixture until the soup has good flavor and has become slightly thickened from the starch in the beans, 25 to 30 minutes. The beans will be tender and broken down and the vegetables will be tender but still have some texture.

3. Stir in the vinegar and season with salt and pepper.

4. Remove and discard the thyme, oregano, and bay leaf. Serve in warm bowls, garnished with tomatoes, sour cream, and cilantro.

**MAKES ABOUT 2 QUARTS**

Asparagus-Edamame Bisque

# Asparagus-Edamame Bisque

This creamy soup is silky-smooth, with light, delicate flavors just perfect for those early spring days. Since frozen soybeans are often more available than fresh, it's perfectly fine to use them in this soup.

2 tbsp olive oil

2 cups thinly sliced leeks (white and light green parts)

2 shallots, minced

2 cloves garlic, minced

6 cups Vegetable Broth (page 287)

1 cup rice

2½ cups shelled edamame (cooked fresh or frozen)

1 pound asparagus spears, cut into 1-inch pieces, tips reserved for garnish

Salt and freshly ground black pepper, as needed

½ cup heavy cream

GARNISH

Reserved asparagus tips, blanched or sautéed in butter

Chopped chives, as needed

1. In a large soup pot, heat the oil over medium heat. Add the leeks, shallots, and garlic, and cook until tender, about 5 minutes.

2. Add the broth, rice, and edamame and bring to a boil. Reduce the heat and simmer the soup until the rice begins to get tender, about 15 minutes.

3. Add the asparagus pieces, season with salt and pepper, and bring back to a boil. Reduce the heat to a simmer, cover the pot, and cook until the vegetables are tender, 10 to 12 minutes.

4. Working in batches if necessary, process the soup in a food processor or blender until smooth. Strain the soup through a fine-mesh sieve and discard any solids.

5. Return the soup to the pot, stir in the cream, and heat through.

6. Serve in warm bowls, garnished with chives and the reserved blanched asparagus tips.

**MAKES ABOUT 2 QUARTS**

VARIATION: **Zucchini and Butter Bean Bisque:** Replace the leeks with an equal amount of sliced yellow onions, the edamame with butter beans or lima beans, and the asparagus stalks with 3 medium zucchini, coarsely chopped. Garnish the soup with finely chopped roasted red peppers.

# Cream of Vegetable Soup

*This is a basic recipe that can be made with any of your favorite vegetables—tomatoes, asparagus, broccoli, peas, or even with an assortment of many varieties. Set aside some of the vegetable to sprinkle on top for garnish.*

¼ cup olive oil

1 medium yellow onion, diced

1 medium carrot, diced

1 stalk celery, diced

1 medium leek (white and light green parts), thinly sliced

2 pounds vegetables, peeled if necessary and diced (see recipe note for suggestions)

¼ cup all-purpose flour

6 cups Vegetable Broth (page 287)

½ cup heavy cream, warm

Salt and freshly ground black pepper, as needed

1. In a large soup pot, heat the oil over medium heat. Add the onion, carrot, celery, leeks, and diced vegetables. Cook, stirring frequently, until the onion is translucent, 6 to 8 minutes.

2. Add the flour and cook, stirring frequently with a wooden spoon, about 5 minutes.

3. Add the broth gradually, whisking well to work out any lumps. Bring the soup to a simmer and cook until flavorful and thickened, about 45 minutes. Stir frequently and skim as needed.

4. Strain the soup, reserving the solids and the broth separately. Purée the solids in a blender or food processor until smooth, adding broth as needed to facilitate puréeing. Or purée in the pot using an immersion blender.

5. Combine the purée with enough of the reserved broth to achieve the consistency of heavy cream. Strain the soup through a fine-mesh sieve, if desired. Return the soup to the pot and bring to a simmer.

6. Heat the cream to a simmer, and stir the cream into the puréed soup. Season with salt and pepper. Serve immediately.

**MAKES ABOUT 2 QUARTS**

# Cheddar and Beer Soup

This soup is a real crowd pleaser—it has great flavor. Be sure to use a good-quality sharp Cheddar cheese. Its flavor will be best complemented by a lager or black and tan–style beer and some crusty rye bread. This soup does not store or reheat well.

¼ cup grapeseed or canola oil

1 cup all-purpose flour

3 cups Vegetable Broth (page 287)

2 tbsp unsalted butter

1 cup minced yellow onion

1 cup diced mushrooms

½ cup diced celery

½ cup diced carrots

1 clove garlic, minced

One 12-ounce bottle beer

2 tbsp dry mustard

6 cups grated sharp Cheddar (about 1½ pounds)

¾ cup heavy cream, warm

Tabasco sauce, as needed

Salt and freshly ground black pepper, as needed

1. In a 1-gallon soup pot, combine the oil and flour over medium heat. Cook, stirring constantly, to make a pale golden roux, about 12 minutes.

2. Gradually add the broth, whisking constantly to work out any lumps. Simmer until the soup has good flavor and a velvety texture, about 45 minutes.

3. Just before you start the next step, heat a medium-size sauté pan over medium heat. Add the butter, and when melted add the onions, mushrooms, celery, carrots, and garlic, and cook until the vegetables are tender, 6 to 8 minutes. Keep warm.

4. While the vegetables are sautéing, whisk the beer and dry mustard together. Pour into the simmering soup, whisking constantly. The beer will foam up a bit—don't worry!

5. Add the cheese into the soup, and stir constantly until the cheese is melted and well incorporated. Stir in the cream, and season with Tabasco, salt, and pepper.

6. Stir the vegetables into the soup and serve immediately.

**MAKES ABOUT 2 QUARTS**

# Corn Chowder

*Nothing beats a comforting, warm chowder. Try spicing it up by adding a minced jalapeño or a pinch of red pepper flakes.*

4 tbsp unsalted butter

½ cup diced onion

¾ cup diced celery

⅓ cup diced green bell pepper

⅓ cup diced red bell pepper

⅓ cup all-purpose flour

3 cups Vegetable Broth (page 287)

2¾ cups corn kernels (fresh or thawed frozen)

2½ cups peeled, diced russet potatoes

1 bay leaf

½ cup heavy cream, warm

½ cup whole milk, warm

Salt and freshly ground black pepper, as needed

Tabasco sauce, as needed

1. In a large soup pot, melt the butter over medium heat. Add the onions, celery, and red and green peppers, and cook until they are tender and the onions are translucent, 4 to 5 minutes.

2. Add the flour and cook, stirring, until the floury taste is gone but it has no color, about 3 minutes.

3. Add 1 cup of the broth and stir until the mixture is well combined. Add the remaining broth, stirring to ensure there are no lumps. Bring to a simmer and cook until the soup thickens, 30 to 40 minutes.

4. In a food processor or blender, purée half of the corn and add it to the soup with the potatoes. Add the remaining corn kernels and the bay leaf. Simmer until the potatoes are tender, about 15 minutes.

5. Stir the cream and milk into the soup and bring the soup to a simmer. Season with salt, pepper, and Tabasco. Remove and discard the bay leaf before serving.

**MAKES ABOUT 2 QUARTS**

Corn Chowder

# Chickpea and Fennel Soup

*The sharp anise flavor of fennel and the creamy, subtle flavor of chickpeas are a great combination. Try replacing the pasta with rice or a cooked grain such as farro or barley.*

2 tbsp olive oil

1 cup diced yellow onion

4 garlic cloves, minced

1 medium fennel bulb, diced

3 cups cooked chickpeas
(see chart, page 131)

One 14.5-ounce can diced tomatoes

5 cups Vegetable Broth (page 287)

1 tsp fennel seeds

¼ tsp red pepper flakes

1 tbsp chopped fresh flat-leaf parsley

1 tbsp chopped rosemary

Salt and freshly ground black pepper, as needed

½ cup short tubular pasta, such as tubetti or ditalini

1. In a large soup pot, heat the oil over medium heat. Add the onion, garlic, and diced fennel, and cook until the vegetables are tender, 5 to 6 minutes.

2. Add the chickpeas, tomatoes, broth, fennel seeds, pepper flakes, parsley, and rosemary. Season with salt and pepper.

3. Bring the soup to a boil, reduce the heat, and simmer until good flavor develops, about 30 minutes.

4. Add the pasta and cook until it is tender, 6 to 8 minutes. Serve in warm bowls.

**MAKES ABOUT 2 QUARTS**

# Collard Green Soup with Black-Eyed Peas and Rice

*All of your favorite Southern side dishes combine for a hearty, healthy soup.*

Salt, as needed

6 cups chopped collard greens, stems removed

Ice water, as needed

2 tbsp olive oil

1 medium yellow onion, chopped

5 cloves garlic, minced

5 cups Vegetable Broth (page 287)

Freshly ground black pepper, as needed

3 cups cooked black-eyed peas (see chart, page 131)

½ cup brown rice

1 tsp Tabasco sauce or as needed

1. Bring a large pot of salted water to a boil over high heat. Fill a large bowl with ice and water to make an ice water bath.

2. Cook the collard greens until tender and bright green, 2 to 3 minutes. Drain the greens and plunge them into the ice water to stop the cooking and cool. Drain thoroughly.

3. In a large soup pot, heat the oil over medium heat. Add the onion and garlic, and cook until the onions are translucent, about 5 minutes.

4. Add the broth and the collard greens, bring to a boil, adjust seasoning with salt and pepper, reduce the heat to low, and add the black-eyed peas and rice. Simmer until the rice is cooked, about 25 to 30 minutes. Season with Tabasco and serve.

**MAKES ABOUT 2 QUARTS**

VARIATION: **Bean and Escarole Soup:** Replace the collard greens with an equal amount of escarole. Do not precool the escarole. Replace the black-eyed peas with an equal amount of white beans. Omit the rice.

# Gazpacho Verde

*This green gazpacho is fresh and delicious, perfect in summer when tomatoes are at their ripest. Try adding other vegetables and herbs such as red peppers, jícama, parsley, and cilantro.*

**SOUP**

2 tbsp minced jalapeño

3 cups cored and cubed tomatoes

½ cup diced green bell pepper

1 cup diced green onion (white and green parts)

1 cup seeded and diced cucumber

1½ cups diced celery

½ cup chopped basil

1 tsp chopped tarragon

2 quarts Vegetable Broth (page 287)

2 tbsp olive oil

3 tbsp balsamic vinegar

Salt and freshly ground white pepper, as needed

Tabasco sauce, as needed

**GARNISH**

Garlic Croutons (page 315), as needed

1. Combine all the soup ingredients and refrigerate until well chilled, at least 30 minutes.

2. Working in batches if necessary, purée the soup in a blender or food processor until it is coarse but even in texture.

3. Serve in chilled bowls, garnished with croutons.

**MAKES ABOUT 3 QUARTS**

VARIATION: **Gazpacho Verde con Aguacate:** Purée 1 avocado into the gazpacho.

Gazpacho Verde (front), Garlic Croutons, page 315 (center), and Gazpacho Verde con Aguacate (rear)

# Caramelized French Onion Soup

*This soup is rich and deeply flavorful. To make a more traditional soup, ladle the soup into oven-safe bowls, top with bread and cheese, and broil until the cheese is golden and melted.*

3 tbsp olive oil

4 large sweet onions, such as Vidalia, thinly sliced

2 cloves garlic, minced

¼ cup Calvados or brandy (optional)

½ cup apple cider

5 cups Vegetable Broth (page 287)

½ tsp dried thyme

1 bay leaf

Salt and freshly ground black pepper, as needed

GARNISH

Baguette sliced approximately ½ inch thick, as needed

Grated Parmesan, as needed

Gruyère cheese, approximately ½ to ¾ cup shredded, as needed

1. In a large soup pot, heat the oil over medium heat. Add the onions and garlic. Cover and cook until beginning to soften, about 2 minutes. Uncover and continue to cook until the onions are very soft, begin to caramelize, and become a deep golden brown, about 15 to 20 minutes.

2. Stir in the Calvados, if using, then the cider, and reduce the liquids by half by gently simmering. Add the broth, thyme, and bay leaf and season with salt and pepper. Bring to a boil, then reduce heat to low and simmer, uncovered, for 45 minutes to 1 hour to allow the flavors to mingle.

3. When ready to serve, preheat the broiler. Arrange 2 bread slices per serving on a baking sheet and top with Parmesan and shredded Gruyère. Place under the broiler until toasted, about 1 minute.

4. Remove the bay leaf from the soup and discard. Ladle the soup into warm bowls, top with the toasted bread and cheese, and serve.

**MAKES ABOUT 2 QUARTS**

# Tom Yum

Tom Yum is a popular soup from Thailand, Malaysia, and Indonesia that is flavored with lemongrass, kaffir lime, and coconut milk. Look for these ingredients at Asian markets or specialty grocery stores—they really make the difference in this soup.

1 medium yellow onion, thinly sliced

2 tbsp minced lemongrass

2 tsp minced fresh ginger

1 tsp red chili paste

3 kaffir lime leaves

3 tbsp soy sauce

6 cups Vegetable Broth (page 287)

½ pound extra-firm tofu, drained and cut into ½-inch dice

2 cups halved cherry tomatoes

2 cups stemmed and thinly sliced shiitake mushrooms

3 tbsp chopped cilantro

1 tbsp fresh lime juice

4 green onions, chopped (white and green parts)

½ cup thin bias-cut snow peas

1 cup unsweetened coconut milk

GARNISH

Chopped cilantro, as needed

Chopped Thai basil, as needed, or Italian basil may be substituted

1. Combine the onion, lemongrass, ginger, chili paste, lime leaves, and soy sauce in a large soup pot. Cook over medium heat until fragrant, about 1 minute.

2. Add the broth. Bring to a boil, reduce the heat to low, and simmer until good flavor develops, 20 to 25 minutes.

3. Strain the broth through a fine-mesh sieve into a clean pot and discard the solids.

4. Add the tofu, tomatoes, mushrooms, cilantro, and lime juice to the broth. Bring to a simmer and cook until the vegetables are tender, 8 to 10 minutes. Add the green onions and snow peas and cook an additional 2 minutes.

5. Stir in the coconut milk and heat through. Serve garnished with cilantro and basil.

**MAKES ABOUT 2 QUARTS**

Tom Yum

Pozole Rojo (front) and Pozole Verde (rear)

# Pozole Rojo

*Pozole is a hearty soup made with hominy. Red pozole is given its color by ancho chiles. Look for dried chiles in the international section of your grocery store or at your local Latin American market.*

4 ancho chiles

2 tbsp grapeseed or canola oil

1 medium yellow onion, sliced thick

1⅓ cups diced tomatoes

2 cloves garlic, minced

3 cups Vegetable Broth (page 287)

2 cups cooked hominy (see chart, page 175)

½ tsp dried Mexican oregano

Salt, as needed

**GARNISH (ENOUGH FOR 8 SERVINGS)**

⅔ cup shredded green cabbage

4 radishes, thinly sliced

½ cup minced red onion

Lime wedges, as needed

1. In a dry cast-iron skillet over medium heat, lightly toast the chiles on both sides just until fragrant. Do not brown or char the chiles. Remove the stems and seeds. Place the chiles in a bowl and cover with warm water. Leave the chiles to soak for 20 to 30 minutes. Drain the chiles and set aside. Discard the soaking water.

2. In a large sauté pan, heat the oil over medium heat. Add the onion, tomatoes, and garlic. Cook until the onions are translucent, 4 to 5 minutes. Add the chiles.

3. In a food processor or blender, purée the mixture until smooth, adding broth as necessary.

4. Transfer the purée to a large soup pot. Add the remaining broth, bring to a simmer, and cook until good flavor develops, 8 to 10 minutes.

5. Stir in the hominy and oregano, season with salt, and simmer for 15 to 20 minutes or until flavor is rich.

6. Serve the soup in warm bowls, garnished with raw cabbage, radishes, and red onion, with lime wedges on the side.

**MAKES ABOUT 2 QUARTS**

VARIATION: **Pozole Verde:** Replace the ancho chiles with 1 to 2 minced serrano chiles, sautéing them with the onions. Replace the tomatoes with an equal amount of tomatillos, and add 2 tbsp lime juice, 2 tbsp chopped fresh flat-leaf parsley, and 3 tbsp chopped cilantro. Garnish the soup with minced red onion, diced avocado, and tortilla strips.

# Beet and Carrot Soup

*This colorful soup is both incredibly flavorful and very nutritious.*

2 beets, trimmed and scrubbed

2 tbsp olive oil, plus more as needed

Salt, as needed

3½ cups peeled and chopped carrots

1 medium yellow onion, chopped

1 medium leek, chopped (white
and light green parts)

2 cloves garlic

5 cups Vegetable Broth (page 287)

2 sprigs thyme

Salt and freshly ground black
pepper, as needed

GARNISH

Crumbled feta cheese, as needed

Chopped cilantro, as needed

1. Preheat the oven to 300°F. Rub the beets with a little olive oil and salt and wrap in aluminum foil. Roast until tender when pierced with a thin knife, 45 minutes to 1 hour. Open the foil and let rest until cool enough to handle.

2. Meanwhile, heat 2 tbsp oil in a large soup pot over medium heat. Add the carrots and cook until soft and light golden brown, 7 to 9 minutes.

3. Add the onions and leeks, cover, and sweat until they are translucent, 3 to 5 minutes more. Add the garlic and cook until fragrant, about 1 minute more. Add the broth and thyme.

4. Bring to a boil, reduce the heat to low, and simmer until good flavor develops, about 20 minutes. Remove the thyme.

5. Peel and coarsely chop the beets, Stir them into the soup. Working in batches if necessary, transfer the soup to a blender and purée until smooth. Or blend in the pot with an immersion blender until smooth.

6. Return the soup to the pot, if necessary. Warm over medium heat. Season with salt and pepper.

7. Serve in warm bowls, garnished with crumbled feta and a sprinkling of cilantro.

**MAKES ABOUT 2 QUARTS**

Salads and sandwiches are quick and simple to make, easy to eat, and both come in many forms. This chapter includes salads and sandwiches that use many different ingredients, textures, temperatures, and flavors, making them ideal for snacks, side dishes, or hearty main courses.

# SALADS AND SANDWICHES

4

# SALADS

Salads are incredibly versatile. Use fresh, seasonal produce and complement them with other ingredients or condiments that will amplify their flavor. The following are just a few types of salads, but the possibilities are truly endless.

## GREEN SALADS

These may also be called tossed, mixed, or garden salads, and are typically made of tender greens coated lightly with dressing. They can be garnished with almost anything ranging from vegetables to croutons to shredded cheese. Green salads offer a great opportunity to highlight the natural flavors and textures in such greens as spicy mustard greens, tender butterhead, and bitter frisée.

## VEGETABLE SALADS

Vegetable salads are slightly heartier. Cut vegetables into approximately the same size pieces for vegetable salads. If the salad is to be served cold, you may need to parcook and cool some of the more fibrous vegetables before you add them to the salad. Vegetables for warm salads may need to be cooked separately to ensure that they are all equally done when the salad is served.

## PASTA AND GRAIN SALADS

Be sure pasta and grains are thoroughly cooked, but be careful not to overcook them. When you add the dressing to the salad, the pasta and grains will absorb some of the moisture in the dressing, and overcooked grains and pasta will then become soggy.

## FRUIT SALADS

Fruits have a variety of characteristics you should consider when using them in salads. Fruits that turn brown easily, such as apples, bananas, and pears, should be tossed with citrus juice, which will prevent oxidation. Fragile fruits, such as berries, should be added at the last minute, as they can break down and bruise easily. Remove any peels, seeds, cores, and any tough membranes and cut the fruits to approximately the same size. These same tips can be applied to savory salads that have fruit in them.

## LEGUME SALADS

Unlike pasta and grains, beans do not soften further after they are cooked. In fact, the acid in salad dressings will make the beans tougher, even if they are fully cooked. Therefore, bean and legume salads should not be held in the dressing for more than four hours.

## WARM SALADS

Warm salads are traditionally made by tossing the salad ingredients in a warm dressing. Toss the salad in the dressing while it is still over the heat, working just until it is heated through, or add the warm dressing to the salad in its serving dish before tossing. Warm dressings provide an excellent opportunity to infuse flavors into the oil, vinegar, or other ingredients.

*One of the attributes of warm salads is using ingredients that must be cooked first, like this broccoli rabe. Peeling off the tough outer skin before cooking, is an excellent way to soften its texture for a salad.*

# HOW TO MAKE IT YOUR OWN: SALADS

When choosing garnishes, use those that will either echo the flavors of the greens and dressing or contrast with them. Garnishes can add a variety of textures and flavors to the salad, so be adventurous and try using a variety of toasted nuts and seeds, fried cubes of tofu, polenta, or potato, roasted vegetables, croutons made from any flavor bread on hand (even banana or pumpkin bread), dried fruits, fresh fruits, roasted or boiled beets, hard-boiled or poached egg, and of course onions of any sort, tomatoes, and cucumbers.

## GREENS AND DRESSINGS

| GREENS | TEXTURE | FLAVOR | APPLICATION | DRESSING |
|---|---|---|---|---|
| **Bitter** Use either a strong vinaigrette to stand up to the flavor of the greens or a mild vinaigrette to allow the flavor of the greens to come through. | | | | |
| **RADICCHIO** | Soft, cabbage-like | Mildly sweet, bitter | Raw, grilled | Balsamic vinaigrette |
| **FRISÉE** | Bristly | Slightly bitter | Raw, grilled | Citrus juice |
| **CURLY ENDIVE** | Bristly, fibrous | Green, bitter | Raw, grilled | Balsamic, sherry vinaigrette; citrus |
| **Neutral** All lettuces in this group are relatively mild in flavor. Almost any vinaigrette or light creamy dressing will work. | | | | |
| **RED OAK** | Tender | Mild | Raw | Warm vinaigrette |
| **RED AND GREEN ROMAINE** | Crisp, succulent | Mild | Raw, grilled | Caesar or creamy Parmesan |
| **RED OR WHITE BABY KALE** | Soft, cabbage-like | Slightly bittersweet | Raw, wilted | Warm vinaigrette |
| **RED OR GREEN BABY CHARD** | Tender but fibrous | Slightly bittersweet | Raw, wilted | Warm vinaigrette |
| **BABY BEET GREENS** | Tender but fibrous | Slightly tannic, beet flavor | Raw, wilted | Warm vinaigrette |
| **ESCAROLE** | Succulent and slightly fibrous | Slightly bitter, nutty | Raw, wilted, grilled, braised | Warm vinaigrette |
| **SPINACH** | Tender but fibrous | Green, slightly tannic | Raw, wilted | Warm vinaigrette |
| **BEET LEAF** | Tender but fibrous | Beet flavor | Raw, wilted | Warm vinaigrette |
| **MÂCHE, LAMB'S LETTUCE, CORN SALAD** | Tender, succulent | Mild nutty | Raw | Warm vinaigrette |
| **SORREL** | Tender, succulent, and slightly fibrous | Slightly tart citrus flavor | Raw, wilted | Citrus vinaigrette |

*continued on next page*

# GREENS AND DRESSINGS cont.

| GREENS | TEXTURE | FLAVOR | APPLICATION | DRESSING |
|--------|---------|--------|-------------|----------|
| **RED OR WHITE BELGIAN ENDIVE** | Crisp, juicy | Nutty, slightly bitter | Raw, braised, or grilled | Balsamic or citrus vinaigrette |
| **ICEBERG** | Crisp, watery | Very mild | Raw | Thousand Island, Catalina, green goddess |
| **BOSTON** | Tender | Very mild | Raw | Light citrus vinaigrette |
| **BUTTER** | Tender | Very mild | Raw | Light citrus vinaigrette |
| **RED OR GREEN LEAF** | Tender, juicy, slightly fibrous | Very mild | Raw | Any flavor |

## Spicy
Use either a strong vinaigrette to stand up to the spiciness or a mild vinaigrette to let the spiciness shine through.

| GREENS | TEXTURE | FLAVOR | APPLICATION | DRESSING |
|--------|---------|--------|-------------|----------|
| **MIZUNA** | Tender, slightly fibrous | Horseradish flavor | Raw | Citrus, white wine vinaigrette |
| **ARUGULA** | Slightly crisp | Peppery | Raw, wilted | Lemon |
| **MUSTARD GREENS** | Tender, slightly fibrous | Spicy mustard flavor | Raw | Citrus, white wine vinaigrette |
| **RED ASIAN MUSTARD** | Tender, slightly fibrous | Spicy mustard flavor | Raw | Rice vinegar, soy sauce |
| **WATERCRESS** | Crisp, juicy | Peppery | Raw, wilted | Citrus |

## Specialty Lettuce Blends
In general, light-textured, mild-flavored (low-acid) dressings work best with these salad blends.

| GREENS | TEXTURE | FLAVOR | APPLICATION | DRESSING |
|--------|---------|--------|-------------|----------|
| **ASIAN MIXED GREENS; ASSORTED BABY ASIAN MIXED GREENS** | Tender, fragile textures | Generally spicy, slightly bitter | Raw | Rice vinegar, citrus |
| **BABY MIXED GREENS; ASSORTED BABY LEAF LETTUCES** | Tender, fragile textures | Generally neutral | Raw | Citrus, Balsamic, white wine vinaigrette |
| **MESCLUN; BABY MIXED GREENS WITH THE AD-DITION OF HERBS OR EDIBLE FLOWERS** | Tender, fragile | Generally neutral, with herbal or floral notes | Raw | Lemon, Balsamic |
| **MICROGREENS: SPROUTS OF VARI-OUS PLANTS SUCH AS BEETS, CORN, ALFAL-FA, AMARANTH** | Very tender, fragile | Has the flavor of the plant for which it is sprouted (e.g., corn sprouts taste of corn) | Raw | Little to no dressing used; mild vinegars, citrus and/or infused oils |

# SANDWICHES

Sandwiches can be made up of any number of ingredients and assembled in a myriad of different ways. They can be hot or cold, small or large, an appetizer or an entrée. They are simple to make, but a little creativity invested in the elements selected can add the crunchy tartness of a pickle, the complexity of a garden-fresh heirloom tomato, or the tangy, rich flavors of a carefully selected cheese. The following are some guidelines that are helpful when building sandwiches.

## BREADS

Bread is the foundation of a sandwich. It can be unobtrusive, serving to unite the other elements, or it can be a major flavor presence. Consider what you want in your final sandwich: Are you toasting the bread? Do you want something crusty or something soft? Will you be applying spreads or adding lots of fillings? Basic store-bought sandwich breads can be tasty, but don't rule out some more unusual choices: biscuits, English muffins, pita bread, tortillas, or a halved baguette. (See Chapter 8 for some recipes.)

## SPREADS

Spreads are functional as well as flavorful. Fat-based spreads like butter or mayonnaise provide a barrier that keeps the bread from getting soggy. They also add moisture to a sandwich and help hold it together as it is picked up and eaten. Traditional condiments such as mustard or ketchup aren't the only ones you can put on a sandwich. Flavorful sauces, compotes, mashed avocado, oil and vinegar, soft cheeses, hummus, and pesto are just a few ideas to kick your sandwich up a notch.

## FILLINGS AND GARNISHES

Typically the filling is the focal point of the sandwich, and typically it is protein based. In the case of vegetarian sandwiches, eggs, tofu, seitan, grains, beans, and a host of vegetables (whether roasted, sautéed, or fried) take center stage as the filling. The only rule for sandwich fillings is that they work well together.

The purpose of a garnish is to add texture, flavor, moisture, eye appeal, and interest. Garnishes can be a very creative way to make a sandwich extra special.

# HOW TO MAKE IT YOUR OWN: SANDWICHES

The bread or base for a sandwich can be almost anything that can be used as a wrapper or platform. Usually a sandwich is one or two slices of bread with a spread, filling, and garnish.

A fun way to change it up a little is to bake, pan fry, or grill a sandwich. So think of your favorite combinations and then try a different preparation technique. For example, the childhood favorite of peanut butter and banana on whole wheat is wonderful cooked on a griddle like a grilled cheese sandwich.

On the following page you will find suggestions for components of sandwiches—you can pair almost any bread with any spread, filling, garnish, and other ingredients and can make them special by grilling or another cooking method.

## CONSTRUCTING A SANDWICH

A sandwich with a slice of bread on the top and bottom is called a "closed sandwich." A "club sandwich" has a third piece of bread in the center. Other sandwiches have only one slice of bread acting as a base; these are called "open-faced sandwiches."

Many types of sandwiches can be made and assembled ahead of time; just be sure to wrap them tightly in plastic wrap or keep them in airtight containers. It is best to hold them for no more than a few hours before serving.

# SANDWICH COMPONENTS

| BREAD OR BASE | SPREAD | FILLING | GARNISHES | COOKING METHODS |
|---|---|---|---|---|
| **BAGUETTE** | Aïoli | Bean patties or burgers | Apples, pears, grapes, or other fruit | Dip the bread in egg batter and pan fry like French toast |
| **BISCUITS** | Bean purée | Breaded and fried eggplant or zucchini | Bacon substitute | Toast on a ridged grill pan such as a Panini Press |
| **FLATBREADS** | Butter | Caponata | Greens, raw or cooked | Lay sandwich open face, top with cheese or a yummy sauce, and brown under the broiler |
| **FOCACCIA** | Chutney or purées | Cheese | Hot peppers, pickled or fresh | Wrap in foil and cook on a charcoal grill |
| **LOAF BREADS** | Cooked vegetable purée | Chopped salad, such as egg or tofu salad | Kimchi | |
| **NATIVE AMERICAN FRYBREAD** | Flavored butter | Cooked greens | Lettuces | |
| **RICE PAPER OR WRAPPERS** | Flavored oils | Fried or poached eggs | Olives | |
| **ROTI** | Harissa | Grilled or roasted onions | Onion, raw or cooked | |
| **TORTILLAS** | Hoisin sauce | Grilled or roasted tomatoes | Pickled vegetables | |
| | Ketchup | Grilled vegetables such as peppers, eggplant, squash, or mushrooms | Pickles | |
| | Marmite | Potato cakes | Rehydrated dried mushrooms or chiles | |
| | Mashed avocado | Rice or alternative protein patties | Roasted peppers | |
| | Mayonnaise | Roasted sweet potatoes | Sauerkraut | |
| | Mustard | Seitan | Sprouts | |
| | Oil and vinegar | TVP | Tomatoes, fresh or sundried | |
| | Olive oil | Vegetable patties | Vegetable chips | |
| | Olives or tapenade | | | |
| | Soft spreadable cheese | | | |
| | Thousand Island dressing | | | |

# Chopped Salad

*This is a basic salad that can be altered to suit any dish it's served with. To start, try it with one of the many salad dressings listed in Chapter 9.*

1 head Bibb or Boston lettuce

1 large red bell pepper, diced

1 medium cucumber, seeded and diced

1 cup corn kernels (for additional flavor, the corn may be roasted before it is removed from the cob)

1 cup minced red onion

1 cup diced plum (Roma) tomatoes

1 cup diced celery

5 medium radishes, thinly sliced (1 cup)

¼ cup capers, rinsed

Red Wine Vinaigrette (page 290), as needed

Salt and freshly ground black pepper, as needed

1. Thoroughly wash and dry the lettuce leaves. Line a large salad bowl or platter with the lettuce leaves.

2. In another large mixing bowl, add the red pepper, cucumber, corn, onion, tomatoes, celery, radishes, capers, and dressing, and toss to coat. Season with salt and pepper, and toss again.

3. Pour the mixed chopped salad into the lettuce-lined bowl or platter and serve immediately.

**MAKES 4 SERVINGS**

NOTE: This salad is delicious with the addition of blue cheese and garlicky croutons as a garnish.

# Crisp Salad with Peppers, Carrots, Jícama, and Oranges

*This salad is sweet, tangy, and juicy. It calms heat, so serve it alongside a spicy entrée.*

## SALAD

1 large red bell pepper, thinly sliced

1 large yellow bell pepper, thinly sliced

1 poblano chile, seeded, thinly sliced

1 medium carrot, thinly sliced

1 medium jícama, peeled, cut into julienne

2 oranges, peeled and cut into suprêmes (see page 321), juice reserved

¼ cup chopped fresh cilantro

## DRESSING

3 tbsp red wine vinegar

2 tbsp reserved orange juice

1 tsp Dijon mustard

2 cloves garlic, minced

1 jalapeño, seeded and minced

1 tsp honey

¼ cup peanut oil

Salt and freshly ground black pepper, as needed

1. In a large bowl, combine all the salad ingredients. Toss to combine.

2. In a small bowl, combine the vinegar, orange juice, mustard, garlic, jalapeño, and honey. Gradually whisk in the oil. Season with salt and pepper.

3. Pour the dressing over the salad. Toss to coat. Serve immediately. Or reserve salad and dressing separately and store refrigerated for up to 2 days. Dress the salad when ready to serve.

**MAKES 4 SERVINGS**

# Cucumber-Yogurt Salad

*This cooling dish is ideal as both a salad and a sauce. Serve it with Falafel (page 117) as either.*

2 medium seedless cucumbers, peeled, seeded, and diced

1 tbsp kosher salt

2 cups Greek-style yogurt

2 cloves garlic, minced

5 green onions, minced (white and green parts)

¼ cup chopped fresh mint

½ tsp ground cumin

Freshly ground black pepper, as needed

1. Toss the cucumbers in a colander with the salt. Allow the cucumber to sit to drain their excess liquid for at least 15 minutes. Press the cucumbers lightly to remove additional moisture.

2. In a medium bowl, combine the cucumbers with the yogurt, garlic, green onions, mint, and cumin. Season with pepper. Cover and chill until needed. Stir before serving.

**MAKES 4 SERVINGS**

# Tabbouleh

*Tabbouleh is a deliciously fresh-tasting parsley salad made with bulgur, tomatoes, and cucumbers. It makes a wonderful crunchy side dish for Falafel (page 117).*

¾ cup bulgur

Boiling water, as needed

1 cup diced tomatoes

1 cup peeled, seeded, and diced cucumber

1 bunch green onions, thinly sliced (white and green parts)

1 cup chopped fresh flat-leaf parsley

¼ cup chopped fresh mint

3 tbsp olive oil

2 tbsp fresh lemon juice

Salt and freshly ground black pepper, as needed

1. Rinse the bulgur in cold water and transfer it into a large bowl. Cover with boiling water by 1 inch and allow to sit until tender, 15 to 20 minutes.

2. Drain any excess water, cover, and refrigerate until chilled.

3. Add the tomatoes, cucumber, green onions, parsley, mint, oil, and lemon juice. Season with salt and pepper and toss to combine. Cover and refrigerate to let the flavors meld. Toss again before serving.

**MAKES 4 TO 6 SERVINGS**

# Warm Lentil Salad with Walnuts

*Serving this salad warm is ideal for enjoying its fragrance and flavors.*

Kosher salt, as needed

1 cup green lentils, picked over, rinsed, and drained

1 medium shallot, halved

1 clove garlic, crushed

2 tbsp white wine vinegar

1 tbsp Dijon mustard

¼ cup olive oil

½ tsp dried oregano

¼ tsp freshly ground black pepper

½ cup finely chopped roasted red bell pepper

½ cup chopped toasted walnuts

¼ cup finely chopped red onion

1 tbsp chopped fresh flat-leaf parsley

1½ tsp chopped fresh tarragon

1½ tsp chopped fresh chives

1. In a medium saucepan, bring salted water to a boil. Add the lentils, return to a boil, and reduce the heat to low. Cover the pot and cook until the lentils are tender, about 45 minutes.

2. Just before the lentils are tender, in a blender or food processor finely chop the shallot and garlic. Add the vinegar, mustard, oil, oregano, ½ tsp salt, and the pepper. Process until well blended.

3. When the lentils are tender, drain well and transfer to a serving bowl. Add the roasted pepper, walnuts, onion, parsley, tarragon, and chives. Add enough dressing to coat and toss gently to combine. Serve warm.

**MAKES 4 SERVINGS**

# Curried Sweet Potato Salad

*The addition of mango and warm spices makes this a perfect salad to serve with any sandwich, but especially the Grilled Vegetable Sandwich with Manchego Cheese on page 123.*

Kosher salt, as needed

2 cups peeled and diced sweet potatoes

2 cups peeled and diced Yukon gold potatoes

½ cup minced red onion

1 mango, peeled, pitted, and diced

½ cup thinly sliced green onions (white and green parts)

1 tbsp curry powder

½ tsp ground cumin

½ tsp ground cardamom

1 cup mayonnaise

¼ cup rice vinegar

Juice of 1 lime

Freshly ground black pepper, as needed

1. Fill 2 medium-sized pots with water, add salt and bring to a boil. Place the diced sweet potatoes in one pot and the diced Yukon gold potatoes in the other. Return to a boil and cook for approximately 8 to 12 minutes, or until the potatoes are tender. (Cooking separately is important because these potatoes have different cooking times.)

2. Drain the potatoes in a colander, and place the drained potatoes on sheet pan to cool to room temperature. Dry very well, blotting with a towel.

3. In a large bowl, toss the cooled potatoes, onion, mango, and green onions to combine.

4. In a small bowl, whisk together the curry powder, cumin, and cardamom, then lightly toast the spices in a warmed sauté pan or toaster oven. Return the toasted spices to the bowl and combine with the mayonnaise, vinegar, and lime juice. Season with salt and pepper.

5. Pour the dressing over the potato mixture and toss to coat. Cover and refrigerate for at least 1 hour before serving.

**MAKES 4 SERVINGS**

# Salad of Leeks, Beets, and Avocado

*This salad is as tasty as it is colorful, and it makes for a great quick lunch or starter to a multicourse meal.*

4 small yellow beets, approximately 2-inch diameter

Salt, as needed

¼ cup olive oil

3 medium leeks, thinly sliced (white and light green parts)

3 small shallots, finely chopped

2 tsp Dijon mustard

1 tbsp white wine vinegar

Freshly ground black pepper, as needed

2 tbsp chopped parsley

2 avocados, thinly sliced

1. In a medium pot, cook the beets in boiling salted water until tender, approximately 30 to 45 minutes. Drain and let cool enough to handle.

2. Peel the beets and thinly slice them. Set aside.

3. In a large sauté pan, heat 1 tbsp oil over medium heat. Add the leeks and sauté until tender, 3 to 5 minutes. Set aside to cool to room temperature.

4. In a blender or food processor, combine the shallots, mustard, and vinegar until smooth. Slowly add the remaining oil. Season with salt and pepper and stir in the parsley.

5. Arrange the beets, leeks, and avocados on a large platter. Pour the vinaigrette over the salad and serve immediately.

**MAKES 4 SERVINGS**

# Marinated Tomato, Cucumber, and Watercress Salad with Candied Walnuts

*Watercress has a peppery, mustardy flavor that makes it an excellent addition to salads. Marinating the vegetables in advance makes this salad easy to assemble at the last moment.*

1½ cups seeded and diced tomatoes

1 tbsp chopped fresh flat-leaf parsley

1 medium seedless cucumber, peeled and diced

1 medium red onion, minced

1½ cups Champagne Vinaigrette (page 290)

Salt and freshly ground black pepper, as needed

½ cup light brown sugar

Pinch cayenne

1½ cups toasted walnuts

1 bunch watercress

⅓ cup crumbled fresh goat cheese

1. In a medium bowl, toss the tomatoes, parsley, cucumber, and onion with ½ cup of the vinaigrette to combine. Season with salt and pepper. Cover and marinate, refrigerated, for at least 20 minutes.

2. Line a baking sheet with waxed paper or a silicone baking mat. In a medium saucepan, bring the sugar, cayenne, and a pinch salt to a boil over medium heat, stirring occasionally. Cook until the mixture is thick and amber-colored and registers about 235°F on a candy thermometer. Add the nuts and quickly toss to coat. Immediately pour the nut mixture onto the baking sheet. Use 2 forks to separate the walnuts slightly. Let cool to room temperature.

3. When you are ready to serve, place the watercress in a large salad bowl. Add the marinated tomato and cucumber, nuts, and goat cheese and toss to combine. Serve immediately.

**MAKES 4 SERVINGS**

NOTE: The marinated tomato and cucumber mixture is also delicious on its own. | Using heirloom tomato varieties creates a dynamic variation to this salad.

Marinated Tomato, Cucumber, and Watercress Salad
with Candied Walnuts

# Fattoush

Fattoush is an Eastern Mediterranean bread salad (much like the Italian bread salad panzanella). This version is made with Pita Bread (page 274) and lots of crisp vegetables.

5 Pita Breads (page 274 or store-bought)

¾ cup plus 2 tbsp extra-virgin olive oil

Salt and freshly ground black pepper, as needed

1 bunch green onions, diced (white and green parts)

⅔ cup chopped parsley

⅔ cup diced plum (Roma) tomatoes

1 medium cucumber, peeled, seeded, and diced

½ cup sliced radishes

1 yellow bell pepper, diced

3 tbsp fresh lemon juice

3 tbsp red wine vinegar

1¾ tsp sugar

2 tbsp chopped thyme

½ tsp cayenne

1. Preheat the oven to 300°F.

2. Cut the pita bread into small wedges. In a medium bowl, toss the pita with 2 tbsp of the oil. Season with salt and pepper. Spread out on a baking sheet and bake until crisp, about 15 minutes. Turn the pita halfway through baking. Remove from the oven.

3. In a large bowl, toss the green onions, parsley, tomatoes, cucumber, radishes, and yellow pepper to combine.

4. In a small bowl, combine the lemon juice, vinegar, sugar, thyme, and cayenne. Slowly whisk in the remaining ¾ cup oil. Season with salt and pepper.

5. Pour the dressing over the vegetables, and toss to coat. Add the pita wedges and toss once more. Serve immediately.

**MAKES 4 SERVINGS**

# Corn, Radish, Lime, and Crème Fraîche Salad

*A little bit of crème fraîche (a thick sour cream–like product) plays nicely off the sweet corn, spicy radish, and sour lime of this salad.*

1 tbsp unsalted butter

1 medium shallot, minced

1 clove garlic, minced

1 jalapeño, seeded and minced

3 cups corn kernels (fresh or thawed frozen)

⅓ cup Vegetable Broth (page 287)

¾ cup thinly sliced radishes

2 green onions, thinly sliced (white and green parts)

¼ cup cilantro leaves, plus more as needed

4 lime suprêmes, whole (see page 321)

3 tbsp fresh lime juice, plus more as needed

¼ cup crème fraîche

2 tbsp grated lime zest

2 tsp sugar

1 tbsp chili powder

Salt and freshly ground black pepper, as needed

1. In a large sauté pan, melt the butter over medium heat. Add the shallot, garlic, and jalapeño, and sauté until the shallots are translucent, 2 to 3 minutes.

2. Add the corn and broth and bring to a simmer. Simmer until the liquid has reduced entirely and the mixture is almost dry. Remove from heat and let cool to room temperature.

3. In a large bowl, combine the corn mixture with the radishes, green onions, cilantro, and lime segments.

4. In a small bowl, combine the lime juice, crème fraîche, lime zest, sugar, and chili powder. Season with salt and pepper.

5. Add the dressing to the corn mixture and toss to combine. Season with salt, pepper, and additional lime juice and cilantro as needed.

**MAKES 4 SERVINGS**

NOTE: If using fresh corn, grilling the corn on the cob ahead of time adds a wonderfully smoky sweetness to this salad.

# Chayote Salad with Oranges

*Chayote is a member of the squash family that's relatively soft skinned. Its mild flavor and crisp texture make it great for salads.*

1 chayote, peeled, pitted, and diced or cut julienne

2 cups peeled jícama, cut julienne

2 cups carrots, cut julienne

2 oranges, cut into suprêmes (see page 321), juices reserved

½ bunch green onions, thinly sliced (white and green parts)

2 tbsp extra-virgin olive oil

2 tbsp fresh lime juice

¾ tsp sugar

Salt and freshly ground black pepper, as needed

2 tbsp fresh cilantro chiffonade

2 tbsp fresh mint chiffonade

1. In a large bowl, toss the chayote, jícama, carrots, oranges, and green onions together to combine.

2. In a small bowl, combine the oil, lime juice, sugar, salt, pepper, and reserved orange juice. Season with salt and pepper. Pour the dressing over the salad.

3. Add the cilantro and mint, and toss the mixture to combine. Serve immediately.

**MAKES 4 SERVINGS**

# Black-Eyed Pea Salad

*Black-eyed peas make this Caribbean-influenced salad out of the ordinary.*

¼ cup olive oil

1 cup minced yellow onion

2 cloves garlic, minced

2 tbsp grated fresh ginger

1 tbsp curry powder

1½ tsp ground turmeric

¼ tsp ground cardamom

2 cups cooked black-eyed peas
(see chart, page 131)

½ tsp minced thyme

¼ cup rice vinegar

Juice of 2 limes

1½ tsp sesame oil

Salt and freshly ground black
pepper, as needed

1½ cups seeded and diced tomatoes

1 bunch green onions, thinly sliced
(white and green parts)

2 cups corn kernels (fresh or thawed frozen)

¼ cup minced cilantro

1. In a large sauté pan, heat the olive oil over medium heat. Add the onions, garlic, and ginger, and cook until the onions are translucent, 4 to 5 minutes. Add the curry powder, turmeric, and cardamom, and cook until fragrant, 1 to 2 minutes more. Stir in the black-eyed peas, thyme, vinegar, lime juice, and sesame oil, and season with salt and pepper. Cook until the mixture is heated through. Remove from the heat and cool to room temperature.

2. Transfer the mixture to a large bowl and toss with the tomatoes, green onions, corn, and cilantro. Let sit for 15 to 20 minutes so that the flavors can combine.

**MAKES 4 SERVINGS**

# Grilled Asparagus Salad with Red-Skin Potatoes

*This salad is the perfect example of how just a few ingredients can make a great dish. This dish contrasts flavors and textures, pairing the crisp asparagus with soft, creamy potatoes.*

2 pounds bliss potatoes

1½ pounds asparagus, trimmed

Olive oil, as needed

Salt and freshly ground black pepper, as needed

¼ cup Shallot-Tarragon Vinaigrette (page 289)

2 cups mixed greens, loosely packed

**GARNISH**

⅓ cup shaved Parmesan

1. Put the potatoes in a saucepan and cover with cold water. Bring to a boil over medium heat and cook until tender, about 15 to 20 minutes. Drain and set aside to cool until cool enough to handle. Cut warm potatoes into wedges.

2. Meanwhile, heat a grill or grill pan until hot. Brush the asparagus lightly with oil. Grill until lightly charred and tender, turning occasionally, 4 to 5 minutes.

3. In a large bowl, combine the asparagus and potatoes. Season well with salt and pepper.

4. Toss with the vinaigrette. Place the greens into a serving bowl or divide onto four individual plates. Arrange the potato asparagus mixture on top of the salad greens. Serve immediately, garnished with shaved Parmesan.

**MAKES 4 GENEROUS SERVINGS**

# Arugula Salad with Figs au Gratin, Parmesan, and Pine Nuts

*The peppery flavor of the arugula and slight sweetness of the figs make this salad perfect as an appetizer, side, or entrée.*

¾ cup pine nuts, toasted

4 tbsp (½ stick) unsalted butter

2 tbsp confectioners' sugar

2 tbsp all-purpose flour

12 figs, halved

2 bunches arugula, washed and dried

¼ cup extra-virgin olive oil

½ cup shaved Parmesan

3 tbsp champagne or Balsamic vinegar

Salt and freshly ground black pepper, as needed

1. Preheat the oven to 400°F. Line a baking sheet with parchment paper.

2. Toast the pine nuts in a small dry sauté pan until golden and fragrant. Transfer to a plate and set aside to cool to room temperature.

3. In a food processor or blender, process ½ cup pine nuts, the butter, sugar, and flour to a coarse meal.

4. Place the figs cut side up on the baking sheet. Spoon some of the pine nut mixture onto each fig, dividing it evenly. Bake the figs until the topping is golden brown and bubbly, 3 to 5 minutes. Let the figs cool slightly.

5. In a large bowl, toss together the arugula, oil, Parmesan, and remaining ¼ cup toasted pine nuts. Place the tossed arugula onto a platter. Arrange the figs on top of the arugula. Drizzle with the vinegar, and season with salt and pepper. Serve immediately.

**MAKES 4 SERVINGS**

Falafel (front), Cucumber-Yogurt Salad, page 103
(center), and Tabbouleh, page 104 (rear)

# Falafel

*These small chickpea patties are crispy on the outside and creamy on the inside. Make larger patties and serve as veggie burgers with Cucumber-Yogurt Salad (page 103) and Tabbouleh (page 104) on the side.*

4 cups dried chickpeas, soaked and drained (see chart, page 131)

1 small yellow onion, roughly chopped

½ bunch fresh flat-leaf parsley, roughly chopped

2 cloves garlic, roughly chopped

1 tbsp ground cumin, toasted

2¼ tsp ground coriander, toasted

2¼ tsp kosher salt

1½ tsp baking powder

½ cup unhulled sesame seeds

Grapeseed or canola oil, as needed for frying

1. In a food processor, process the chickpeas, onion, parsley, garlic, toasted cumin, toasted coriander, salt, and baking powder until they form a coarse meal. Add the sesame seeds and pulse just to combine.

2. Divide the mixture into 2-tbsp portions and use your hands to flatten them into patties. (For burger-size patties, use ½-cup portions.)

3. Heat ¼ inch oil in a heavy-bottomed skillet. Add the patties and pan fry until golden brown on each side, 4 to 6 minutes. Drain on paper towels and serve warm.

**MAKES ABOUT 30 SMALL PATTIES OR 6 TO 8 BURGERS**

# Veggie Burger

*These patties freeze well and can be made in advance, thawed, and cooked when you're ready to eat them, making them perfect for a quick dinner or dinner for one.*

½ pound tempeh, cubed

¾ cup chopped yellow onion

2 cloves garlic, minced

¾ cup chopped walnuts

½ cup old-fashioned or quick-cooking rolled oats

1 tbsp chopped fresh flat-leaf parsley

½ tsp dried oregano

½ tsp dried thyme

½ tsp kosher salt

¼ tsp freshly ground black pepper

3 tbsp olive oil

Dijon mustard, as needed

4 sandwich buns, split

GARNISH

Leaf lettuce, as needed

Sliced tomato, as needed

Sliced red onion, as needed

Sliced avocado, as needed

1. In a medium saucepan of simmering water or vegetable broth, cook the tempeh for 30 minutes. Drain and set aside to cool to room temperature.

2. In a food processor, mince the onion and garlic together. Add the tempeh, walnuts, oats, parsley, oregano, thyme, salt, and pepper. Process until well blended. Shape into 4 equal patties.

3. In a large sauté pan, heat the oil over medium heat. Add the burgers and cook until cooked thoroughly and browned on both sides, about 7 minutes per side.

4. Spread desired amount of mustard onto each half of the buns. Place a burger on each bun. Garnish with lettuce, tomato, red onion, and avocado, as desired. Serve immediately.

**MAKES 4 BURGERS**

VARIATION: **Tofu Veggie Burger:** Skip Step 1 and replace the tempeh with ½ pound firm tofu.

NOTE: To freeze these burgers, form the patties and lay on a parchment paper–lined tray. Place in the freezer. Once the patties have become firm, individually wrap in plastic wrap and store in a zipper freezer bag.

Veggie Burger

# Brown Rice Burger

*The natural starches in the rice are what keep this patty together. It can be flavored in a number of ways—try cayenne, chili powder, and cumin in place of the parsley and chives, to taste.*

⅔ cup short-grain brown rice

2 cups Vegetable Broth (page 287)

¼ cup minced yellow onion

1 clove garlic, minced

2 tbsp chopped fresh flat-leaf parsley

¼ cup chopped toasted pecans

2 tbsp minced fresh chives

Salt and freshly ground black pepper, as needed

Unseasoned dry bread crumbs, or panko, as needed

Grapeseed or canola oil, as needed for cooking

1. In a small saucepan, combine the rice and broth. Cook over medium heat until rice is tender and has absorbed the broth, about 20 to 30 minutes. Cool slightly.

2. In a food processor, pulse the rice, onion, garlic, parsley, pecans, and chives until nearly smooth. Season with salt and pepper.

3. Form the mixture into 4 patties and dredge them in bread crumbs to coat. Press the bread crumbs firmly onto the surface of the patties.

4. In a large sauté pan, heat ¼ inch oil over medium heat.

5. Cook the burgers until golden brown on each side and heated through, 3 to 5 minutes per side.

6. Serve burgers on your favorite whole grain rolls with any cheese, veggie garnishes, or condiments.

**MAKES 4 SERVINGS**

VARIATIONS: **Quinoa Burger:** Replace the rice with 2½ cups cooked quinoa, rinsed thoroughly and drained. **Barley Burger:** Replace the rice with 2½ cups cooked barley.

# Black Bean Burger

*Black beans have a creamy texture and rich flavor that make this burger compatible with any topping, especially salsa, avocado, and spicy cheeses.*

3 tbsp olive oil

½ cup minced yellow onion

1 clove garlic, minced

1½ cups cooked black beans
(see chart, page 131)

1 tbsp chopped fresh flat-leaf parsley

½ cup unseasoned dry bread crumbs

¼ cup vital wheat gluten

1 tsp smoked paprika, either sweet or hot

½ tsp dried thyme

Salt and freshly ground black pepper, as needed

4 sandwich buns, split

GARNISH

Lettuce, as needed

Sliced tomato, as needed

1. In a small skillet, heat 1 tbsp of the oil over medium heat. Add the onion and garlic and cook until soft, about 5 minutes.

2. Transfer the onion mixture to a food processor. Add the beans, parsley, bread crumbs, gluten, paprika, and thyme. Season with salt and pepper.

3. Process until well combined, leaving some texture. Shape the mixture into 4 equal patties and refrigerate for 20 minutes.

4. In a large sauté pan, heat the remaining oil over medium heat. Add the burgers and cook until browned on both sides, turning once, about 5 minutes per side.

5. Serve the burgers on the buns, garnished with lettuce and tomato.

**MAKES 4 SERVINGS**

Grilled Vegetable Sandwich with Manchego Cheese
(left), and Curried Sweet Potato Salad (page 106)

# Grilled Vegetable Sandwich with Manchego Cheese

*Be sure to cut the vegetables evenly so that they are roughly the same size. Not only will this make them easier to cook, it will make for an easy-to-assemble and easy-to-eat sandwich.*

¾ cup olive oil

2 tbsp chopped fresh thyme

2 tbsp chopped fresh oregano

1 clove garlic, minced

½ jalapeño, seeded and minced

2 tbsp Dijon mustard

Salt and freshly ground black pepper, as needed

8 slices eggplant, ½-inch thick

8 slices red onion, ¼-inch thick

1 large red bell pepper, halved and seeded

2 poblano chiles, halved and seeded

2 large or 4 small portobello mushroom caps

4 whole-wheat hard rolls, split *or* 2 whole-wheat baguettes, halved and split

⅓ cup Tapenade (page 14)

8 slices tomato

8 slices Manchego cheese (about 4 to 6 ounces)

1. Heat a grill or grill pan until hot.

2. In a large bowl, combine oil, thyme, oregano, garlic, jalapeño, and mustard. Season with salt and pepper. Brush the eggplant slices with the marinade, then toss the onion, red peppers, chiles, and mushrooms with remaining marinade to coat. Allow to marinate for approximately 10 minutes.

3. Working in batches if necessary, grill the vegetables, draining off excess marinade before placing each vegetable on the grill. Grill until the vegetables are lightly charred and tender. Let cool slightly.

4. Thinly slice the red pepper, chiles, and mushrooms once cool enough to handle.

5. Spread a thin layer of tapenade onto each roll. Layer the eggplant, onion, red peppers, chiles, and mushrooms on the rolls, dividing the vegetables evenly among the rolls. Top each sandwich with 2 slices tomato and 2 slices cheese.

6. If desired, warm the sandwiches in a 250°F oven before serving.

**MAKES 4 SERVINGS**

# Vegetable Satay Roll-Ups

*To make the tortillas easier to roll, heat them briefly in a dry skillet or sauté pan.*

½ pound extra-firm tofu, drained well and patted dry

⅔ cup creamy peanut butter

1 tbsp soy sauce

1 tbsp fresh lime juice

½ tsp grated fresh ginger

1 clove garlic, minced

¼ tsp ground cayenne

4 Flour Tortillas (page 271 or store-bought)

2 cups shredded romaine lettuce

¼ cup chopped toasted peanuts

½ cup bean sprouts

1 large red bell pepper, cut into julienne

1 large carrot, grated

½ seedless cucumber, peeled and thinly sliced

1. In a food processor, combine the tofu, peanut butter, and soy sauce and process until smooth. Add the lime juice, ginger, garlic, and cayenne and process until smooth.

2. Set aside at room temperature for 30 minutes to let all of the flavors blend together.

3. To assemble the wraps, place 1 tortilla on a work surface and spread with about ½ cup of the tofu mixture. Sprinkle with one-quarter of the lettuce, peanuts, bean sprouts, red pepper, carrots, and cucumber. Roll up tightly and cut in half diagonally. Repeat with the remaining ingredients and serve.

**MAKES 4 SERVINGS**

# Spicy Tomato-Bulgur Sandwich

*This saucy sandwich is made with a flavorful tomato sauce and bulgur. It's delicious, healthy, and kid-friendly.*

1 cup medium-grind whole grain bulgur

Salt, as needed

1 tbsp olive oil

1½ cups minced red onion

½ cup minced red bell pepper

½ cup minced mushrooms

2 cups canned crushed tomatoes

1 tbsp sugar

1 tbsp spicy brown mustard

2 tsp soy sauce

1 tbsp chili powder

Freshly ground black pepper, as needed

4 sandwich rolls, split

1. In a large saucepan, bring 1¾ cups water to a boil over high heat. Stir in the bulgur and salt lightly. Cover, remove from the heat, and set aside until the bulgur absorbs the water and softens, about 20 minutes.

2. Meanwhile, in a large sauté pan, heat the oil over medium heat. Add the onion, red peppers, and mushrooms, cover, and cook until soft, about 7 minutes. Stir in the tomatoes, sugar, mustard, soy sauce, and chili powder. Season with salt and pepper. Simmer, stirring frequently, until flavor is well developed, about 10 minutes.

3. Add the bulgur to the cooked mixture and return to a simmer. Adjust the seasoning with salt and pepper to taste. Spoon the bulgur mixture onto the bottom half of each roll, cover with the top half, and serve.

**MAKES 4 SERVINGS**

# Muffaletta Sandwiches

*Traditionally, muffaletta sandwiches are wrapped in deli or butcher's paper and allowed to rest so the juices can be absorbed into the bread.*

1 cup pitted and chopped Kalamata olives

1 cup chopped pimiento-stuffed green olives

½ cup chopped pepperoncini
(pickled peppers)

½ cup chopped roasted red peppers

2 tbsp capers, rinsed

3 green onions, chopped
(white and green parts)

3 plum (Roma) tomatoes, chopped

⅓ cup chopped fresh flat-leaf parsley

½ tsp chopped fresh marjoram

½ tsp chopped fresh thyme

¼ cup olive oil

2 tbsp white wine vinegar

Salt and freshly ground black
pepper, as needed

1 baguette, split lengthwise, or one
large ciabatta loaf, sliced horizontally

1. In a medium bowl, combine the Kalamata and green olives, pepperoncini, roasted pepper, capers, green onions, tomatoes, parsley, marjoram, thyme, oil, and vinegar. Season with salt and pepper. Set aside.

2. Pull out some of the inside of the bread to make room for the filling. Spoon the filling mixture into the bottom half of the bread, packing lightly. Top with remaining baguette half, slice, and serve.

**MAKES 4 SERVINGS**

VARIATION: Try adding a few slices of provolone to the sandwich as well.

Muffaletta Sandwich

# Spicy Chickpea Patties

*These patties are perfect to serve on top of a salad or sandwiched inside a bun. Try them with Pita Bread (page 274) and Cucumber-Yogurt Salad (page 103).*

1 tbsp olive oil, plus more
as needed for frying

1 medium yellow onion, diced

1½ tsp chili powder

1 tsp cayenne

Salt and freshly ground black
pepper, as needed

1 cup cooked chickpeas (see chart, page 131)

1 tbsp chopped fresh flat-leaf parsley

½ cup vital wheat gluten

⅓ cup unseasoned dry bread crumbs

1. In a large sauté pan, heat the oil over medium heat. Add the onion and sauté until translucent, 4 to 5 minutes. Stir in the chili powder and cayenne and season with salt and pepper. Remove from the heat.

2. In a food processor or blender, process the chickpeas, parsley, gluten, bread crumbs, and onion mixture to combine. Mix until the mixture can be formed into patties but is not entirely smooth. Using your hands, form the mixture into 4 patties.

3. Heat about ¼ inch oil in a large sauté pan over medium heat. Add the patties and cook until they are evenly browned on both sides, about 5 minutes per side. Serve warm.

**MAKES 4 SERVINGS**

The major sources of protein in the vegetarian diet are beans, tofu, tempeh, seitan, and eggs. This chapter is all about how to use these ingredients—how to prepare and cook them, but more importantly, how to develop and flavor them to make memorable meals.

5

# BEANS, TOFU, TEMPEH, SEITAN, AND EGGS

# BEANS AND OTHER LEGUMES

Beans are available dried and canned. Canned beans have been fully cooked and can be used immediately, but dried beans must be soaked and cooked until tender before they are eaten. Sort dried beans by spreading them into a single layer and removing any stones and other debris and any moldy beans. Rinse the beans with cold water to remove any dust. Put the beans in a container and cover them with cold water. Remove any that float to the surface; they are too dry to be eaten. After soaking, drain the beans and cook them. This technique works for other legumes as well. Beans, peas, and lentils are in the plant family known as legumes. Beans are typically kidney or oval in shape, and other legumes, such as peas and lentils, are round or elliptical in shape. Soaking beans and legumes will soften their skins, allowing them to hydrate slightly; this makes for faster and more even cooking. There are two methods of soaking:

## The Long-Soak Method

1. Sort and rinse the beans or legumes.

2. Place them in a large container and add enough water to cover them by 2 inches.

3. Let the legumes soak in the refrigerator for 4 hours to overnight, depending on the type of legume (see chart, facing page).

## The Short-Soak Method

1. Sort and rinse the beans or legumes.

2. Place them in a large pot and add enough water to cover them by 2 inches.

3. Bring the water to a simmer.

4. Remove the pot from heat, cover, and let the beans steep for 1 hour.

Most bean recipes specify to soak the beans, then to drain and discard the soaking liquid and start the cooking process with fresh water or stock. However, you may opt to use the soaking liquid for the cooking process because a small amount of the nutrients, flavor, and color are leached into the water, and using the liquid will retain these in the final dish.

The amount of liquid used to cook beans and legumes varies based on their size and type. Beans and legumes need to be covered by liquid at all times throughout cooking. Salt should be added near the end of cooking, or the beans will be tough. Beans and legumes are finished cooking when they are completely tender and creamy in texture but still retain their shape.

## MORE ON SOAKING BEANS AND LEGUMES

Most recipes use only some of the soaking liquid in the cooking process, if they use it at all. In addition to some nutrients and flavor leaching into the soaking water, many of the indigestible complex sugars present in beans and legumes do as well. These sugars are the part of beans known to cause flatulence. Therefore, using the soaking water to cook the beans means adding those sugars back into the beans.

# HOW TO MAKE IT YOUR OWN: DRIED BEANS AND LEGUMES

## DRIED BEANS AND LEGUMES

| LEGUME | SOAKING TIME | COOKING TIME | COOKING METHODS/USES | FLAVORING SUGGESTIONS |
|---|---|---|---|---|
| **BLACK BEANS** | 4—8 hours | 1½ hours | ○ Usually simmered<br>○ Can be used in chilies, stews, soups, stuffings | Onion, garlic, cumin, oregano, Mexican herbs such as epazote and hoja santa |
| **BLACK-EYED PEAS** | Overnight | 45 minutes—1 hour | ○ Usually simmered<br>○ Can be used in chilies, stews, soups, stuffings<br>○ In Southern U.S. cuisine | Onion, garlic, smoky flavors, mushrooms |
| **CHICKPEAS** | 4—8 hours | 2—2½ hours or more | ○ Usually simmered<br>○ Can be used in hummus, falafel, salads, pasta dishes | Lemon, rosemary, garlic, onion, fennel, cumin, coriander, curry |
| **FAVA BEANS** | 12 hours | 3 hours | ○ Usually simmered<br>○ Can be used in purées, succotash, salads, pasta dishes, falafel, stews | Olive oil, herbs such as tarragon, chervil, and chives, fennel, mushrooms, roasted peppers |
| **GREAT NORTHERN/CANNELLINI/ WHITE BEANS** | 4—8 hours | 1 hour | ○ Usually simmered<br>○ Can be used in Tuscan-style beans, purées, soups | Garlic, onion, rosemary, oregano, basil, tarragon, herbes de Provence |
| **KIDNEY BEANS (RED OR WHITE)** | 4 hours | 1 hour | ○ Usually simmered<br>○ Can be used in chilies, stews, salads, soups, stuffings | Latin and Mexican spice combinations; vinaigrettes |
| **LENTILS\*** | N/A | 30—40 minutes | ○ Usually simmered<br>○ Can be used in soups, purées<br>○ Green lentils in salads or pilaf | Middle Eastern spice blends, curry, herbes de Provence, onion, garlic, walnuts, mushrooms, goat cheese |
| **LIMA / BUTTER BEANS** | 4—8 hours | 1—1½ hours | ○ Usually simmered<br>○ Can be used in succotash, soups, salads, stuffings | Butter, olive oil, herbs, onion, green onion, chives |

*continued on next page*

# DRIED BEANS AND LEGUMES cont.

| LEGUME | SOAKING TIME | COOKING TIME | COOKING METHODS/USES | FLAVORING SUGGESTIONS |
|---|---|---|---|---|
| **NAVY BEANS** | 4 hours | 2 hours | ○ Usually simmered<br>○ Can be used in chilies, stews, soups, stuffings, baked beans | Molasses, brown sugar, onion, garlic, all types of herbs and vegetables |
| **SPLIT PEAS\*** | N/A | 30 minutes | ○ In soups, purées | Vegetables such as carrots, onion, leek, garlic, smoky flavors, cumin, mint, tarragon |
| **WHOLE PEAS** | 4 hours | 40 minutes | ○ In soups, stuffings, with rice, purées | Vegetables such as carrots, onion, leek, garlic; smoky flavors, cumin, tarragon, mint |
| **PIGEON PEAS** | 4 hours | 30 minutes | ○ Usually simmered<br>○ Can be used in braised dishes, stews, soups, stuffings | Curry, herbs, onion, garlic, carrots, celery, mushrooms |
| **PINK BEANS** | 4—8 hours | 1 hour | ○ Usually simmered<br>○ Can be used in chilies, stews, soups, stuffings, combined with rice | Latin and Mexican spice combinations, vinaigrettes |
| **PINTO BEANS** | 4—8 hours | 1½—2 hours | ○ Usually simmered<br>○ Can be used in chilies, stews, soups, refried, mashed<br>○ In Southwestern and Southern U.S. cuisine | Latin and Mexican spice combinations, vinaigrettes, garlic, onions, smoky flavors |
| **SOYBEANS: BLACK, GREEN, WHITE** | 12 hours | 3—3½ hours | ○ In homemade tofu, stuffings, stews, salads, chilies, soups | Asian spices and sauces, all types of vegetables, sesame oil, ginger, green onions |

\*Soaking not necessary

# TOFU

Tofu is made from soybeans that are soaked, ground into a paste, cooked, and filtered as soy milk. This milk is then curdled, and the curds are removed from the whey and pressed. The pressing removes any excess whey and forms the tofu.

Tofu is generally sold in bricks, stored in water. Store your purchased tofu similarly—in fresh water (changed daily), refrigerated—until you are ready to use it. When packed in aseptic boxes, it can be stored unopened without refrigeration. Tofu is quite perishable; once opened, it should be used within 1 week.

Tofu is available in the following varieties:

**SILKEN** A very soft, creamy, almost custard-like tofu. Ideal for use in desserts and for puréed items.

**SOFT** Just firm enough to be sliced, but still very soft and creamy in texture.

**FIRM** Firm enough to be sliced and used in a variety of cooking methods. Sometimes grocery stores also sell "extra-firm" tofu, which is even denser.

**DRIED TOFU** The firmest available tofu, it can be sliced or crumbled. It has a very chewy texture.

Tofu may also be sold frozen (though it usually changes the texture), pickled, in flavored varieties, smoked, fried, and more.

# HOW TO MAKE IT YOUR OWN: TOFU

The many different varieties of tofu, along with its readiness to absorb flavor, make it one of the most versatile proteins. Besides varying by type, different brands of tofu will vary slightly in flavor and texture as well.

## TOFU

| TYPE | TEXTURE | FLAVOR | APPLICATION |
|---|---|---|---|
| **Japanese-Style**<br>Usually packed in aseptic boxes | | | |
| **SILKEN** | ○ Purées and mashes easily<br>○ Does not hold shape well when diced or sliced | Overall, bland; readily takes on the flavor of other ingredients and seasonings | Best suited for smooth preparations such as smoothies, sauces, soups, custards, salad dressings, baked goods such as cheesecake |
| **SOFT** | Like soft custard | Bland | Smoothies |
| **MEDIUM** | Like medium-firm custard | Bland | Soft fillings and purée soups |
| **FIRM** | Like firm custard | Bland | Soft fillings and purée soups |
| **EXTRA-FIRM** | Like extra-firm or dense custard | Bland | Cheesecake |
| **SOME FLAVORED VARIETIES AVAILABLE** | | Flavored varieties include smoked, curry, hot and spicy, and 5-spice | |

*continued on next page*

# TOFU cont.

| TYPE | TEXTURE | FLAVOR | APPLICATION |
|---|---|---|---|
| **Chinese-Style** Generally packed in water in clamshell containers or sold loose; found in the produce or refrigerator section | | | |
| **REGULAR** | Texture is generally drier than the silken varieties and more dense. When cut, these types hold their form, especially if pressed first. | Generally bland, readily takes on the flavor of other ingredients and seasonings | ○ Generally best used to stir-fry, pan fry, roast, bake, grill, deep-fry, as soup garnish<br>○ Crumbled, diced, or sliced<br>○ Breaded, battered; coated in seeds, nuts, spices and spice rubs |
| **SOFT** | If crumbled, like ricotta cheese | Bland, readily takes on the flavor of other ingredients and seasonings | |
| **MEDIUM** | If crumbled, like scrambled eggs | Bland, readily takes on the flavor of other ingredients and seasonings | |
| **FIRM** | If crumbled, like egg salad | Bland, readily takes on the flavor of other ingredients and seasonings | ○ Very good to sauté, grill, or pan fry<br>○ Can be marinated or dry-rubbed |
| **EXTRA-FIRM** | If crumbled, mock chicken salad | Bland, readily takes on the flavor of other ingredients and seasonings | ○ Very good to sauté, grill, or pan fry<br>○ Can be marinated or dry-rubbed |
| **SOME FLAVORED VARIETIES AVAILABLE** | | Flavored varieties include smoked, 5-spice, Italian seasoning, teriyaki, Cajun seasoning, mock turkey, and mock bacon | |

## MARINATING ALTERNATIVE PROTEINS

Tempeh, seitan, and tofu all respond very well to marinating. Because their textures are similar to meat, they are able to absorb the flavors of a marinade. Marinades can be as simple as flavored oils, vegetable or fruit juices, or a mixture of spices, or you can use the marinade recipes in Chapter 9. Refer to specific recipes for instructions, but marinate the protein in a shallow dish. Turn it occasionally for best results.

## TEXTURED VEGETABLE PROTEIN (TVP)

TVP is produced from soy flour from which the soybean oil has been extracted. The flour is pressure cooked, extruded, and dried, and the resulting mixture has both a texture and flavor similar to that of meat. This product is dried and can be stored in an airtight container for up to six months without spoiling. It can replace meat in a variety of cooking techniques and recipes. Before use, it can be rehydrated by adding three-quarters of its weight in water.

# TEMPEH

Like tofu, tempeh is made from soybeans, but it undergoes a fermentation process that gives it an altogether different flavor and texture. Tempeh is firmer than tofu, and is higher in protein and fiber. Originally from Indonesia, tempeh can be used in a variety of cooking techniques, such as steaming, boiling, frying, and so on. When tightly wrapped and refrigerated, tempeh can be stored for up to 10 days, and frozen for 2 months. It will occasionally have a white bloom on its surface, but this is normal. A few black and gray spots are also to be expected, but if the tempeh ever gains a yellow, blue, or pink hue, it has most likely overfermented and is spoiled.

# SEITAN

Seitan is made from vital wheat gluten that has been cooked and pulled or kneaded to create a meat-like product, firm in texture and high in protein. Because its texture is so similar to that of meat, it can be used in a variety of preparations: it can be baked, braised, stir-fried, grilled, and more. Seitan also takes on other flavorings easily, making it ideal for marinating. When making your own seitan, you can flavor it with anything—dried herbs, (see also page 161) spices, or even nuts. Refrigerated, it will keep up to ten days.

## Making Seitan

1. Place the vital wheat gluten into a food processor or mixer and add water. Mix until the water is absorbed.

2. Continue to mix until it forms a smooth dough.

3. Pull or knead the dough and then divide into two pieces.

4. Stretch and pull the dough into logs.

5. Place into simmering liquid.

6. Cook, turning occasionally, for 45 minutes to 1 hour.

Pull or knead the seitan until it's uniform in texture.

Divide the seitan and simmer it in the broth. It will swell in size as it cooks.

# HOW TO MAKE IT YOUR OWN: ALTERNATIVE PROTEINS

## ALTERNATIVE PROTEINS

| PROTEIN TYPE | TEXTURE | COOKING METHODS | PREPARATION | MARINADE |
|---|---|---|---|---|
| **TOFU** | Varies from smooth and creamy (silken) to dense and curd-like (firm, pressed) | Sauté, grill, pan fry, deep-fry, roast, braise, scramble | ○ May be eaten raw, cold <br> ○ Coat with flour, bread crumbs, crushed tortilla chips, crushed flake cereal before cooking | Will take on flavors readily so anything goes, from Asian spice blends to Cajun rubs, Latin flavors, etc. |
| **TEMPEH** | Firm, can be diced or sliced; can be crumbly | Boil first, then use in a host of ways: grill, sauté, crumble and brown | ○ Can be incorporated into loaves, "meatless" balls, or patties <br> ○ Excellent in veggie burgers, stir-fries, stews, casseroles | Any ethnic flavor or spice profile will work, especially Asian and Indian |
| **TVP** | Usually sold dehydrated in ground "meat" texture, or diced as for stew | Reconstitute first, then brown or sauté | ○ Excellent in tomato sauce, chili, veggie burgers, stews <br> ○ Can be used as a replacement in any way that ground beef or stew meat would be used | Takes on almost any spice or seasoning blend |
| **SEITAN** | Smooth texture but somewhat chewy or meat-like; texture similar to cooked portobello mushroom | Boil first if made from scratch, then sauté, grill, pan fry, brown as for stew | ○ May be breaded, diced, chopped, ground <br> ○ Useful in "meatless" loaves, stews, layered casseroles | Handles strong flavors and spice rubs well; excellent with tomato sauce or roasted peppers |

# EGGS

Eggs are incredibly versatile and are a naturally good source of protein. Eggs are available in varying sizes (small, medium, large, and extra-large), colors (brown, white, and even pastel shades), and grades (AA is the top grade, indicating very fresh eggs). It is very important to cook eggs correctly, regardless of the technique being used, because when eggs are overcooked, they excessively coagulate, forcing water out and making them dry and unappealing.

Eggs cooked in the shell should be cooked in simmering water. Time will depend on size of egg and desired doneness. Poached eggs are prepared by slipping eggs directly into barely simmering water and gently cooking until the egg holds its shape. Fried eggs can be cooked in oil or butter, and they should be made in heavy-bottomed steel or nonstick pans for best results. Scrambled eggs can be made one of two ways: They can be stirred constantly over low heat for a soft, creamy texture or stirred less frequently for a stiff, firm texture.

## THE GREEN RING

The green ring that forms around the yolk of a hard-boiled egg is the result of a chemical reaction between the iron and sulfur naturally present in eggs, which form green iron sulfide. Heat speeds up this reaction, so the best way to prevent the ring from forming is to watch cooking time closely and not allow the eggs to cook longer than necessary. Rapidly cooling the eggs also helps.

Beans Bourguignon

# Beans Bourguignon

*In this recipe, beans are cooked slowly on the stovetop in red wine, much like the rich beef bourguignon originally from France.*

2 tbsp unsalted butter

2 tbsp all-purpose flour

1 tbsp olive oil

3 medium shallots, diced

4 medium carrots, sliced

2 cloves garlic, minced

¾ pound cremini mushrooms, quartered

1 sprig fresh thyme

1 sprig fresh rosemary

1 bay leaf

1 cup canned crushed tomatoes

½ cup Vegetable Broth (page 287)

1 cup dry red wine

3 cups cooked kidney beans
(see chart, page 131)

Salt and freshly ground black pepper, as needed

1. In a small bowl combine the butter and flour, mixing with a fork until the two are thoroughly blended. Set aside.

2. In a large sauté pan, heat the oil over medium heat. Add the shallots, carrots, and garlic, and cook until the shallots are translucent, 3 to 4 minutes.

3. Stir in the mushrooms and cook until the mushrooms start to become tender, 4 to 5 minutes more.

4. Stir in the thyme, rosemary, bay leaf, flour mixture, tomatoes, broth, and half of the wine. Bring to a boil, reduce heat to low, and simmer until the vegetables are tender, 20 to 25 minutes.

5. Add the rest of the wine and the beans and season with salt and pepper. Simmer until good flavor develops, 10 to 15 minutes more. Remove and discard the thyme, rosemary, and bay leaf before serving.

**MAKES 4 SERVINGS**

# Molasses Baked Beans

*Slow-baked beans may take a while, but their flavor is worth the wait.*

2 tbsp grapeseed or canola oil

2½ cups minced yellow onions

2 cloves garlic, minced

2 cups dried navy beans

1 cup diced tomatoes

1 cup ketchup

One 12-ounce bottle ale

2 tbsp dry mustard

2 tbsp pure maple syrup

¼ cup molasses

1 bay leaf

2 tbsp apple cider vinegar

3 cups Vegetable Broth (page 287), plus more as needed

Salt and freshly ground black pepper, as needed

1. Preheat the oven to 300°F.

2. In a large ovenproof pan with tight-fitting lid or Dutch oven, heat the oil over medium heat. Add the onions and garlic and sauté until the onions are lightly browned, about 10 minutes.

3. Add the beans, tomatoes, ketchup, ale, mustard, maple syrup, molasses, bay leaf, vinegar, and broth and bring to a simmer. Cover the pot and transfer to the oven.

4. Bake the beans, stirring occasionally, until they begin to become tender, about 5 hours. Stir in more broth as the beans cook if they appear to be drying out.

5. Uncover and bake until the beans are completely tender, 45 minutes to 1 hour more. Add salt and pepper to taste. Remove and discard bay leaf before serving.

**MAKES 4 TO 8 SERVINGS**

# Frijoles à la Charra

*This is a good basic bean dish with lots of great flavor and a hint of spice. For borracho (drunken) beans, add a 12-ounce bottle of beer in place of 1½ cups of the broth used to cook the beans.*

2 cups dried black beans, soaked and drained (see chart, page 131)

1 quart Vegetable Broth (page 287)

1¼ tsp ground cumin, toasted

⅔ tsp dried oregano

1¼ tsp paprika, toasted

⅔ tsp dried thyme

2 tsp tomato paste

Freshly ground black pepper

1 tbsp grapeseed or canola oil

¾ cup minced yellow onion

1 serrano chile, seeded and minced

1 clove garlic, minced

1 cup diced tomatoes

Salt, as needed

1. In a large saucepan, cover the beans with the broth. Add the cumin, oregano, paprika, thyme, tomato paste, and pepper. Simmer over medium heat, covered, until the beans start to become tender, 30 to 40 minutes.

2. In a medium sauté pan, heat the oil over medium heat. Add the onion, chile, garlic, and tomatoes. Cook until the onions are tender, 6 to 8 minutes. Stir into the beans.

3. Cook until the beans are very tender, about 10 to 20 minutes more. Season with salt.

**MAKES 4 TO 8 SERVINGS**

# Puerto Rican–Style Red Beans

*Coconut milk and butternut squash give these beans a delicious rich and creamy flavor. Serve simply with rice for a great meal.*

1½ tbsp vegetable oil

¾ cup minced yellow onion

1 clove garlic, minced

2 cups chopped tomatoes

1½ cups dried red kidney beans, soaked and drained (see chart, page 131)

1 bay leaf

Vegetable Broth (page 287), as needed

2 cups peeled, seeded, and diced butternut squash

½ cup unsweetened coconut milk

½ bunch green onions, chopped (white and green parts)

2 tsp chopped fresh thyme

¼ cup chopped fresh cilantro

Salt and freshly ground black pepper, as needed

1. In a large saucepan, heat the oil over medium heat. Add the onion and cook until translucent, 4 to 5 minutes. Add the garlic and cook until fragrant, about 1 minute more. Add the tomatoes, lower the heat, and cook, stirring frequently, until the tomatoes "melt" into a paste, about 20 minutes.

2. Stir in the beans and bay leaf. Add enough broth to cover the beans by 1 inch. Bring to a simmer and cook until the beans are nearly tender, 45 to 50 minutes.

3. Stir in the squash and coconut milk. Simmer until the squash is tender, 10 to 15 minutes more.

4. Stir in the green onions, thyme, and cilantro and simmer until good flavor develops, 5 to 10 minutes more. Season with salt and pepper. Remove and discard bay leaf before serving.

**MAKES 4 TO 8 SERVINGS**

NOTE: For a smoky flavor, add 1 tbsp of smoked sweet paprika, aka pimento dulce.

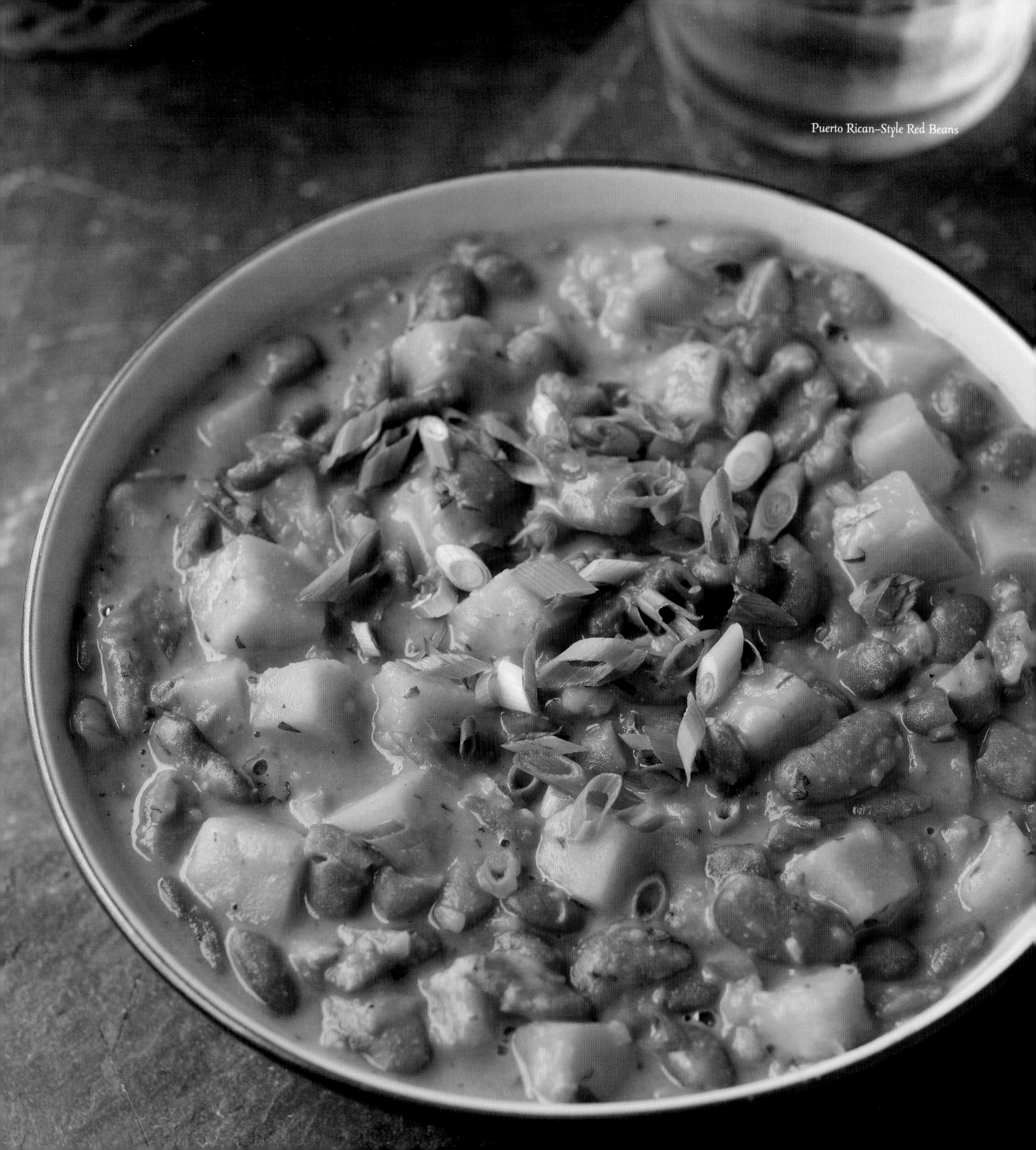

Puerto Rican–Style Red Beans

# Chipotle Baked Tofu

Canned chipotle chiles in adobo sauce are generally available in the international section of most grocery stores. This recipe uses both the chiles and the sauce they're packaged in.

Nonstick spray, as needed for the pan

½ cup all-purpose flour

2 large eggs

3 tbsp adobo sauce

3 cups finely crushed tortilla chips

1 pound extra-firm tofu, drained well and sliced

3 tbsp soy or tamari sauce

2 canned chipotle chiles, with seeds

1 tbsp grapeseed or canola oil

1. Preheat the oven to 350°F. Spray a baking sheet with nonstick spray.

2. Prepare a breading station by setting up three shallow bowls: one with the flour, one with the eggs (beaten lightly with 2 tbsp of the adobo sauce), and one with the tortilla chip crumbs. Dredge the tofu slices to coat completely in the flour, then in the eggs, and finally in the crumbs. Place the tofu on the baking sheet. Spray liberally with nonstick spray.

3. Bake the tofu until the crust is golden brown, 12 to 15 minutes.

4. Meanwhile, make the sauce: In a food processor or blender, combine the soy sauce, chiles, the remaining 1 tbsp adobo sauce, and the oil until smooth.

5. Transfer the tofu to plates and serve with the chipotle sauce.

**MAKES 4 SERVINGS**

# Ma Po Dofu

*This Sichuan dish is composed of lightly fried tofu in a chili and bean–based sauce. It is best served simply with steamed white rice.*

Grapeseed or canola

1 pound firm tofu, cut in ¼-inch-thick triangles

**SAUCE**

3 tbsp peanut or soybean oil

2 tsp minced fresh ginger

2 cloves garlic, minced

1 green onion, thinly sliced (white and green parts)

1 tbsp hot bean paste

1 tbsp black bean sauce

2 tsp Korean chili powder

1 cup stemmed and thinly sliced shiitake mushrooms

1 cup halved snow peas (2 to 3 ounces)

1 cup thinly sliced red bell pepper

½ cup bean sprouts

1 tbsp vegetarian oyster sauce

1 tbsp toasted sesame oil

1 tbsp chopped cilantro

1 tsp ground Sichuan peppercorns

Salt, as needed

1. Fill a deep, heavy pot half-full with oil. Heat over medium heat until it registers 350°F on a deep-fry thermometer. Working in batches if necessary, deep-fry the tofu until golden brown. Drain well on paper towels and set aside.

2. To make the sauce, heat the oil in a wok over high heat. Add the ginger, garlic, and green onion, and stir-fry until fragrant, 2 to 3 minutes.

3. Add the bean paste, bean sauce, and chili powder. Stir until well combined, about 1 minute. Add the mushrooms, snow peas, red peppers, and bean sprouts, and stir-fry until the vegetables are tender, 3 to 4 minutes.

4. Add the tofu, oyster sauce, sesame oil, cilantro, and Sichuan pepper. Season with salt. Stir-fry until heated through, about 2 minutes. Serve immediately.

**MAKES 4 SERVINGS**

# Tofu à la Veracruzana

*This dish gets a great briny flavor from capers and olives, and it pairs perfectly with Tostones (page 45).*

Salt, as needed

8 new potatoes, peeled

1 tbsp extra-virgin olive oil, plus more as needed for frying

½ cup minced yellow onions

2 cloves garlic, minced

4 cups minced tomatoes

1 cup thinly sliced or diced roasted red peppers

10 green olives, pitted and chopped

2 tbsp capers, rinsed

1 small cinnamon stick

3 tbsp coarsely chopped blanched almonds

1 bay leaf

3 tbsp raisins

1 pound extra-firm tofu, sliced into four equal pieces

Salt and freshly ground black pepper, as needed

All-purpose flour, as needed for dredging

GARNISH

2 pickled jalapeños, thinly sliced

¼ cup chopped fresh flat-leaf parsley

2 tbsp capers, rinsed

15 green olives, rinsed, halved, and pitted

1. In a medium pot, cover the potatoes with cold salted water by 2 inches and bring to a boil. Cook until the potatoes are tender, 15 to 18 minutes. Drain and set aside.

2. In a large sauté pan, heat the oil over medium heat. Add the onions and garlic, and sauté until the onions are translucent, 4 to 5 minutes.

3. Add the tomatoes, roasted peppers, olives, capers, cinnamon stick, almonds, bay leaf, and raisins. Bring to a simmer and cook until reduced slightly, about 10 minutes. Add the potatoes and keep warm. Remove the bay leaf and cinnamon stick.

4. Season the tofu with salt and pepper and dredge in flour to coat. Heat ¼ inch oil in a large sauté pan. Add the tofu and sauté until golden on each side, 3 to 4 minutes per side.

5. Arrange the sautéed tofu on a warmed platter and spoon the sauce over it. Garnish with the jalapeños, parsley, capers, and olives.

**MAKES 4 SERVINGS**

Tofu à la Veracruzana

# Ginger Tofu with Citrus-Hoisin Sauce

*Tofu has very little flavor of its own but takes on the flavors of marinades and sauces very well.*

1 pound extra-firm tofu, cubed

2 tbsp soy or tamari sauce

1 tbsp plus 1 tsp cornstarch

1 tbsp canola oil

2 tsp toasted sesame oil

2 tsp minced fresh ginger

½ cup hoisin sauce

½ cup Vegetable Broth (page 287)

¼ cup fresh orange juice

1½ tbsp fresh lime juice

1½ tbsp fresh lemon juice

Salt and freshly ground black pepper, as needed

5 green onions, minced (white and green parts)

1. Place the tofu in a medium bowl. Add the soy sauce and toss to coat. Add 1 tbsp cornstarch and toss to coat again.

2. In a large sauté pan, heat the canola oil over medium heat. Add the tofu and cook, turning occasionally, until golden on all sides, 8 to 10 minutes. Remove the tofu from the pan and set aside.

3. In the same pan, heat the sesame oil over medium heat. Add the ginger and cook until fragrant, about 1 minute. Stir in the hoisin sauce, broth, and orange juice and bring to a simmer. Cook until the liquid is reduced slightly, about 3 minutes.

4. In a small bowl, combine the remaining cornstarch with the lime and lemon juices. Add to the sauce. Stir until the sauce thickens slightly. Season with salt and pepper.

5. Return the tofu to the sauté pan and cook, turning it gently, until it is coated with the sauce. Stir in the green onions and serve immediately.

**MAKES 4 SERVINGS**

# Asian Tofu Salad

*This recipe calls for baked tofu. It's also ideal for leftover Ginger Tofu with Citrus-Hoisin Sauce (facing page) or any tofu that has been marinated and baked.*

2 cups shredded cabbage

½ cup shredded carrots

¼ cup minced green onions
(white and green parts)

2 tbsp chopped fresh cilantro

1 clove garlic, crushed

1 tsp minced fresh ginger

2 tbsp mirin

1 tsp red pepper flakes

1 tbsp rice vinegar

2 tbsp Vegetable Broth (page 287)

1 tbsp fresh lime juice

1 tbsp toasted sesame oil

2 tbsp soy sauce

¾ pound baked marinated tofu,
chopped or shredded

⅓ cup chopped toasted unsalted peanuts

1. In a large bowl, toss the cabbage, carrots, green onions, and cilantro to combine.

2. In a small bowl, combine the garlic, ginger, mirin, pepper flakes, vinegar, broth, lime juice, sesame oil, and soy sauce. Pour the dressing over the vegetables and toss to coat.

3. Add the tofu and peanuts and toss to combine. Serve immediately, while warm.

**MAKES 4 SERVINGS**

Tempeh in Coconut Curry Sauce

# Tempeh in Coconut Curry Sauce

*A classic coconut curry sauce is nicely accentuated by the crispy coconut tempeh.*

1 pound tempeh, sliced ¼ inch thick

2 tbsp grapeseed or canola oil, plus more as needed for greasing

1 cup unsweetened dried coconut

1 medium yellow onion, diced

3 cloves garlic, minced

1 red bell pepper, diced

1 green bell pepper, diced

1 jalapeño, seeded and minced

1 tbsp curry paste, red or massaman

2 cups diced fresh tomatoes

1¾ cups unsweetened coconut milk

Salt and freshly ground black pepper, as needed

### GARNISH

½ cup toasted peanuts or cashews, coarsely chopped

¼ cup chopped fresh cilantro

1. Bring a medium pot of water to a simmer. Add the tempeh and cook until tender, 20 to 25 minutes. Drain completely.

2. Meanwhile, preheat the oven to 350°F. Lightly grease a baking sheet.

3. Dredge the cooked tempeh in the coconut and place on the baking sheet. Bake until the tempeh is golden brown, 12 to 15 minutes. Keep warm.

4. Heat the oil in a large sauté pan over medium heat. Add the onions, garlic, red and green peppers, and jalapeños. Sauté until the peppers are tender-crisp, 4 minutes.

5. Stir in the curry paste, tomatoes, and coconut milk. Reduce heat to medium-low, and simmer until the sauce has reduced and thickened slightly, 15 to 20 minutes. Season with salt and pepper.

6. Serve the sauce over the baked tempeh, garnished with the peanuts and cilantro.

**MAKES 4 SERVINGS**

# Glazed Kibbeh Skewers

*Traditionally, the Mediterranean dish kibbeh is formed into balls and either sautéed or fried. In this meatless version, the kibbeh is formed around skewers before being glazed and grilled.*

½ cup bulgur

9½ ounces tempeh, precooked, cut into cubes

⅔ cup onion, diced

2 cloves garlic

¼ cup toasted pine nuts

2 jalapeños, minced

2 tsp plain Greek-style yogurt

2 tbsp olive oil, plus more as needed for the grill

1 tbsp chopped fresh flat-leaf parsley

1 tbsp chopped fresh cilantro

2 tsp chopped fresh mint

1 tbsp ground cumin, toasted

¼ tsp ground allspice, toasted

Pinch ground cinnamon

¼ tsp freshly ground black pepper, or more to taste

Pinch cayenne

Twelve 6-inch wooden skewers, soaked in water for 30 minutes

1 tbsp honey

1 tbsp soy or tamari sauce

1. Rinse the bulgur and place it in a medium bowl. Cover with warm water by 1 inch and soak for 10 to 15 minutes. Pour into a fine-mesh strainer and drain for 15 to 20 minutes. Press to remove any excess moisture.

2. Heat a grill or grill pan until hot.

3. In a food processor or blender, process the bulgur, tempeh, onion, garlic, pine nuts, jalapeño, yogurt, 1 tbsp of the oil, the parsley, cilantro, mint, cumin, allspice, cinnamon, pepper, and cayenne until the mixture is smooth. Mold evenly onto the skewers.

4. In a small bowl, combine the honey, soy sauce, and the remaining 1 tbsp oil. Brush the bulgur mixture generously with the glaze.

5. Brush the grill lightly with oil. Grill the skewers until golden brown and cooked through, 3 to 5 minutes per side. Serve immediately while hot.

**MAKES 12 SKEWERS**

NOTE: Mixture or assembled skewers may be stored in the refrigerator up to 2 days.

Glazed Kibbeh Skewers

Pineapple-Glazed Tempeh and Sweet Potatoes

# Pineapple-Glazed Tempeh and Sweet Potatoes

*Seasoning the tempeh before frying makes it incredibly flavorful, even before the vegetables and sauce are added.*

1 pound tempeh, cubed

3 tbsp soy or tamari sauce

1 tsp ground coriander, toasted

½ tsp ground turmeric

3 tbsp grapeseed or canola oil

Cornstarch, as needed for dredging

1 green bell pepper, thinly sliced

2 tbsp minced shallots

2 medium sweet potatoes, peeled and diced

2 tsp grated fresh ginger

2 star anise pods

1 cup water chestnuts

2 cups pineapple juice

Juice of 1 lime

1 tsp red pepper flakes

1. Bring a medium pot of water to a simmer. Add the tempeh and cook until tender, 25 to 30 minutes. Drain.

2. Transfer the tempeh to a large bowl. Add the soy sauce, coriander, and turmeric, and toss to coat.

3. In a large sauté pan, heat the oil over medium heat. Dredge the seasoned tempeh in cornstarch and shake off excess. Add the tempeh to the oil and cook until evenly browned, 6 to 7 minutes. Remove from the pan and set aside.

4. Add the green peppers, shallots, and sweet potatoes to the oil. Cover the pan and cook until the vegetables are slightly softened and evenly browned, 10 to 12 minutes, turning once. Potatoes should be about half cooked.

5. Add the ginger, star anise, water chestnuts, and pineapple juice, and bring to a simmer. Add the tempeh, cover, and cook until the potatoes are soft, 10 minutes more.

6. Remove the star anise and stir in the lime juice and pepper flakes. Serve immediately.

**MAKES 4 SERVINGS**

# Tempeh-Cashew Noodles

*This dish can easily be made with lots of other vegetables—try adding mushrooms, bean sprouts, snow peas, or green onions.*

¾ cup unsalted toasted cashews

2 cloves garlic

¼ cup soy or tamari sauce

3 tbsp rice vinegar

2 tsp light brown sugar

1 tbsp toasted sesame oil

1 tbsp red chili paste

Salt, as needed

10 ounces udon noodles

2 tbsp grapeseed or canola oil

1 pound tempeh, precooked, diced

1 medium yellow onion, diced

1 red bell pepper, diced

1 large zucchini, thinly sliced into rounds

1 cup green beans, halved

4 cloves garlic, minced

GARNISH

Chopped fresh cilantro, as needed

Chopped toasted cashews, as needed

1. In a food processor or blender, combine the cashews, 2 cloves garlic, soy sauce, vinegar, sugar, sesame oil, and chili paste until smooth. Set aside.

2. Bring a pot of lightly salted water to a boil. Add the noodles and cook until tender, 7 to 9 minutes. Drain.

3. In a large sauté pan or wok, heat the oil over medium heat. Stir-fry the tempeh, onions, and red peppers until the onions are translucent, 4 to 5 minutes.

4. Add the zucchini and green beans and stir-fry until the beans are tender, 3 to 5 minutes more. Add the minced garlic and stir-fry until fragrant, about 1 minute.

5. Add the noodles and toss to combine. Add the cashew sauce and toss to coat. Heat through, about 5 minutes.

6. Serve immediately, garnished with cilantro and cashews.

**MAKES 4 SERVINGS**

# Tempeh Reuben

This sandwich has all the flavors of a traditional Reuben. The longer the tempeh is marinated, the stronger the flavor will be.

1 pound tempeh, precooked

3 tbsp soy sauce

½ cup red wine vinegar

½ cup Vegetable Broth (page 287)

⅓ cup minced yellow onions

3 cloves garlic, minced

⅓ tsp freshly ground black pepper

⅔ tsp sweet paprika

12 slices rye bread, toasted

⅓ cup Thousand Island dressing

1 cup drained sauerkraut, warm

12 slices Swiss cheese, optional

1. With a sharp knife, gently slice the tempeh into 12 thin pieces.

2. In a shallow baking pan, combine the soy sauce, vinegar, broth, onion, garlic, pepper, and paprika. Add the tempeh slices, turning to coat. Cover, refrigerate, and marinate at least 2 hours and up to overnight, turning occasionally.

3. Remove the tempeh from the refrigerator and preheat the oven to 350°F.

4. Bake the tempeh in the marinade until lightly browned, 15 to 20 minutes.

5. Spread the bread with dressing and layer with the tempeh and sauerkraut. Serve warm.

**MAKES 6 SERVINGS**

NOTES: If using cheese, place cheese slices on the bread, then sliced tempeh, dressing, and sauerkraut. | After assembly, this sandwich is delicious cooked on a griddle as for a grilled cheese!

# Sesame Tempeh Sticks with Apricot Dipping Sauce

*These tempeh sticks make a great appetizer, but served alongside Coconut Rice (page 28) they become a satisfying meal.*

6 tbsp toasted sesame seeds

10½ ounces tempeh, precooked

2 green onions, chopped
(white and green parts)

1 tbsp sesame oil

1 tbsp soy sauce

1½ tsp cornstarch

2 tsp minced fresh ginger

1 clove garlic, minced

6 sheets phyllo dough, thawed
overnight in the refrigerator

4 tbsp (½ stick) unsalted butter, melted

Egg Wash (see page 315), as needed

Kosher salt, as needed

**APRICOT DIPPING SAUCE**

½ cup apricot preserves, warm

2 tbsp fresh lime juice

1 tsp Dijon mustard

1 tsp minced fresh ginger

2 tbsp rice vinegar

1½ tsp soy or tamari sauce

¼ tsp red pepper flakes

1. Preheat the oven to 350°F. Line a baking sheet with parchment paper.

2. In a blender or food processor, blend ¼ cup of the sesame seeds, tempeh, green onions, sesame oil, soy sauce, cornstarch, ginger, and garlic until the mixture forms a coarse paste.

3. Lay out the phyllo dough on the work surface and cover with plastic wrap and then a dampened kitchen towel. Only remove 1 sheet to work with at a time.

4. Brush 1 sheet generously with butter. Stack another sheet on top and brush with butter again. Repeat with one last piece of phyllo and butter.

5. Cut the stack of buttered phyllo sheets in half lengthwise to make two stacks. Arrange one stack with the long side nearest you.

6. With dampened fingers, shape about 3 to 4 tbsp of the sesame-tempeh mixture into a narrow rope along the edge near you. Roll the phyllo away from you tightly to form a long, thin roll.

7. Repeat with the other half of the phyllo stack, and then repeat the whole process with remaining 3 sheets of phyllo dough.

8. Lightly brush the top of the sticks with egg wash and sprinkle with the remaining sesame seeds and with kosher salt.

9. Using a sharp knife, cut each roll into 4 sticks and place, seam side down, on the prepared baking sheet. Bake until the phyllo is golden brown, 12 to 15 minutes. Cool slightly.

10. In a small bowl, combine the ingredients for the dipping sauce with 1 tbsp water. Serve the sticks warm with the dipping sauce.

**MAKES ABOUT 16 STICKS**

*Sesame Tempeh Sticks with Apricot Dipping Sauce*

# Tempeh Sausage Patties

*These flavorful sausage substitutes are great for breakfast, lunch, or dinner. Pair a patty with scrambled eggs and cheese on an English muffin for a tasty sandwich.*

1 pound tempeh

1 cup minced yellow onion

1 clove garlic, minced

Pinch cayenne

Salt, as needed

1 tbsp chopped fresh chives

1 tbsp chopped fresh sage

2 tbsp chopped fresh flat-leaf parsley

2 tbsp olive oil, plus more as needed for cooking

Panko bread crumbs, as needed

1. Cook the tempeh in simmering water until tender, about 20 minutes. Drain. Transfer the tempeh to a large bowl and use a fork or potato masher to mash it until smooth.

2. Add the onion, garlic, cayenne, salt, chives, sage, parsley, and oil and mix to combine. Form the mixture into patties and refrigerate until firm, 15 to 20 minutes.

3. Dredge the patties in the panko.

4. Heat ¼ inch oil in a large sauté pan over medium heat. Add the patties and cook until they are golden brown and heated through, 3 to 5 minutes per side.

**MAKES 4 SERVINGS**

# Seitan

*Try adding other seasonings to the liquid you cook the seitan in. Herbs, spices, or garlic will all help to make your seitan more flavorful.*

¾ cup vital wheat gluten

4½ cups Vegetable Broth (page 287) or Mushroom Broth (page 287)

¼ cup soy or tamari sauce

2 tbsp dry sherry (optional)

1. Place the vital wheat gluten into a food processor or a stand mixer fitted with a dough hook. Add ⅔ cup water and mix until it is absorbed, about 2 minutes. The mixture will be thick but should all come together.

2. Continue to mix until it forms a smooth dough, about 1 minute more. Transfer the dough from the food processor to a bowl. Cover the dough and let it rest to relax the gluten, 15 to 20 minutes.

3. When the dough is rested, use your hands to pull it into 2 pieces. Stretch and pull each piece until it forms a log.

4. In a large saucepan, bring the broth, soy sauce, and sherry (if using) to a simmer over medium-low heat. Place the logs in the simmering liquid and lower the heat to low. Cover the pot and cook, turning the seitan occasionally, for 45 to 55 minutes, or until it can be easily sliced with a knife. Cool the seitan in the liquid until it reaches room temperature.

5. Drain the seitan for immediate use or store refrigerated in the cooking liquid for up to 2 days. Cooked seitan may also be frozen in the cooking liquid and stored in the freezer for up to 3 months. The cooking liquid is reusable for cooking additional seitan or as an additive or partial replacement for broth in some recipes.

**MAKES ABOUT 1 POUND**

# Pan-Seared Seitan with Artichokes and Olives

*This dish gets wonderful briny flavor from olives and capers, which are a perfect match with the tender artichoke hearts.*

2 tbsp olive oil

1 pound Seitan (page 161), cooked, sliced into 4 thick or 8 thinner slices

2 garlic cloves, minced

2 cups diced tomatoes

1½ cups thinly sliced canned artichoke hearts

⅓ cup halved and pitted oil-cured black olives

1 tbsp capers, rinsed

3 tbsp chopped fresh flat-leaf parsley

Salt and freshly ground black pepper, as needed

GARNISH

1 cup crumbled feta cheese

Chopped fresh flat-leaf parsley, as needed

1. In a large sauté pan, heat 1 tbsp of the oil over medium heat. Add the seitan and cook, turning once, until evenly browned on both sides, about 5 minutes. Keep warm.

2. In the same sauté pan, heat the remaining oil over medium heat. Add the garlic and cook until fragrant, about 1 minute.

3. Add the tomatoes, artichokes, olives, capers, and parsley. Season with salt and pepper and cook until the mixture is heated through, 3 to 5 minutes.

4. Pour the sauce over the seitan, sprinkle with the cheese and parsley, and serve.

**MAKES 4 SERVINGS**

# Rustic Cottage Pie

*Try adding other herbs to this pie, or using a variety of wild mushrooms for different flavors and textures.*

## TOPPING

3 tbsp unsalted butter, plus more for greasing pan

4 medium Yukon gold potatoes, peeled and diced

Salt, as needed

¼ cup milk

Freshly ground black pepper, as needed

## FILLING

1 tbsp olive oil

1 medium yellow onion, diced

1 medium carrot, diced

2 large celery stalks, diced

1 pound Seitan (page 161), sliced ¼ inch or diced ½ inch

1½ cups Mushroom Sauce (page 303)

1½ cups thinly sliced mushrooms

1 cup green peas (fresh or thawed frozen)

1 cup corn kernels (fresh or thawed frozen)

2 tsp rosemary

1 tsp oregano

1 tsp dried thyme

1. Preheat the oven to 350°F. Lightly grease a 9 by 13-inch baking pan.

2. Place the potatoes in a medium pot and cover with cold salted water. Bring to a boil and cook until the potatoes are tender, 15 to 20 minutes. Drain completely and return to the pot.

3. Add the butter and milk and season with salt and pepper. Use a fork or potato masher to coarsely mash the potatoes. Set aside.

4. In a large sauté pan, heat the oil over medium heat. Add the onion, carrot, and celery and sauté until the vegetables are tender, 6 to 8 minutes.

5. Stir in the seitan, mushroom sauce, mushrooms, peas, corn, rosemary, oregano, and thyme. Season with salt and pepper. Bring to a simmer. Transfer the mixture to the prepared baking pan.

6. Top the seitan mixture with an even layer of mashed potatoes. Bake until the potatoes have evenly browned and the filling is bubbly and cooked through, 30 to 40 minutes.

7. Rest the finished product in a warm place for 10 minutes, then serve while hot.

**MAKES 6 TO 8 SERVINGS**

# Seitan Fajitas

*The marinade can be added to the peppers and onions. Cook the mixture over low heat until the marinade has reduced to almost no liquid. This will give the peppers and onions an extra boost of flavor.*

1 pound Seitan (page 161)

MARINADE

½ cup fresh lime juice

¼ cup chopped fresh cilantro

1 jalapeño, seeded and minced

2 cloves garlic, minced

2 tbsp olive oil

1 tsp ground cumin, toasted

1 tsp ground coriander, toasted

½ tsp cayenne

Salt and freshly ground black pepper, as needed

FAJITAS

2 tbsp olive oil

1 red bell pepper, thinly sliced

1 green bell pepper, thinly sliced

1 medium red onion, thinly sliced

Warm Corn or Flour Tortillas (pages 273 and 271, or store-bought), as needed

GARNISH

Lime wedges, as needed

Salsa Roja (page 308), as needed

Sour cream, as needed

1. In a large bowl, combine the marinade ingredients and season with salt and pepper. Slice the seitan crosswise into 4 pieces and place in the bowl with the marinade.

2. Turn the seitan over in the marinade to coat well. Cover and marinate the seitan, refrigerated, for at least 1 hour and up to overnight, turning occasionally. Remove from the refrigerator 30 minutes before cooking.

3. Heat the olive oil in a large sauté pan over medium heat. Add the red and green peppers and onion, and season with salt and pepper. If using the marinade, drain the seitan and add the marinade to the peppers and onion. Cook until the peppers are tender, 6 to 8 minutes, and the liquid is almost entirely reduced. Keep warm.

4. Preheat the broiler. If not yet done, remove the seitan from the marinade and place it on a baking sheet. Broil until the seitan is heated through and lightly browned, turning once, about 3 minutes per side.

5. Slice the seitan thinly, and toss it with the peppers and onions. Wrap a portion of the seitan and vegetable mixture in each tortilla. Garnish with lime wedges, salsa, and sour cream.

MAKES 4 SERVINGS

# Seitan Satay

*This satay has great flavor and makes a perfect healthy snack.*

1 tbsp olive oil

1 medium shallot, diced

½ jalapeño, seeded and minced

2 garlic cloves, minced

2 tsp minced fresh ginger

3 tbsp soy or tamari sauce

3 tbsp fresh lime juice

1 tbsp toasted sesame oil

2 tbsp honey

1 tbsp coarsely chopped fresh cilantro

¾ pound Seitan (page 161),
cut into ¼-inch strips

Twelve 6-inch wooden skewers,
soaked in water for 30 minutes

Peanut Dipping Sauce (page 301), as needed

1. Heat the oil in a small sauté pan over low heat. Add the shallot and jalapeño and sauté until softened, about 2 minutes. Add the garlic and ginger and sauté until aromatic, about 1 minute more. Transfer to a blender or food processor.

2. Add the soy sauce, lime juice, sesame oil, honey, and cilantro. Pulse until smooth. If the mixture is too thick and paste-like, add water 1 tbsp at a time to create a thick but fluid marinade.

3. Transfer the marinade to a shallow dish, add the seitan, and stir to coat. Cover and marinate, refrigerated, for at least 1 hour and up to overnight. Remove from the refrigerator 30 minutes before cooking.

4. Heat a grill or grill pan until hot.

5. Thread the seitan onto the skewers. Grill until the seitan is nicely browned and cooked through, 3 to 4 minutes on each side. Serve with the peanut sauce.

**MAKES 4 SERVINGS**

# Tandoori-Style Seitan

*Warm spices make this a hearty, satisfying meal.*

1 medium yellow onion, diced

½ cup canned crushed tomatoes

¾ cup plain Greek-style yogurt

2 tbsp fresh lemon juice

1 tbsp minced fresh ginger

2 cloves garlic, minced

¼ tsp cayenne

2 tsp ground cumin, toasted

2 tsp ground coriander, toasted

1 tbsp garam masala, toasted

¼ tsp ground cinnamon

1 tbsp chopped fresh cilantro

Salt and freshly ground black pepper, as needed

1 pound Seitan (page 161), diced

Twelve 6-inch wooden skewers, soaked in water for 30 minutes

Nonstick spray, as needed

**GARNISH**

Chopped cilantro, as needed

1. In a blender or food processor, combine the onion, tomatoes, yogurt, lemon juice, ginger, and garlic until smooth.

2. Transfer to a large bowl and stir in the cayenne, cumin, coriander, garam masala, cinnamon, and cilantro. Season with salt and pepper. Add the seitan and toss to coat. Cover and marinate, refrigerated, for at least 30 minutes and up to 2 hours. Remove from the refrigerator 30 minutes before cooking.

3. Heat a grill or grill pan until hot.

4. Thread the seitan onto the skewers. Grease the grill lightly with nonstick spray. Grill until evenly browned, 2 to 3 minutes per side. Serve immediately, garnished with cilantro.

**MAKES 4 SERVINGS**

# Tofu-Seitan Cutlets

*These cutlets are very versatile and are great on sandwiches, chopped and tossed with salads, or on their own with any of the flavorful sauces in Chapter 9.*

6 ounces firm tofu, drained and crumbled

3 tbsp soy or tamari sauce

1 tsp sweet paprika

¾ tsp onion powder

¾ tsp garlic powder

½ tsp freshly ground black pepper

¾ cup vital wheat gluten

Grapeseed or canola oil, as needed for cooking

1. In a food processor, combine the tofu, soy sauce, paprika, onion powder, garlic powder, pepper, and vital wheat gluten. Process until well mixed.

2. Transfer the mixture to a work surface and shape into a cylinder. Divide the cylinder into 6 equal pieces. Place each piece in between two pieces of plastic wrap, and use a rolling pin to flatten them into very thin cutlets, no more than ¼ inch thick.

3. In a large sauté pan, heat the oil over medium heat. Add the cutlets without crowding the pan, in batches if necessary. Cook until nicely browned on both sides, 5 to 6 minutes per side. Serve immediately with your favorite sauce. Or cool and store refrigerated for 2 to 3 days.

**MAKES 4 SERVINGS**

Seitan and Lentil Loaf

# Seitan and Lentil Loaf

This is a simple, quick dinner. If you prefer to have a neat, even-looking loaf, use a loaf pan, but simply forming the loaf on a baking sheet creates more exposed surface area, allowing you to brush the loaf with olive oil or sauce to keep it moist during cooking.

Olive oil, as needed

1 pound seitan, coarsely chopped

1 cup dry lentils, cooked (see chart, page 131)

1 medium yellow onion, minced

3 cloves garlic, minced

1 large egg, lightly beaten

3 tbsp soy or tamari sauce

1 tbsp white wine vinegar

2 tbsp tomato paste

2 tsp ground cumin

1 tsp ground coriander

2 tsp paprika

Freshly ground black pepper

¾ cup unseasoned bread crumbs

1. Preheat the oven to 350°F. Lightly grease a loaf pan or baking sheet.

2. In a food processor or blender, process the seitan and cooked lentils until smooth. Transfer to a large bowl. Add the remaining ingredients and mix until thoroughly combined.

3. Transfer the mixture to the loaf pan, or form into a loaf on the baking sheet. Brush with olive oil. Bake until the loaf is browned on the surface and cooked through, 20 to 25 minutes. Serve immediately while hot, or cool and serve sliced as a sandwich filling.

**MAKES 6 SERVINGS**

# Migas

This Spanish dish was traditionally served for breakfast with refried beans, tortillas, and salsa. Served with rice and stewed beans, it makes for a hearty lunch or dinner.

⅓ cup olive oil

¼ cup minced yellow onion

3 cloves garlic, minced

1 jalapeño, seeded and minced

6 Corn Tortillas (page 273 or store-bought), torn into 1-inch pieces

12 large eggs, lightly beaten

Salt and freshly ground black pepper, as needed

GARNISH

¼ cup grated *queso Chihuahua* or Monterey Jack cheese

¾ cup Salsa Roja (page 308)

6 Corn Tortillas (page 273 or store-bought), warmed

1. In a large sauté pan, heat the oil over medium heat. Add the onions, garlic, and jalapeño. Sauté until the onion is translucent, 3 to 4 minutes.

2. Add the torn tortillas, raise the heat to high, and cook until the tortillas are golden and crispy, 2 to 3 minutes.

3. Add the eggs; do not stir the eggs until you see them begin to coagulate around the edges.

4. Stir the egg mixture until the eggs are completely cooked but still slightly soft. Serve immediately, topped with cheese and salsa, with warmed tortillas on the side.

**MAKES 6 SERVINGS**

VARIATION: **Matzo Brei:** Omit the garlic and jalapeño and replace the tortillas with 3 large matzos, broken into 1-inch pieces. Follow the recipe as instructed, replacing the cheese and salsa with ½ cup sour cream and 2 thinly sliced green onions for garnish. Serve with additional matzo and jam.

Grains, pasta, noodles, and dumplings have long been considered a major part of a vegetarian diet. This chapter includes not only basic preparations of commonly used grains and pastas, but also a variety of dishes featuring specialty or less common grains that are considered to have a rich nutritional profile, thus increasing their importance in a meal and allowing many of these dishes to stand alone, not merely be served as a side dish.

6

# GRAINS, PASTA, NOODLES, AND DUMPLINGS

Grains can be simmered in various liquids to impart flavor, such as broth or vegetable juice. Grains can also be simmered simply in water, and aromatics can be added to give the grains flavor during simmering.

# GRAINS

Grains are dried and must be properly rehydrated by cooking in broth, water, or other liquid before they can be eaten. Many grains are combined with the cooking liquid before bringing it to a boil, but some, such as quinoa or polenta, are added to the liquid after it has come to a boil. Some grains are soaked prior to cooking. Whole grains such as barley, wheat berries, and rye berries benefit from soaking, which softens the outer layer of bran. Steep grains like bulgur and couscous in boiling liquid for several minutes, until the grain softens enough to be chewed easily.

Use a pot large enough to accommodate the liquid and the grains as they expand. Grains will be done when they are tender to the bite but not overly soft.

## Simmering Grains

1. Bring the liquid to a rolling boil. Add the grain.

2. Reduce the heat and simmer the grain until it reaches the desired doneness.

3. Drain, season, garnish if desired, and serve.

## Steaming Grains

1. Place the grain over simmering or boiling liquid.

2. Steam until the grain reaches the desired doneness.

3. Season, garnish if desired, and serve.

# CEREALS AND MEALS

Cereals and meals are grains that have been milled (broken down) to a finer texture. Depending on the grain, the texture can range from coarse (cracked wheat) to very fine (cornmeal). Other varieties of cereals include oats, buckwheat groats, and bulgur; other varieties of meals include grits, polenta, and Cream of Rice. The type of milling and processing grains undergo affects both the flavor and nutritional content of the cereals and meals. Regardless of type and texture, they should all have a fresh aroma. The natural oils present in these grains make them prone to spoilage and becoming rancid, so always check your cereals and meals before using.

Use a heavy-bottomed pot large enough to accommodate the liquid and grains while cooking.

## Cooking Cereals or Meals

1. Depending on the grain, bring the liquid to a rolling boil and add the cereal or meal in a constant stream, stirring constantly. Other grains can be combined with the liquid and then brought to a boil.

2. Cook the grains, stirring occasionally, until they are liquid enough to pour while still warm.

3. Season, garnish if desired, and serve, or let cool before beginning a secondary preparation.

# PILAFS

Originally from the Middle East, pilaf is a dish in which a grain (typically rice) is first heated in fat in a pan, then combined with hot liquid and cooked either on the stovetop or in the oven. Pilafs can be simple side dishes or can also include other ingredients such as vegetables, nuts, spices, and dried fruits, making them much more substantial.

Broth is generally the preferred cooking liquid, because it creates a flavorful pilaf. Another way to boost the flavor of the pilaf is to add an onion or other aromatic to the cooking liquid. Use a heavy-bottomed pot with a lid that is large enough to accommodate the liquid and the grains.

## Pilaf Method

1. Heat the fat or oil. Add the onions or other aromatics, and sweat until tender.

2. Add the grains and sauté a minute more, being sure to coat the grains evenly with the hot fat or oil.

3. Add the hot liquid and any remaining aromatics. Bring to a simmer.

4. Cover the pot and cook until the grain reaches the desired doneness. All liquid should be absorbed by the time the grain is cooked.

5. Season, garnish if desired, and serve.

Add warm broth to the rice in stages and cook over low heat, stirring constantly, until the liquid has been absorbed.

The finished risotto will be thick, tender, and creamy.

# RISOTTO

A classic risotto is a rich, creamy dish. The rice or other grain is parched as for a pilaf, in hot fat or oil, but the liquid is added and absorbed gradually while the grain is stirred constantly. Starch is released slowly during the cooking process, producing the dish's signature creamy texture.

Although risotto is traditionally made with Arborio or Carnaroli rice, other grains such as brown rice, barley, and wheat berries make delicious risottos as well. A wide, heavy-bottomed pot is best for making risotto. Traditional additions are onions or other aromatics, cheese, and butter.

## Risotto Method

1. Heat the fat or oil. Add the onion or other aromatics and sweat until tender.

2. Add the grains and cook until they have a glazed, pearl-like appearance.

3. Add the simmering liquid in three parts, stirring constantly as the grain absorbs each addition of the liquid.

4. Season, garnish if desired, and serve immediately.

# HOW TO MAKE IT YOUR OWN: GRAINS

All long- and medium-grain rice varieties, as well as any whole or cracked grains, can also be cooked in a rice cooker. Using a rice cooker usually produces a light, fluffy finished product.

# GRAINS

| GRAIN | RATIO OF GRAIN TO LIQUID (CUPS) | APP. YIELD (CUPS) | COOKING TIME | COOKING METHODS | FLAVORING SUGGESTIONS |
|---|---|---|---|---|---|
| **PEARL BARLEY** | 1:2 | 4 | 35—45 minutes | Boil or pilaf method | Herbs, mushrooms, sun-dried tomatoes, wilted greens |
| **BARLEY GROATS** | 1:2½ | 4 | 50 minutes—1 hour | Boil or pilaf method | Mushrooms, herbs, sautéed vegetables |
| **BUCKWHEAT GROATS (KASHA)** | 1:1½—2 | 2 | 12—20 minutes | Boil or pilaf method | Mushrooms, carrots, onions, garlic |
| **COUSCOUS*** | 1:2 pilaf method | 2—3 | Steam for 60 minutes, fluffing every 20 minutes; 20 minutes cooked pilaf method | Steam or pilaf method | Butter, herbs, small-diced pre-cooked vegetables |
| **WHOLE HOMINY**** | 1:4—6 | 3 | 2½—3 hours | Boil or cook in pressure cooker | Cooked onions, cooked garlic, cilantro, diced precooked vegetables |
| **HOMINY GRITS** | 1:4 | 3 | 25 minutes | Polenta method (see Cooking Cereals or Meals, page 173) | Cheddar cheese, cooked onions, garlic |
| **MILLET** | 1:2 | 3 | 30—35 minutes | Boil or pilaf method | Onions, garlic, mushrooms |
| **OAT GROATS** | 1:2 | 2 | 45 minutes—1 hour | Boil | Can be savory or sweet, so vegetables such as carrots, onions, garlic, or cinnamon, dried fruits |
| **POLENTA, COARSE GRIND CORNMEAL** | 1:4 | 3—4 | 35—45 minutes | Simmer on stovetop or bake in oven | Cheese, butter, cream, onions, garlic, sun-dried tomatoes, chopped olives, herbs |
| **QUINOA** | 1:2 | 2 | 10—12 minutes | Generally made in the pilaf method | Any sautéed vegetables, herbs, aromatics such as onion and garlic |
| **ARBORIO RICE, CARNAROLI RICE, VALENCIA RICE** | 1:3—4 | 3 | 20—30 minutes | Simmer or risotto method | Herbs, cheese, garlic, onions, mushrooms, asparagus, sun-dried tomatoes |
| **BASMATI RICE** | 1:1½ | 3 | 25 minutes | Simmer, boil, or pilaf method | Herbs, diced cooked vegetables such as carrots, dried fruits such as currants and apricots, coconut, curry spices |

*continued on next page*

# GRAINS cont.

| GRAIN | RATIO OF GRAIN TO LIQUID (CUPS) | APP. YIELD (CUPS) | COOKING TIME | COOKING METHODS | FLAVORING SUGGESTIONS |
|---|---|---|---|---|---|
| **CONVERTED RICE** | 1:1¾ | 4 | 25—30 minutes | Boil, pilaf method, or steam | Adapts to almost any application of flavor |
| **LONG-GRAIN BROWN RICE** | 1:3 | 4 | 40 minutes | Boil, pilaf method, or steam | Earthy flavors are best, although this rice can also be used for a hearty rice pudding |
| **LONG-GRAIN WHITE RICE** | 1:1½—1¾ | 3 | 18—20 minutes | Boil, pilaf method, or steam | Adapts to almost any application of flavor |
| **SHORT-GRAIN WHITE RICE** | 1:1—1½ | 3 | 20—30 minutes | Boil or steam | Usually starchy or sticky; using flavored liquids to cook the rice does the best job of imparting flavors. Garnishes should be kept simple to avoid overworking the rice |
| **WILD RICE** | 1:3 | 4 | 30—45 minutes | Boil | Toasted nuts such as pecans, pine nuts; mushrooms; herbs such as savory, rosemary, thyme, bay leaf |
| **WHEAT BERRIES\*\*** | 1:3 | 2 | 1 hour or more | Boil or steam | Herbs, tomatoes, wilted greens, mushrooms, vinaigrettes; dried fruits such as cherries, cranberries, apricots; toasted nuts such as pecans, walnuts, pine nuts, almonds |
| **BULGUR\*\*\* AVAILABLE IN MEDIUM AND COARSE GRIND, POLISHED OR WHOLE GRAIN** | 1:4 | 2 | 2 hours | Generally soaked in hot liquid, then drained, or simmered approx. 5—10 minutes, then drained | Herbs, mushrooms, tomatoes, cucumbers, dried fruits, vinaigrettes |
| **CRACKED WHEAT\*\*\*\*** | 1:2 | 3 | 20 minutes | | Herbs, tomatoes, wilted greens, mushrooms, vinaigrettes; dried fruits such as cherries, cranberries, apricots; toasted nuts such as pecans, walnuts, pine nuts, almonds |

\*From 1 cup of uncooked grain.

\*\*Grain should be briefly soaked in warm water, then drained before it is cooked.

\*\*\*Grain should be soaked overnight in cold water, then drained before it is cooked.

\*\*\*\*Grain may be cooked by covering it with boiling water and soaking it for 2 hours, or via the pilaf method.

# PASTA, NOODLES, AND DUMPLINGS

Fresh pasta is simple to make and can be flavored in a number of ways (see also page 197). It is often more delicate and tender in texture and has a fresher flavor than dried pasta. Fresh pasta or noodles can be made ahead, then covered and refrigerated for up to 2 days. Once the pasta is rolled out or formed and is waiting to be cooked, sprinkle it lightly with cornmeal or coarse semolina flour, then lay it carefully onto trays lined with plastic wrap or parchment paper. You can also dry fresh pasta by storing it on racks in a warm, dry place until it has hardened. Good-quality store-bought dried pasta can be substituted for fresh pasta in most of the recipes.

Cook pasta, noodles, and dumplings in a large amount of salted water. Depending on their shape and size, some varieties cook very quickly while others take several minutes to cook properly. Use a large pot that is taller than it is wide for long pasta and noodles, and a pot that is wider than it is tall for smaller, flat pasta such as lasagna noodles, dumplings, and filled pastas. Drain cooked pasta and, when possible, serve immediately.

## Making Fresh Pasta

1. Blend all the dry ingredients and mound in a large bowl or on a clean surface. Make a well in the center.

2. Combine all the wet ingredients. Pour them into the well.

3. Working quickly, pull the dry ingredients into the wet ingredients, mixing them together to form a rough dough.

4. Knead the dough until smooth and let rest 1 hour, covered, before rolling.

Mix the dough until it forms a shaggy mass.

Knead the finished dough until smooth and uniform.

## Cooking Pasta

1. Bring a large pot of salted water (1 gallon with 1 ounce of salt per pound of pasta being cooked) to a rolling boil.

2. Add the pasta and stir briefly to separate.

3. Cook until the pasta is tender but not soft.

4. Drain, sauce and garnish if desired, and serve. Do not rinse the pasta, as this washes off the surface starches. The surface starch is critical to the sauce adhering.

# HOW TO MAKE IT YOUR OWN: PASTA

Pasta is one of the most versatile foods in your culinary arsenal. It can be a starter or a meal, served hot, warm, or cold, sauced with or without vegetables, or marinated and served at room temperature or cold! Let your imagination run wild. Be sure to look for different varieties such a multigrain, whole wheat, brown rice, or corn and Jerusalem artichoke.

## ROLLING OUT FRESH PASTA

After the pasta dough has rested, break off a workable piece of pasta dough and flatten it in your hands into a thin rectangle.

If you're using a pasta machine, set the gauge to the widest opening and roll the pasta through the machine. Fold the dough in thirds and roll it through the machine again. Set the gauge at the next widest opening and roll the sheet through the machine. Continue doing this, setting the gauge lower and lower until the desired thickness is reached. Then cut into the desired shapes.

If you're rolling the dough out by hand, use a rolling pin in a back-and-forth stretching motion to roll the pasta into an evenly thin piece. Let the sheet of pasta dry until the surface is no longer sticky to the touch. Use a sharp knife or pizza cutter to cut the pasta into the desired shapes.

*Roll out pasta dough in a pasta machine. Begin with the machine on its widest setting and work down until the pasta is at the desired thickness.*

# PASTA AND SAUCES

| PASTA SHAPE | TYPE OF SAUCE/USE | GARNISHES |
|---|---|---|
| **LONG FLAT PASTA SUCH AS LINGUINE, FETTUCCINE** | Any type of sauce but especially olive oil, butter, and wine-based or creamy sauces | Small pieces of cooked vegetables, sliced mushrooms, or wilted greens; herbs, nuts, tofu, TVP, seitan |
| **LONG ROUND PASTA SUCH AS ANGEL HAIR, SPAGHETTI, BUCATINI** | Tomato sauce or vegetable purée sauces; pesto | Small pieces of cooked vegetables, sliced mushrooms, or wilted greens; herbs, nuts, tofu, TVP, seitan |
| **SHORT HOLLOW PASTA SUCH AS TUBETTI, PENNE, CAMPANELLE, CAVATELLI, RIGATE, ZITI, MOSTACCIOLI, TORTIGLIONI** | Thick and chunky sauces, creamy sauces | Chunky cooked vegetables, cooked beans and legumes, herbs, cheeses |
| **CURLY PASTA SUCH AS ELBOWS, FUSILLI, ROTINI, CAVATAPPI; TWISTED PASTA SUCH AS GEMELLI** | Excellent for casseroles such as macaroni and cheese or cold pasta salads. Serve with smooth or creamy sauces | Wilted greens, sliced cooked mushrooms, cooked beans, cooked grains such as wheat berries |
| **SMALL PASTA SHAPES SUCH AS ACINI DI PEPE, ANELLINI, FIDEOS, ALPHABET, ORZO** | Best used for soup garnishes | Chopped herbs and vegetables such as wilted spinach or broccoli rabe and olive oil |
| **FLAT OR BROAD SHAPES SUCH AS BOW TIES OR FARFALLE** | Use as a side dish with simple creamy or purée sauces; equally delicious with butter sauces, chopped herbs, or pesto | Small pieces of cooked vegetables, sliced mushrooms or wilted greens, herbs, nuts, tofu, TVP, seitan |
| **RIBBON PASTA SUCH AS REGINETTE, TAGLIATELLE** | Butter or olive oil sauces, wine sauces, pesto, light-textured tomato sauce | Herbs, thin slices of vegetables, mushrooms, crumbled cheeses or tofu |
| **STUFFING PASTA SUCH AS LARGE SHELLS, LASAGNA, CANELLONI** | Smooth vegetable sauces such as tomato sauce, purée of butternut squash, creamy sauces such as Alfredo, or mushroom sauce | Fill with seasoned, minced cooked vegetables, cheeses such as ricotta, cooked grains, beans, or bean purée |
| **SPECIAL SHAPES SUCH AS ORECCHIETTE, SMALL AND MEDIUM SHELLS, CAPPELLETTI, WAGON WHEELS** | Best with chunky, creamy, or "clingy" sauces. Pesto is also excellent | Small pieces of cooked vegetables, sliced mushrooms or wilted greens, herbs, nuts, crumbled tofu, TVP, seitan |
| **FILLED PASTA SUCH AS TORTELLINI, RAVIOLI** | Butter sauces, olive oil sauces, or smooth vegetable sauces such as tomato sauce or pesto | Toasted nuts, cheese, fresh or fried herbs, toasted coarse bread crumbs, cooked vegetables such as mushrooms, wilted greens |

# Mixed Grain Pilaf

*This stovetop grain mix is incredibly healthful and can be made with any combination of your favorite grains.*

1 cup rye berries

1 cup wheat berries

½ cup wild rice

½ cup pearl barley

2 tbsp unsalted butter or olive oil

½ cup minced red onion or shallot

6¾ cups Vegetable Broth (page 287)

Salt and freshly ground black pepper, as needed

1. Rinse all the grains together in a strainer.

2. In a large pot, sauté the onions or shallots in butter. Add the rinsed grains and toss to coat with the fat. Add the broth. Bring to a boil over medium heat, cover, reduce the heat to low, and simmer until soft, about 1½ hours. If the liquid is not entirely absorbed, increase the heat and cook uncovered for 5 to 10 minutes longer, stirring gently but frequently. Add salt and pepper to taste. Serve immediately.

**MAKES 6 TO 8 SERVINGS**

# Quinoa Pilaf

*Quinoa adds a distinct flavor to the everyday pilaf.*

1 quart Vegetable Broth, warm (page 287)

2 tbsp butter or olive oil

1 medium shallot, minced

2 cloves garlic, minced

2⅔ cups quinoa, rinsed and thoroughly drained

1 bay leaf

1 sprig fresh thyme

Salt and freshly ground black pepper, as needed

1. Preheat the oven to 350°F. Preheat the broth.

2. Heat a flameproof casserole over medium heat. Sauté the shallot and garlic in butter. Add the rinsed quinoa and toss to coat with the fat. Add the hot broth, the bay leaf, and thyme. Season with salt and pepper. Bring to a boil. Stir to combine.

3. Cover the pot tightly and transfer to the oven. Bake until the quinoa is tender and has absorbed all the liquid, about 8 to 10 minutes. Remove from the oven and rest for 5 minutes.

4. Fluff the quinoa and remove the bay leaf and thyme before serving.

**MAKES 6 TO 8 SERVINGS**

# Quinoa à la Jardinera

*This flavorful side dish works well with nearly any grain. Try it with couscous or wild rice. See the chart on pages 175–76 for cooking times for other grains.*

⅔ cup quinoa, rinsed thoroughly and drained

2 tbsp unsalted butter

1 serrano chile, seeded and minced

1 cup small diced green bell pepper

1 cup small diced red bell pepper

1 medium shallot, minced

1½ tsp finely minced fresh ginger

½ cup small diced carrots

½ cup small diced celery

Salt and freshly ground black pepper, as needed

Vegetable Broth (page 287), as needed (optional)

GARNISH

2 green onions, minced (white and green parts)

1 tbsp chopped fresh flat-leaf parsley

2 tsp chopped fresh thyme

2 tbsp chopped fresh basil

1. In a large pot, heat 1 quart water to a boil. Add the quinoa, return to a simmer, and cook until it is barely cooked, 4 to 5 minutes. Drain the quinoa in a fine-mesh sieve. Spread the quinoa on a large baking sheet, and cool to room temperature. Use a fork to fluff the quinoa occasionally.

2. Melt the butter in a large sauté pan over medium heat. Add the serrano chile, green and red peppers, shallot, ginger, carrots, and celery. Season with salt and pepper. Cover and sweat the vegetables for 3 to 5 minutes. Vegetables will be about half-cooked and should generate a few tablespoons of liquid.

3. Stir in the quinoa and cook until heated through. (Add a few more tablespoons of water or vegetable broth to help the reheating process.) The cooking liquor from sweating the vegetables along with a few tablespoons of water or broth will complete the cooking of the quinoa.

4. Serve hot, garnished with the green onions, parsley, thyme, and basil.

**MAKES 4 SERVINGS**

Quinoa and Leek Tart

# Quinoa and Leek Tart

This tart has a little bit of everything—lots of complementary flavors that work together to make a great tart. Try making this with leftovers you have in your fridge, such as White Beans with Lemon, Fennel, and Avocado (page 42) (pile on top of a baked crust) or Grits with Corn and Hominy (page 33) (top with Cheddar cheese and bake until the cheese melts).

All-purpose flour, as needed for rolling

1 recipe Tart Dough (page 282)

3 tbsp unsalted butter

1½ cups peeled and diced McIntosh apples

1 cup diced red peppers

1½ tsp ground ginger

1 tbsp chopped tarragon

2½ cups thinly sliced leeks (white and light green parts)

1½ cups halved chanterelle mushrooms

Salt and freshly ground black pepper, as needed

⅔ cup quinoa

1 cup coarsely chopped hazelnuts

**GARNISH**

¾ cup crumbled fresh goat cheese

1. Preheat the oven to 350°F.

2. Place the quinoa in a sieve and wash until the liquid runs clear. Combine the washed quinoa with 4 cups of water. Bring to a simmer and cook for 4-5 minutes, until quinoa is barely cooked. Pour the cooked quinoa into a strainer and drain the excess water. Transfer the quinoa to a large sheet tray, spread it out, and allow to cool. Use a fork to fluff the quinoa occasionally.

3. On a floured surface, roll out the tart dough to about ¼ inch thick. Gently transfer the dough to a 10-inch tart pan. Chill for 10 to 15 minutes.

4. Dock the base of the shell generously with a fork. Bake the shell until it just begins to brown, 8 to 10 minutes. Remove from the oven and set aside, leaving the oven on.

5. In a large sauté pan, melt 1 tbsp of the butter over medium heat. Add the apples and peppers and sauté until lightly caramelized, 6 to 8 minutes. Add the ginger and tarragon. Transfer the mixture to a large bowl, and set aside.

6. Melt the remaining 2 tbsp butter in the same pan. Add the leeks and sauté until translucent, 3 to 4 minutes. Add the mushrooms and cook until they are softened and the leeks are golden, 4 to 5 minutes more. Add to the apple mixture, season well with salt and pepper, and toss to combine.

7. Spread the apple-mushroom mixture into an even layer in the tart shell. Spread the quinoa into an even layer on top of the apple mixture. Sprinkle with the hazelnuts. Bake until the filling is heated through and the crust is golden, 8 to 10 minutes more.

8. Garnish the finished tart with the goat cheese. Serve warm or at room temperature.

**MAKES ONE 10-INCH TART**

# Wheat Berry Salad with Oranges, Cherries, and Pecans

*Sweet and savory—a mixture of herbs is ideal for this dish.*

1 orange, peeled and cut into suprêmes (see page 321), juice reserved

1 tsp each, chopped thyme, sage, or rosemary

¼ cup extra-virgin olive oil, plus more as needed

2 tbsp red wine vinegar

Salt and freshly ground black pepper, as needed

2 cups wheat berries, cooked (see chart, page 176)

1 medium red onion, halved and thinly sliced

½ cup dried cherries, plus extra for garnish, as needed

½ cup toasted pecans, plus extra for garnish, as needed

1. In a large bowl, combine the orange juice, herbs, oil, and vinegar. Whisk well to combine and season with salt and pepper.

2. Add the wheat berries, onion, ½ cup cherries, ½ cup pecans, and the orange segments. Toss to combine.

3. Garnish with additional cherries and pecans, if desired.

**MAKES 4 SERVINGS**

CLOCKWISE FROM TOP RIGHT:
Wheat Berry Salad with Oranges, Cherries, and Pecans; Cracked Wheat and Tomato Salad (page 186); Barley Salad with Cucumber and Mint (page 187); Sweet and Spicy Bulgur (page 188)

# Cracked Wheat and Tomato Salad

*Cracked wheat is made from whole wheat kernels that have been crushed to form smaller pieces. It can take longer to cook than some other grains, but it has a great nutty flavor and a hearty texture.*

2 cups cracked wheat

3 cups chopped tomatoes

1 medium red onion, diced

½ cup crumbled feta cheese

2 tbsp red wine vinegar, plus more as needed

¼ cup extra-virgin olive oil, plus more as needed

2 tbsp chopped oregano

1 tsp red pepper flakes

Salt and freshly ground black pepper, as needed

1. In a medium pot, combine the cracked wheat with 1 quart water, bring to a boil, lower the heat, and simmer until tender, 30 to 35 minutes. Remove from heat and drain in a fine-mesh sieve, pressing to release any excess moisture. Cool to room temperature.

2. In a large bowl, toss the tomatoes, onion, feta, vinegar, oil, oregano, and pepper flakes to combine. Season with salt and pepper.

3. Add the wheat and toss well to combine. Serve at room temperature or chill until needed.

**MAKES 6 SERVINGS**

# Barley Salad with Cucumber and Mint

*A fresh, light salad, ideal for summer—it makes a great side, or add some marinated tofu for a quick lunch.*

1 pound pearl barley

Kosher salt, as needed

2 cups peeled, seeded, and chopped tomatoes

2 cups peeled, seeded, and chopped cucumbers

2½ cups chopped fresh flat-leaf parsley

½ cup chopped mint

¼ cup thinly sliced green onions (white and green parts)

1 cup extra-virgin olive oil

½ cup fresh lemon juice

Freshly ground black pepper, as needed

1. Place the barley in a bowl and cover with cold water. Let stand for 30 minutes.

2. Drain the barley well. Place the drained barley in a medium sauce-pan, cover by 2 inches with salted water, and bring to a boil over high heat. Reduce the heat to low and simmer until tender, 40 to 50 minutes.

3. Drain the barley and rinse with cold water. Drain again well and cool to room temperature.

4. In a large bowl, toss the barley, tomatoes, cucumbers, parsley, mint, and green onions.

5. In a small bowl, whisk together the oil and lemon juice. Pour over the salad and toss to coat. Season with salt and pepper and toss again. Serve immediately or chill until needed.

**MAKES 10 SERVINGS**

# Sweet and Spicy Bulgur

*This dish can be made a little sweeter by adding more honey, but be careful not to add too much—some honeys have a very strong flavor. Taste along the way to achieve the right balance of sweet and spicy.*

1 tbsp olive oil, plus more as needed

2 cups cherry tomatoes, halved

½ cup minced sun-dried tomatoes

Salt, as needed

2 cloves garlic, minced

1½ cups bulgur

¼ tsp red pepper flakes

2 tbsp fresh lemon juice

2 tsp honey

Freshly ground black pepper, as needed

1. Heat the oil in a large sauté pan over medium-high heat. Add the cherry tomatoes and sauté until softened, about 5 minutes.

2. Add the sun-dried tomatoes and continue cooking until softened, 2 to 3 minutes longer. Season with salt.

3. Reduce the heat to medium-low. Add the garlic and bulgur and sauté until fragrant, 1 to 2 minutes.

4. Add 2 cups water, raise the heat to medium, and bring to a boil. Reduce the heat to low and simmer until the bulgur is tender, 20 to 25 minutes.

5. Fluff the bulgur and stir in the pepper flakes, lemon juice, and honey. Season with black pepper and more salt if needed. Serve warm.

**MAKES 6 SERVINGS**

# Bulgur Cereal with Dried Apricots, Prunes, and Lemon Zest

*Try replacing the bulgur with wheat berries. Soak wheat berries for 4 to 6 hours, then simmer until tender, about 30 minutes.*

¼ tsp kosher salt

2 tbsp unsalted butter

1 tbsp light brown sugar

1 cup bulgur

Grated zest and juice of 1 lemon

¼ cup pitted prunes, sliced

¼ cup dried apricots, sliced

1. Preheat the oven to 325°F.

2. In a flameproof casserole, combine 3 cups water, the salt, butter, and sugar and bring to a boil. Add the bulgur and bring to a simmer, stirring gently but constantly.

3. Cover and transfer the casserole to the oven. Bake until the bulgur is tender, 25 to 30 minutes.

4. Fluff the bulgur with a fork and set aside to keep warm.

5. In a small saucepan, bring the lemon zest and juice to a boil. Stir in the prunes and apricots, and, with the heat off, let them steep until the fruits are slightly plumped, about 10 minutes.

6. Stir the fruit and any remaining liquid into the bulgur cereal. Serve immediately.

**MAKES ABOUT 4 SERVINGS**

# Mushroom, Spinach, and Kasha Pie

*Kasha, also called buckwheat groats, is a whole grain from a grass. It has a nutty flavor and is great paired with mushrooms in this pie.*

2 tbsp unsalted butter, plus more as needed for the pan

2½ cups chopped mushrooms

1 tbsp minced shallot

1 cup minced yellow onion

Salt and freshly ground black pepper, as needed

1 cup cooked kasha (see chart, page 177)

2 cups spinach, packed

2 tbsp chopped flat-leaf parsley

2 tsp chopped thyme

2 tsp chopped fresh rosemary

3 large eggs

1 cup whole-milk plain Greek-style yogurt

2 tbsp olive oil

½ tsp baking powder

1¼ cups all-purpose flour

1. Preheat the oven to 375°F. Lightly butter a 9 by 13-inch baking pan.

2. In a large sauté pan, melt the butter over medium heat. Add the mushrooms, shallot, and onion and season with salt and pepper. Sauté until the mushrooms have softened and the onions are translucent, 5 to 7 minutes. Add the kasha and mix to heat through, about 1 minute.

3. Remove from the heat. Stir in the spinach, parsley, thyme, and rosemary. Toss to wilt the spinach. If necessary, return the mixture to the heat briefly.

4. In a large bowl, combine the eggs, yogurt, and oil. Add the baking powder and flour, and mix until smooth. Spread half the batter in the prepared baking pan. Top with the mushroom mixture. Spread with the remaining batter.

5. Bake until the top is lightly browned, about 45 minutes. Let cool and serve warm or at room temperature.

**MAKES 6 TO 8 SERVINGS**

# Wild Rice and Millet Croquettes

*Try these dipped in Blackberry Ketchup (page 312) or Creamy Garlic Dressing (page 293).*

¾ cup millet, cooked (see chart, page 177)

½ cup wild rice, cooked (see chart, page 178)

3 tbsp olive oil

1 medium shallot, minced

1 stalk celery, minced

¼ cup shredded carrot

⅓ cup all-purpose flour

¼ cup chopped flat-leaf parsley

Salt and freshly ground black pepper, as needed

Canola or peanut oil, as needed for deep-frying

1. In a large bowl, toss the millet and wild rice to combine.

2. In a small sauté pan, heat the olive oil over medium heat. Add the shallot, celery, and carrot. Sauté until the vegetables have softened, 4 to 5 minutes.

3. Add the vegetables to the cooked grains, and mix to combine. Add the flour and parsley, and season with salt and pepper. Mix until well combined. Cover and refrigerate until chilled, 15 to 20 minutes.

4. Fill a deep, heavy pot about half-full with oil. Heat the canola oil over medium heat until it registers 350°F on a deep-fry thermometer.

5. Use your hands to shape the mixture into 1½-inch diameter small balls. Working in batches if necessary, add the croquettes to the oil and fry until they are golden brown and float to the surface of the oil, 4 to 6 minutes. Drain briefly on paper towels. Sprinkle with salt and serve hot.

MAKES 4 SERVINGS, TK CROQUETTES

# Soft Polenta

*This recipe is for a smooth, soft polenta. For a basic firm polenta recipe that can be grilled, sautéed, or fried, see the recipe for Parmesan-Herb Polenta on page 192.*

5 cups Vegetable Broth (page 287) or water

1½ tsp kosher salt

1 cup polenta

2 tbsp unsalted butter

Freshly ground black pepper, as needed

1. Bring the broth or water to boil in a heavy saucepan and add the salt. Stream the polenta gradually into the boiling liquid, whisking constantly. Reduce the heat. Simmer, stirring frequently, until the polenta pulls away from the side of the pot but isn't overly thick, about 45 minutes.

2. Remove the polenta from the heat and stir in the butter. Season with pepper. Serve immediately.

MAKES 4 SERVINGS

VARIATION: **Blue Cheese Polenta:** Reduce the liquid to 4 cups. When adding the butter, stir in ½ tsp freshly grated nutmeg, 1 tbsp chopped rosemary, 1 tbsp chopped thyme, and ½ cup crumbled blue cheese. Pour the polenta into a lightly oiled 9-inch square baking pan, level the surface, cover with plastic wrap, and refrigerate until set, about 2 hours. Cut into the desired shapes. For frying instructions, see page 192, Step 4.

# Parmesan-Herb Polenta

*Try other herbs, spices, and cheeses to make a variety of flavorful polentas.*

2 cups milk

1 sprig thyme

1 sprig oregano

1¼ tsp kosher salt

2 tbsp olive oil, plus more
as needed (optional)

1 cup polenta

1¼ cups grated Parmesan

All-purpose flour, as needed (optional)

1. In a medium pot, bring 2 cups water, the milk, thyme, oregano, salt, and oil to a simmer over medium heat. Simmer for about 5 minutes, then remove and discard the herbs.

2. Stream the polenta gradually into the boiling liquid, whisking constantly to prevent any lumps. Reduce the heat to very low and simmer, stirring often until the polenta pulls away from the sides of the pot but isn't overly thick, about 45 minutes. The more frequently you stir the polenta, the creamier it will be.

3. Remove the pot from the heat and whisk in the cheese. Pour the polenta into a lightly oiled 9-inch square baking pan, level the surface and cover with plastic wrap and refrigerate until set, about 2 hours or more, but overnight is best to allow the polenta to become very firm. This is important for grilled polenta; it helps prevent sticking to the grill.

4. Cut the set polenta into shapes and grill, fry, or reheat in the oven. To grill, brush lightly with oil and place on a hot grill or grill pan until heated through and grill marks develop, turning once. To fry, heat 2 tbsp olive oil in a medium sauté pan over medium heat. Dredge the polenta in flour and cook until evenly browned and heated through, 3 to 5 minutes per side. To reheat in the oven, place on a lightly oiled baking sheet and bake at 400°F until browned and crisp (baking time will depend on size and shape).

5. Serve immediately.

**MAKES 4 SERVINGS**

# "Succotash" Risotto with Lima Beans, Corn, Butternut Squash, and Dry Jack Cheese

*This classic succotash with a sophisticated twist is elegant enough to serve as an appetizer in a multicourse meal or stand on its own as an entrée.*

1 tbsp unsalted butter

1⅓ cups peeled, seeded, and diced butternut squash

Salt and freshly ground white pepper, as needed

2 tsp olive oil

½ cup minced yellow onion

1¼ cups Arborio rice

1 quart Vegetable Broth (page 287), warm

1½ cups cooked corn kernels (fresh or thawed frozen)

1 cup cooked lima beans (fresh or thawed frozen)

GARNISH

2 tbsp toasted pumpkin seeds

3 tbsp grated dry Jack cheese

2 green onions, thinly sliced (white and green parts)

1. In a large sauté pan, melt the butter over medium heat. Add the squash and sauté until lightly browned and tender, 6 to 8 minutes. Season with salt and pepper and set aside.

2. In a medium saucepan, heat the oil over medium heat. Add the minced onion, cover, and sweat until translucent, 4 to 5 minutes. Add the rice and mix until well combined, about 30 seconds. Gradually add the broth by ladlefuls, stirring the risotto until the rice has absorbed nearly all of the liquid before adding more. Cook until the rice is tender and has absorbed all of the liquid, about 25 minutes.

3. Stir in the corn, lima beans, and squash. Cook, stirring occasionally, until everything is heated through.

4. Serve the risotto in warm bowls, garnished with pumpkin seeds, cheese, and green onions.

MAKES 4 SERVINGS

VARIATION: **Sweet Corn Risotto:** Omit the squash, lima beans , and pumpkin seeds. Increase the amount of corn to 2½ cups and replace the dry Jack cheese with an equal amount of grated Parmesan. Start at Step 2 and follow recipe to the end.

Casserole of Polenta, Mushrooms, Seitan, and Broccoli

# Casserole of Polenta, Mushrooms, Seitan, and Broccoli

*Soft polenta is perfect for a casserole—it provides a creamy base layer that you can season any way you like!*

Nonstick spray, as needed

2 tbsp olive oil

½ cup minced yellow onion

2 cloves garlic, thinly sliced

2½ cups thinly sliced mushrooms

2 cups broccoli florets

½ pound Seitan (page 161), thinly sliced

¼ cup white wine

1 tbsp chopped thyme

2 tsp chopped rosemary

Salt and freshly ground black pepper, as needed

2 cups milk

¾ cup Vegetable Broth (page 287)

2 cloves garlic, minced

½ cup polenta

1 tbsp unsalted butter

⅓ cup grated Fontina

¾ cup grated Gruyère

1. Preheat the oven to 400°F. Grease a 9-inch square baking pan lightly with nonstick spray.

2. In a large sauté pan, heat the oil over medium heat. Add the onion and sliced garlic and sauté until they are golden brown, 5 to 6 minutes.

3. Add the mushrooms and broccoli and sauté until the mushrooms begin to soften, 2 to 3 minutes. Add the seitan and cook until the seitan is lightly browned and the vegetables are tender, 4 to 6 minutes.

4. Add the wine. Simmer over medium heat until the liquid has evaporated. Stir in the thyme and rosemary and season with salt and pepper. Keep warm.

5. In a medium saucepan, bring the milk and broth to a boil. Remove the pan from the heat, and add the minced garlic and polenta, stirring constantly until well blended.

6. Return the pan to low heat and cook, stirring occasionally, until the polenta has thickened, 7 to 9 minutes. Stir in the butter and half of each cheese, and season with salt and pepper. Combine the remaining cheeses.

7. Spread a thin, even layer of about one-third the polenta in the bottom of the prepared baking pan. Spoon half the vegetable mixture over the polenta and top with one-third of the cheese mixture. Repeat with half of the remaining polenta, all the remaining vegetable mixture, and half of the remaining cheese. Finish the layering with the remaining polenta and cheese.

8. Bake until the top is golden brown and the filling is bubbly, 20 to 25 minutes. Let stand for 5 to 10 minutes before slicing and serving.

**MAKES 4 SERVINGS**

# Creamy Risotto with Orange Suprêmes

*This risotto is great as breakfast or even dessert. Try it with other fruits, such as apples in the fall or berries in the summer.*

1 orange

3 tbsp unsalted butter

1 tbsp minced fresh ginger

1 cup Arborio rice

1¼ cups whole milk

Salt, as needed

¼ cup fresh orange juice (add to the reserved juice as needed)

2 tbsp light brown sugar

1. Preheat the oven to 350°F.

2. Grate the orange zest and set aside 2 tbsp for garnish. Peel the orange and cut it into suprêmes (see page 321). Set aside the suprêmes for garnish.

3. In a large ovenproof saucepan, melt 2 tbsp of the butter over low heat and cook until it develops a light brown color. Add the ginger, cover, and sweat for 10 seconds. Stir in the rice until it is thoroughly coated with butter. Add 1 cup milk and season lightly with salt. Bring to a boil, cover, and transfer to the oven. Bake until the rice is tender and the liquid has been absorbed, about 45 minutes.

4. Remove from the oven and stir in orange juice to adjust the risotto's thickness.

5. Add the remaining butter and milk and the brown sugar. Taste and adjust seasoning with salt as needed. Stir until butter melts and the brown sugar is incorporated. Serve immediately in warm bowls, garnished with orange zest and orange segments.

**MAKES 4 SERVINGS**

# Fresh Pasta Dough

*This pasta dough is the perfect base for all your favorite sauces, vegetables, and proteins. Try adding herbs or spices to the dough for different colors and flavors.*

**2 cups all-purpose flour, plus more for kneading**

**½ tsp kosher salt**

**2 large eggs**

**1 tsp olive oil**

**2 tbsp water, plus more as needed**

1. In a large bowl, combine the flour and the salt. Make a well in the center the size of a fist.

2. Whisk together the eggs, olive oil, and water, and add to the flour. Mix the flour and wet ingredients together until a shaggy mass forms. Add more water as needed, to form a dough that is pliable but not overly sticky.

3. Knead the dough on a lightly floured surface until it is smooth. Wrap the dough in plastic and let it rest at room temperature for 1 hour.

4. Divide the dough into four equal pieces. Working one piece at a time and keeping the unused portions covered, roll the dough into thin sheets with a pasta machine. Let paste dough sheets rest for 10 to 15 minutes before cutting into desired shapes by hand or machine.

5. The pasta can be cooked now, or sprinkle the cut pasta with corn meal to prevent the raw pasta from clumping together. Cover and refrigerate for up to 2 days.

**MAKES 1 POUND DOUGH**

# Pappardelle with Butter Bean and Tomato Ragù

*Fresh green lima beans, as shown in the photo, make this dish feel a little lighter than dry beans would.*

Salt, as needed

Pappardelle made from ½ recipe Fresh Pasta Dough (page 197) or 12 ounces dried

1½ cups halved grape tomatoes

3 tbsp olive oil

1 medium yellow onion, minced

2 cloves garlic, minced

3 tbsp tomato paste

1 cup cooked butter beans or large lima beans

¼ cup Vegetable Broth (page 287)

1 tbsp chopped thyme

1 tsp chopped rosemary

3 tbsp chopped basil

Freshly ground black pepper, as needed

GARNISH

⅓ cup grated ricotta salata cheese

1. Bring a large pot of salted water to a boil over high heat. Add the pappardelle and cook until tender, 2 to 3 minutes if fresh, 7 to 9 minutes if dried. Drain thoroughly but do not rinse the pasta, reserving 1 cup plus 3 tbsp of the cooking water. Set aside the pasta. While pasta is cooking, start steps 2 and 3.

2. In a food processor or blender, process ¾ cup of the tomatoes until smooth. Set aside.

3. In a large sauté pan, heat the oil over medium heat. Add the onion and cook until translucent, 4 to 5 minutes. Add the garlic and sauté until fragrant, about 1 minute more. Stir in 3 tbsp of the reserved pasta water. Stir in the tomato paste, the puréed tomatoes, beans, and broth. Add the thyme, rosemary, and basil, and reduce the heat to a simmer. Simmer until the liquid has reduced to a thick, chunky sauce, 10 to 15 minutes.

4. Stir in the remaining tomato halves. Season with salt and pepper. Add the pappardelle and the remaining pasta water, and toss to coat. Portion the pasta onto warm plates, and serve garnished with grated ricotta salata.

MAKES 4 SERVINGS

Pappardelle with Butter Bean and Tomato Ragù

# Individual Spinach, Asparagus, and White Bean Lasagnas

*This recipe calls for fresh pasta, but it could also be made with store-bought lasagna noodles. Boil the noodles until tender, then cut them in half before assembling the lasagnas as directed.*

Salt, as needed

1 lb asparagus, cut into 1-inch pieces

1 recipe Fresh Pasta Dough (page 197)

All-purpose flour, as needed for cutting

1 cup cooked white beans
(see chart, page 131)

1 clove garlic, lightly crushed

1 tbsp chopped rosemary

¼ cup plus 2 tbsp extra-virgin olive oil

Freshly ground black pepper, as needed

¼ cup minced shallots

3 cloves garlic, minced

2 cups baby spinach, packed

2 tbsp Madeira

¼ cup green peas (cooked
fresh or thawed frozen)

2 tbsp chopped sage

GARNISH

Extra-virgin olive oil, as needed

Grated Parmesan, as needed

1. Bring a large pot of salted water to a boil over high heat. Fill a large bowl with ice and water to make an ice water bath. Cook the asparagus until bright green and barely tender, about 1 minute. Remove with a skimmer or slotted spoon and plunge the asparagus into the ice water to stop the cooking and chill. Drain thoroughly and set aside. Reduce the heat and leave the water on a low boil.

2. Roll out the pasta dough into thin sheets. On a lightly floured surface, cut the sheets into 12 large, even 4 by 4-inch or 6 by 6-inch squares. Cover with plastic wrap until needed.

3. In a food processor or blender, purée the beans, crushed garlic, rosemary, and ¼ cup of the oil until smooth. Season with salt and pepper and set aside.

4. In a large sauté pan, heat the remaining oil over medium heat. Add the shallots, minced garlic, and spinach, and sauté until the shallots are translucent and the spinach is wilted, 2 to 3 minutes. Add the Madeira and simmer until almost no liquid remains.

5. Add the asparagus and peas and toss to combine and heat through, about 1 minute. Stir in the sage. Keep warm over low heat.

6. Return the water to a boil over medium-high heat. Cook the pasta until tender, 2 minutes for fresh pasta. Drain.

7. Place 1 sheet of pasta on each plate. Top with some of the white bean purée and some of the vegetable mixture. Repeat this layering twice more with the remaining pasta, purée, and vegetables.

8. Garnish the lasagnas with a drizzle of olive oil and a sprinkling of Parmesan and serve immediately.

**MAKES 4 SERVINGS**

# Caramelized Onion Ravioli with Portobello Mushroom Sauce

*Mascarpone cheese is an excellent way to finish or sauce pasta dishes—it has a wonderful creamy texture and a hint of sweetness.*

**RAVIOLI**

5 tbsp olive oil

1 medium yellow onion, thinly sliced

1 cup thinly sliced leeks (white and light green parts)

¼ cup thinly sliced shallots

5 cloves garlic, minced

2½ cups Vegetable Broth (page 287)

Salt and freshly ground black pepper, as needed

1 recipe Fresh Pasta Dough (page 197)

All-purpose flour, as needed for cutting

Corn meal, as needed for dusting

**SAUCE**

¾ cups diced yellow onion

3 cups stemmed, halved, and thinly sliced portobello mushrooms

1 bay leaf

1 tbsp chopped flat-leaf parsley

2 tbsp chopped thyme

2 tbsp grated lemon zest

**GARNISH**

¼ cup mascarpone cheese

1. In a large sauté pan, heat 3 tbsp of the oil over medium heat. Add the sliced onions, leeks, and shallots and sauté until translucent, 4 to 5 minutes. Reduce heat to low and cook until the onions are golden and caramelized, 6 to 8 minutes more.

2. Add half of the garlic and sauté until fragrant, about 1 minute. Add ½ cup of the broth and bring to a simmer. Simmer until the liquid has reduced almost entirely. Season with salt and pepper. Cool to room temperature.

3. Using a pasta machine, roll the dough out very thin, about ⅛ inch thick. On a lightly floured surface, cut the pasta into 60 2½-inch squares.

4. Brush the edge of a pasta square lightly with water. Spoon a few teaspoons of the onion filling onto the center of half of the pasta squares. Top with remaining pasta squares, keeping the edges of the dough lined up. Lightly press the edges of the dough together, being careful to force out any trapped air pockets from around the filling. Crimp the edges with a fork to seal them. Hold the ravioli in a single layer dusted with corn meal, covered, on a parchment paper—lined baking sheet. Set aside.

5. In a large saucepan, heat the remaining oil over medium heat. Add the diced onion and sauté until translucent, 4 to 5 minutes. Add the remaining garlic and sauté until fragrant, about 1 minute more. Add the mushrooms and sauté briefly, 2 to 3 minutes. Add the remaining broth and the bay leaf and bring to a simmer. Simmer until the liquid has reduced to about ¾ cup, 15 to 20 minutes.

6. Remove and discard the bay leaf and stir in the parsley, thyme, and lemon zest. Season with salt and pepper. Keep warm.

7. Bring a large pot of salted water to a boil over high heat. Add the ravioli, reduce the heat to medium, and simmer until tender, 2 to 3 minutes if fresh, 6 to 8 minutes if dried. Remove the ravioli from the water with a skimmer or slotted spoon and add to the mushroom sauce. Turn gently to coat.

8. Divide the ravioli and sauce among 4 warm plates. Top each with a dollop of mascarpone and serve immediately.

**MAKES 4 SERVINGS**

Butternut Squash and Sage Ravioli

# Butternut Squash and Sage Ravioli

*Butternut squash and sage is a classic combination, perfectly delicious when colder weather sets in. This recipe finishes the pasta with sage butter and cheese, but any other thin, lightly flavored sauce would be good, too.*

1 large butternut squash (about 2 pounds), halved lengthwise and seeded

7 tbsp unsalted butter

2 tbsp chopped sage

1¼ cups grated Parmesan

2 tbsp grated lemon zest

½ tsp freshly grated nutmeg

Salt and freshly ground black pepper, as needed

½ recipe Fresh Pasta Dough (page 197)

All-purpose flour, as needed for cutting

Corn meal, as needed for dusting

16 sage leaves

1. Preheat the oven to 350°F.

2. Place the butternut squash cut side up in a baking pan. Cover the pan with foil and bake until the flesh is tender, 45 minutes to 1 hour. Remove from the oven, uncover, and set aside to cool slightly.

3. In a small sauté pan, melt 3 tbsp of the butter with the chopped sage over medium heat. Cook until very hot and lightly browned, 3 to 4 minutes. Remove from the heat and set aside.

4. Scoop the flesh out from the squash and discard the skin. Using a blender or food processor, purée the squash, sage butter, 1 cup of the cheese, the lemon zest, and nutmeg until smooth. Season with salt and pepper.

5. Using a pasta machine, roll out the pasta dough into sheets about ⅛ inch thick. On a lightly floured surface, cut the sheets into forty 2- to 3-inch squares. Cover with plastic wrap until ready to be filled.

6. Brush the edge of a pasta square lightly with water. Spoon approximately 1 tbsp of the squash filling in the center of the square.

7. Top with another square, keeping the edges of the dough lined up. Lightly press the edges of the dough together, being careful to force out any trapped air pockets from around the filling. Crimp the edges with a fork to seal them. Hold the ravioli in a single layer dusted with corn meal, covered, on a parchment paper—lined baking sheet. Repeat with remaining pasta squares and filling to make 20 ravioli.

8. Bring a large pot of salted water to a boil over high heat. Add the ravioli, reduce the heat to medium, and simmer until tender, 2 to 3 minutes if fresh, 5 to 7 minutes if dried. Drain.

9. In a large sauté pan, melt the remaining butter over medium heat. Add the ravioli and toss lightly to coat. Add the sage leaves and the remaining Parmesan and toss to coat. Heat the mixture through, about 1 minute. Serve immediately.

**MAKES 4 SERVINGS**

NOTE: If desired, save the seeds from the squash. Wash them and toast for a garnish.

# Pasta with Cilantro Pesto

*Pesto is a fragrant and flavorful herb-based sauce or dip. Using cilantro in lieu of the traditional basil gives this pasta dish a unique twist.*

Salt, as needed

1 clove garlic

2 tbsp minced fresh ginger

¼ tsp red pepper flakes

¼ cup roasted unsalted macadamia nuts

1 tbsp fresh lime juice

1 cup cilantro leaves

2 tbsp extra-virgin olive oil,
plus more as needed

Freshly ground black pepper, as needed

½ pound dried pasta, such as farfalle

GARNISH

Grated dry Jack cheese, as needed

1. Bring a large pot of salted water to a boil over high heat.

2. In a food processor or blender, process the garlic, ginger, pepper flakes, nuts, lime juice, and cilantro to form a coarse paste. With the machine running, drizzle in the olive oil (and more as needed) to form a slightly smoother paste. Season with salt and pepper.

3. Cook the pasta in the boiling water until tender, 7 to 9 minutes.

4. Drain, reserving 2 tbsp of the pasta water. Transfer the pasta to a large bowl. Pour the pesto over the warm pasta and add the pasta water. Toss to combine. Serve warm, in warm bowls, garnished with cheese.

**MAKES 4 SERVINGS**

# Penne with Eggplant-Tomato Sauce, Wilted Greens, and Asiago

*Adding greens such as spinach, arugula, radicchio, or mâche to pasta is a great way to eat them. They taste fantastic warm, and tossing them with the hot pasta cooks them just enough to make them tender.*

Salt, as needed

2⅓ cups penne

3 tbsp olive oil

1 medium eggplant, diced

1 cup minced shallots

2 cloves garlic, minced

2 tbsp tomato paste

¼ cup red wine

1 cup diced tomatoes

1 bay leaf

2 tbsp grated lemon zest

¼ cup diced sun-dried tomatoes

2 tbsp chopped flat-leaf parsley

Freshly ground black pepper, as needed

½ cup Vegetable Broth (page 287)

5 cups spinach leaves

1 head radicchio, cored and cut in chiffonade

¼ cup chopped basil

3 tbsp chopped oregano

GARNISH

1 cup grated Asiago cheese, plus more as needed

1. Bring a large pot of salted water to a boil over high heat. Cook the penne until tender, 6 to 8 minutes. Drain, reserving 3 tbsp of the pasta water, and set aside.

2. In a large sauté pan, heat the oil over medium heat. Add the eggplant, shallots, and garlic, and sauté until golden brown and tender, 10 to 15 minutes.

3. Stir in the tomato paste and wine. Simmer until the liquid has reduced almost entirely, about 10 minutes.

4. Stir in the diced tomatoes, bay leaf, lemon zest, and sun-dried tomatoes. Simmer over low heat until good flavor has developed, 15 to 20 minutes.

5. Remove and discard the bay leaf, stir in the parsley, and season with salt and pepper. Keep warm.

6. In a large sauté pan, heat the broth over medium heat. Add the spinach and radicchio, reduce heat to low, and toss until slightly wilted and the liquid has evaporated, about 2 minutes. Remove from the heat. Stir in the basil and oregano.

7. Portion the pasta onto warm plates. Top with the eggplant-tomato sauce and a spoonful of wilted leaves. Garnish with grated Asiago and serve warm.

MAKES 4 SERVINGS

# Orzo with Broccoli Rabe, Tomato, and Poached Egg

Salt, as needed

1 cup orzo

¼ cup olive oil

Grated zest and juice of 1 lemon

2 tbsp chopped basil

1 bunch broccoli rabe, trimmed and chopped

2 cloves garlic, thinly sliced

1 cup cherry tomatoes, halved

¾ cup grated Parmesan

Freshly ground black pepper, as needed

2 tsp balsamic or red wine vinegar

4 large eggs

1. Bring a large pot of salted water to a boil over high heat. Fill a large bowl with ice and water to make an ice water bath.

2. Cook the orzo until tender, 5 to 7 minutes. Using a sieve, scoop the orzo out of the water, drain, and transfer to a medium bowl. Stir in 1 tbsp of the oil, the lemon zest and juice, and the basil. Set aside.

3. Bring the water back to a boil. Add the broccoli rabe and cook until it begins to become tender, 3 to 4 minutes. Drain the broccoli rabe and plunge it into the ice water to stop the cooking and cool. Drain again thoroughly.

4. In a large sauté pan, heat the remaining oil over medium heat. Add the garlic and broccoli rabe and sauté until the broccoli rabe is tender, 4 to 5 minutes.

5. Stir in the tomatoes and orzo and cook until everything is heated through, 1 to 2 minutes. Stir in the Parmesan and season with salt and pepper. Keep warm.

6. In a large, deep skillet, bring about 3 inches water to a gentle simmer. Season with salt and add the vinegar. Adjust the heat as needed to prevent a full boil, as large bubbles will break the eggs.

7. Crack each egg first into a small cup or bowl, then gently slide the egg into the poaching liquid. Cook until the whites are set, 3 to 4 minutes. Remove with a slotted spoon and blot briefly on paper towels.

8. Spoon the orzo mixture into warm bowls and top each with a poached egg. Season with salt and pepper and serve immediately.

**MAKES 4 SERVINGS**

Orzo with Broccoli Rabe, Tomato, and Poached Egg

Gnocchi with
Oven-Dried
Tomatoes,
Zucchini, and Pesto

# Gnocchi with Oven-Dried Tomatoes, Zucchini, and Pesto

*Gnocchi are tender potato dumplings that are as easy to make as mashed potatoes. For more rustic gnocchi, simply spoon small pieces of the dough into simmering water rather than cutting it into even pieces.*

2 cups cherry tomatoes

Kosher salt and freshly ground black pepper, as needed

1½ pounds russet potatoes, peeled and cut in half

1 tbsp unsalted butter

1½ cups all-purpose flour, plus more for rolling

1 large egg

1 large egg yolk

2 tbsp olive oil

1 cup button mushrooms, quartered

2 medium zucchini, thinly sliced

2 medium yellow squash, thinly sliced

1 cup Pesto (page 297)

¼ cup grated dry Jack Cheese

1. Preheat the oven to 250°F.

2. Cut the cherry tomatoes in half and place on a fine-mesh wire rack over a baking sheet, cut side up. Season with salt and pepper. Bake until dried, 15 to 20 minutes. Remove from the oven and set aside.

3. Meanwhile, in a large pot, cover the potatoes with cold salted water by 1 inch. Bring to a boil over medium-high heat and cook until the potatoes are tender, 15 to 20 minutes. Drain well.

4. Using a potato masher or food mill, mash the potatoes until smooth. Transfer to a large bowl. Add the butter, flour, egg, egg yolk, 1 tbsp oil, 1 tsp salt, and ¼ tsp pepper, and mix until the mixture forms a smooth dough.

5. Line a baking sheet with parchment or waxed paper. Bring a large pot of salted water to a simmer over medium heat.

6. On a floured surface, divide the dough into three even pieces. Roll one of the pieces into a rope about ½ inch thick. Cut the rope into ½-inch pieces and set the pieces aside on the baking sheet. Repeat with the remaining dough.

7. Cook the gnocchi until tender, 7 to 9 minutes. Drain and set aside.

8. In a large sauté pan, heat the remaining oil over medium heat. Add the mushrooms and sauté until almost tender, 5 to 6 minutes. Add the zucchini and squash and sauté until all the vegetables are tender, 3 to 4 minutes more.

9. Stir in the pesto and the gnocchi. Add the cheese and tomatoes and toss to combine. Season well with salt and pepper and serve immediately in warm bowls.

**MAKES 6 SERVINGS**

# Ricotta and Goat Cheese Gnocchi with Tuscan Cabbage Sauce

*Cheese-based gnocchi are easier and quicker to make than the well-known potato dumplings. All ingredients simply need to be combined before forming into dumplings—no precooking or mashing involved.*

⅓ cup ricotta

⅓ cup crumbled fresh goat cheese

3 tbsp grated Pecorino Romano

1 large egg

1 large egg yolk

Kosher salt, as needed

Pinch freshly grated nutmeg

½ cup all-purpose flour, plus more as needed for rolling

3 tbsp extra-virgin olive oil

¼ cup minced shallots

1 cup Vegetable Broth (page 287)

2¾ cups chiffonade Lacinato (Tuscan) kale

Freshly ground black pepper, as needed

4 tbsp (½ stick) unsalted butter

**GARNISH**

Poppy seeds, as needed

1. In a large bowl, combine the ricotta, goat cheese, and Pecorino. Mix well.

2. In a small bowl, lightly beat together the egg, egg yolk, ¼ tsp salt, and the nutmeg.

3. Fold the egg mixture into the cheeses. Stir in the flour just until the dough is well combined and a large pinch holds together when pressed. Do not overwork the dough. Cover and refrigerate until the dough is firm, about 1 hour.

4. Bring a large pot of salted water to a boil over medium-high heat. Line a baking sheet with parchment or waxed paper.

5. On a floured surface, roll the dough into ropes about ¼ inch thick. Cut the ropes into dumplings about ½ inch long. Set aside on the baking sheet.

6. Cook the gnocchi until they are tender and rise to the surface, 2 to 4 minutes. Drain and set aside.

7. In a large sauté pan, heat the olive oil over medium heat. Add the shallots and sauté until translucent, 2 to 3 minutes. Add the broth and bring to a simmer. Add the kale and cook until it is tender and the liquid has been reduced by three-quarters, about 10 minutes. Season with salt and pepper and keep warm.

8. In another large sauté pan, melt the butter over medium heat. Add the gnocchi and sauté to heat through, about 1 minute. Add the kale sauce and toss to combine.

9. Portion the gnocchi into warm bowls and garnish with a sprinkling of poppy seeds.

**MAKES 4 SERVINGS**

Vegetables are, of course, a major part of any vegetarian diet. And while vegetables can easily be selected to enhance another dish or used in an appetizer, soup, or salad, they are often the focal point of an entrée preparation. When cooking vegetables, it's important to consider the desired texture and flavor you want in your finished dish, as each method will produce different results.

7

# VEGETABLES

# GENERAL GUIDELINES FOR COOKING VEGETABLES

Carefully handled vegetables maintain their flavor, color, and texture longer. Rinse leafy or delicate vegetables carefully to avoid bruising them, and dry them thoroughly. Scrub hardier vegetables before peeling. Be sure to remove all traces of dirt or grit.

There are variances in how tender a vegetable should be when it is properly cooked. Some vegetables—broccoli and green beans, for example—are not considered properly cooked until they are quite tender. Others, such as snow peas and sugar snap peas, should always retain some bite (fully cooked but still firm). Preferences regarding the correct doneness of certain vegetables may vary from one cook to another, and different cooking techniques will produce different results. Stir-frying,

for example, results in a crisp texture, while baking or braising produces very tender vegetables.

## Boiling Vegetables

1. Bring the liquid to a full boil. Add any seasonings or aromatics.

2. Add the vegetable.

3. Cook to the desired doneness.

4. Drain the vegetable.

5. Serve the vegetable or use in a secondary preparation.

## Steaming Vegetables

1. Bring the liquid to a full boil. Add the seasonings and aromatics.

STEAMING VEGETABLES: Pan Steaming is ideal for tender or fragile vegetables. Here, spinach is added to a small amount of simmering water, which gently cooks it.

ROASTING AND BAKING VEGETABLES: Different vegetables can be roasted or baked together as long as they are of uniform size and cooking time.

2. Add the vegetable to the steamer basket in a single layer.

3. Steam the vegetable to the desired doneness.

4. Serve the vegetable or use in a secondary preparation.

Pan steaming is a method that requires a shallow pan with a lid and requires a very small amount of water. This method is commonly used for asparagus, spinach, or any other tender vegetable.

## Roasting or Baking Vegetables

1. Prepare the vegetable. If desired, toss with fat or seasonings.

2. Place the vegetable in a hot or moderate oven.

3. Roast to the desired doneness.

4. Serve the vegetable or use in a secondary preparation.

## Sautéing and Stir-Frying Vegetables

1. Place the pan over medium heat. Pour in the cooking fat and heat until it shimmers or becomes mildly aromatic.

2. Add the vegetable.

3. Sauté the vegetable, keeping it in motion.

4. Add the aromatics, seasonings, or glaze and heat thoroughly.

5. Serve the vegetable or use in a secondary preparation.

## Pan Frying Vegetables

1. Heat the cooking fat.

2. Add the vegetable.

3. Cook until its exterior is lightly browned and crisp.

STIR-FRYING VEGETABLES: *Stir-fry any aromatics first, then add vegetables to the hot wok or pan.*

*A finished stir-fry will be brightly colored, and all vegetables will be tender.*

PAN FRYING VEGETABLES: Bread or batter vegetables as desired, then add them to the hot oil. Cook the vegetables until they are golden brown on all sides.

GRILLING VEGETABLES: Different vegetables can be grilled together, even if they are different sizes or require different cooking times. Just remember to rotate vegetables as necessary to cook them evenly.

4. Blot on paper towels.

5. Season and serve immediately.

## Deep-Frying Vegetables

1. Coat the vegetable with breading or batter, if desired.

2. Heat the oil in a deep fryer.

3. Add the vegetable.

4. Fry the vegetable until evenly browned or golden.

5. Remove from the oil and blot on paper towels.

6. Season and serve immediately.

## Grilling and Broiling Vegetables

1. Heat the grill or broiler.

2. Marinate the vegetable, if desired, or brush with oil.

3. Grill or broil the vegetables until tender.

4. Serve the vegetable or use in a secondary preparation.

## Stewing and Braising Vegetables

1. Heat the oil or broth.

2. Combine the vegetable and seasonings.

3. Add vegetable to the liquid and bring to a simmer.

4. Cook until the vegetable is tender.

5. Adjust the seasoning and finish the dish according to the recipe.

6. Serve the vegetable or use in a secondary preparation.

# TYPES OF VEGETABLES

Vegetables are the edible roots, tubers, stems, leaves, stalks, seeds, and heads of plants. Some foods that are considered vegetables are actually classified as fruits, such as tomatoes.

## CABBAGE FAMILY

Some members of this family, such as cauliflower and green cabbage, are referred to as "heading cabbages." Others, such as bok choy, form loose heads, while still other varieties do not form a head but are used for their roots. Members of this family include: broccoli; Brussels sprouts; green, red, Napa, and savoy cabbage; kohlrabi; kale; collard greens; and broccoli rabe.

## GOURDS

### Soft-Shell Squash, Cucumber, and Eggplant

These vegetables are all members of the gourd family. They are all picked when they are immature to ensure delicate flesh, tender seeds, and thin skins. Soft-shell squash and eggplant varieties cook rather quickly, while cucumbers are often eaten raw. Select products that are on the smaller side, firm, brightly colored, and without bruising. These vegetables should all be refrigerated.

### Hard-Shell Squash

Hard-shell squashes, also members of the gourd family, are characterized by their hard, thick rinds and seeds. The thick skins and yellow-to-orange flesh require longer cooking than their soft-shell counterparts. Select squashes that are heavy for their size, with a hard, unblemished stem and bottom. Hard-shell squashes may be stored in a cool place for many weeks without deteriorating in quality. Varieties of hard-shell squash include: acorn, butternut, Hubbard, pumpkin, spaghetti, and delicata.

# LETTUCES, BITTER SALAD GREENS, AND COOKING GREENS

Each of the thousands of lettuce varieties can be classified into one of the following categories: leaf, romaine, butterhead, or crisphead. Each of these categories is characterized by specific leaf shape, the presence of a "head" or not, and the tenderness or crispness of the leaf texture. Select lettuce that is crisp, never wilted or bruised. Lettuce should not be washed, cut, or torn until you are ready to serve it. Store it in the refrigerator, covered loosely with damp paper towels. Wash and dry lettuce very carefully to remove any dirt or grit. Varieties of lettuces include: Boston, Bibb, iceberg, romaine, red leaf, and green leaf. Varieties of bitter greens include: arugula, Belgian endive, frisée, radicchio, and watercress. Varieties of cooking greens include: beet greens, mustard greens, spinach, and Swiss chard.

# HOW TO MAKE IT YOUR OWN: COOKING GREENS

All cooking greens have a certain fibrous quality, and for the most part will require cooking before being eaten. Most often the cooking process will involve the use of water or broth, although some types of greens may be sautéed or grilled from the raw state. Bitter greens are often briefly blanched first in salted boiling water , then shocked in ice-cold water, pressed to remove the excess moisture, then sautéed. Blanching the greens first minimizes the bitterness. All greens are appropriate for use in soups and some in stews.

# COOKING GREENS

| TYPE OF GREENS | FLAVOR PROFILE | COOKING METHODS |
|---|---|---|
| **KOHLRABI** | Mild | Sauté from raw state or braise |
| **BOK CHOY** | Mild | Sauté, stir-fry, grill |
| **SPINACH** | Slightly tannic | Sauté from raw state, or blanch then sauté |
| **BROCCOLI RABE** | Bitter | Blanch then sauté, braise |
| **SWISS CHARD** | Mild | Sauté from raw state if young greens are used, or braise |
| **COLLARD GREENS** | Mild to slightly bitter | Sauté from raw state using very high heat, or braise |
| **ASIAN MUSTARD GREENS** | Spicy | Sauté from raw state or braise |
| **MUSTARD GREENS** | Spicy | Sauté from raw state, or blanch then sauté, braise |
| **BEET GREENS** | Mildly tannic | Sauté, or blanch then sauté |
| **KALE** | Mildly bitter | Sauté from raw state, or blanch then sauté |
| **SORREL** | Mildly tart or sour | Sauté from raw state, or blanch then sauté |
| **CABBAGES (GREEN, RED, NAPA, CHINESE, OR SAVOY)** | Mild, sweet | Sauté, stir-fry, or braise |
| **ESCAROLE** | Mildly bitter | Sauté, braise, or grill |

## MUSHROOMS

Mushrooms are a fungus and exist in thousands of varieties. Select mushrooms that are firm, without blemishes or breaks. Mushrooms should be stored in the refrigerator, in a single layer, covered with damp paper towels. When you want to use them, wipe them with a damp paper towel or rinse them very quickly. Available varieties include: white, porcini, chanterelle, cremini, morel, portobello, oyster, and shiitake.

## ONIONS

Onions fall into two main categories: dry and green (fresh). Select dry onions that are heavy for their size and have tight-fitting skins. Store in a cool, dry place for up to several weeks. Green onions should be crisp, not wilted; store in the refrigerator. Varieties in this family include: pearl, cipollini, Spanish, and sweet onions; shallots; leeks; ramps; and green onions.

## PEPPERS

There are two basic types of peppers: sweet (bell) peppers and chiles. Chiles are available in many sizes, colors, and levels of heat. Generally, the smaller the chile, the hotter it is. The white ribs (membranes) and seeds have the highest concentration of capsaicin (the compound that gives chiles their heat). Take precautions when handling chiles: Thoroughly wash cutting surfaces and knives, and always avoid contact with your eyes or other sensitive body parts. Pepper varieties include: bell peppers and Anaheim, poblano, jalapeño, serrano, Thai bird, Scotch Bonnets and habanero chiles, as well as dried chiles, just to mention a few.

## POD AND SEED VEGETABLES

This group includes fresh legumes (peas, beans, etc.) as well as corn and okra. All varieties are best eaten young, when they are at their sweetest and most tender. Select vegetables that are crisp, brightly colored, and free of discoloration. Varieties include: corn, green beans, romano beans, Chinese long beans, lima beans, fava beans, edamame, snow peas, sugar snap peas, and English peas.

## ROOT VEGETABLES

Roots serve as a food-storage area for plants and therefore are rich in sugars, starches, vitamins, and minerals. Store root vegetables dry and unpeeled. If they come with greens attached, the greens should appear fresh and not wilted. Varieties include: carrots, celery root, lotus root, parsnip, salsify, turnip, rutabaga, radishes, and beets.

## TUBERS

Tubers are vegetables that are connected to the root system by an underground stem. They should be stored dry and unpeeled, away from excess light and heat. If they get wet or overly warm, they will sprout and wrinkle. Varieties include: yuca, ginger, galangal, jícama, sunchoke, and boniato, as well as all varieties of potatoes.

## SHOOTS AND STALKS

Shoots and stalk vegetables should be firm, fleshy, and full, with no evidence of browning or wilting. Store these vegetables in the refrigerator and wash just prior to cooking. Varieties include: asparagus, fennel, fiddlehead ferns, celery, and artichokes.

## TOMATOES

Tomatoes are actually a fruit, but because of their many savory cooking applications are often considered a vegetable. Select brightly colored tomatoes that are free of soft spots and blemishes. They should be heavy for their size but not overly firm. Tomatoes should not be refrigerated because the cold makes their texture mushy and halts ripening, affecting flavor. Varieties include: beefsteak, plum (Roma), cherry, grape, currant, pear, heirloom, and tomatillos.

# HOW TO MAKE IT YOUR OWN: STUFFINGS AND FILLINGS

Stuffings can be made using all sorts of grains and vegetables. It is important to remember that all components should be at least three-quarters (if not completely) cooked before using in stuffing. Stuffings are generally made with a starchy base (such as grains or bread), vegetables, legumes, spices, and herbs.

## STUFFING VEGETABLES AND OTHER WRAPPERS

| ITEM TO BE STUFFED | PREPARATION FOR STUFFING | FILLINGS/STUFFINGS | COOKING METHODS |
|---|---|---|---|
| Vegetables | | | |
| **LARGE FLAT-LEAF GREENS SUCH AS COLLARDS, MUSTARD GREENS, KALE, OR CABBAGE** | Separate leaves, blanch, shock in cold water, and lay flat | Grains, vegetables, potatoes, or yams | Braise |
| **BELL PEPPERS, FRESH CHILES** | ○ Remove stem, core, seeds, and membranes<br>○ If desired, blanch or roast before filling | Grains, legumes, or vegetables | Bake, braise, fry |

*continued*

# STUFFING VEGETABLES AND OTHER WRAPPERS cont.

| ITEM TO BE STUFFED | PREPARATION FOR STUFFING | FILLINGS/STUFFINGS | COOKING METHODS |
|---|---|---|---|
| **DRIED CHILES** | Toast, remove stem, seeds, and membranes, soak | Legumes, beans, cheese, grains, or vegetables | Bake, braise, fry |
| **SUMMER SQUASH** | ○ Split in half and remove seeds<br>○ If desired, blanch or roast before filling | Grains, vegetables, cheese, fresh herbs | Bake |
| **WINTER SQUASH** | ○ Cut in half or into wedges, remove stem and seeds<br>○ If desired, blanch or roast before filling | Grains, vegetables, cheese, dried fruits, nuts, herbs, greens, corn, potatoes, or yams | Bake, braise |
| **MUSHROOMS** | Remove stems and gills | Grains, vegetables, cheese, bread, dried fruit, sun-dried tomatoes, herbs, greens, or nuts | Bake, braise, fry |
| **ONIONS** | Cut in half, remove center layers | Cheese, bread, herbs, vegetables, or grains | Bake, braise, fry |
| **TOMATOES** | Remove stem and seeds | Vegetables, bread, grains, herbs, cheese, or nuts | Bake, braise |
| Other Edible Wrappers | | | |
| **LARGE PASTA SHELLS** | Soak or par cook in boiling water | Bread, vegetables, cheese, greens, or herbs | Bake |
| **LASAGNA OR PASTA SHEETS** | Soak or par cook in boiling water | Vegetables, cheese, bread, nuts, or greens | Bake |
| **WONTON OR EGGROLL WRAPPERS** | No advance prep necessary | Vegetables, greens, nuts, grains, or cheese | Steam, braise, fry |
| Inedible Wrappers | | | |
| **CORN HUSKS** | Soak in warm water to soften | Masa harina, vegetables, beans, cheese, nuts, dried fruits, or grains | Steam |
| **BANANA LEAVES** | Blanch in water or pass over an open flame to singe each side | Masa harina, vegetables, beans, cheese, nuts, dried fruits, or grains | Steam |

# Black Bean and Quinoa–Stuffed Zucchini

*Quinoa makes a great base for stuffing vegetables—try using it with peppers, onions, or mushrooms.*

4 medium zucchini, halved lengthwise

2 tbsp olive oil

Salt and freshly ground black pepper, as needed

1 cup cooked black beans (see chart, page 131)

¾ cup grated Cheddar

⅔ cup Oven-Steamed Quinoa (page 000)

½ jalapeño, seeded and minced

½ tsp ground cumin, toasted

½ tsp ground coriander, toasted

1 tbsp chopped cilantro

1 tbsp chopped marjoram

2 tsp chopped oregano

1. Preheat the oven to 350°F.

2. Place the quinoa in a sieve and wash until the liquid runs clear. Combine the washed quinoa with 4 cups of water. Bring to a simmer and cook for 4-5 minutes - until it is barely cooked. Pour the cooked quinoa into a strainer and drain the excess water. Transfer the quinoa to a large sheet tray, spread it out and allow to cool. Use a fork to fluff the quinoa occasionally.

3. Use a spoon to scoop about three-quarters of the flesh and seed from the center of the zucchini and set aside for other uses. Leave a substantial shell. Transfer the zucchini shells to a baking sheet cut side up, brush with the oil, and season with salt and pepper.

4. In a medium bowl, combine the beans, cheese, quinoa, jalapeño, cumin, coriander, cilantro, marjoram, and oregano. Season with salt and pepper. Spoon into the zucchini, pressing to make sure it stays in place.

5. Bake until the zucchini are tender, 20 to 30 minutes. Serve immediately.

**MAKES 4 SERVINGS**

Aztec Vegetable Casserole

# Aztec Vegetable Casserole

*This is a great, easy casserole that can easily be assembled in advance and baked when you're ready. It freezes well, too.*

2 tbsp grapeseed or canola oil, plus more for greasing the casserole

1 cup diced yellow onions

1 clove garlic, minced

2¾ cups tomato purée

2 tsp chopped oregano

Salt and freshly ground black pepper, as needed

2 poblano chiles, roasted, peeled, seeded, and thinly sliced

1 jalapeño, seeded and minced

2 cups seeded and diced zucchini

1 cup thinly sliced mushrooms

1 cup green onions (white and green parts), sliced into ¼-inch pieces

2 cloves garlic, minced

1¼ cups corn kernels (fresh or thawed frozen)

¾ cup green peas (fresh or thawed frozen)

1 cup seeded and diced tomatoes

1 cup cooked brown rice (see chart, page 176)

8 Corn Tortillas (page 273 or store-bought)

⅓ cup crème fraîche

1½ cups grated Manchego cheese (about 6 ounces)

1. Preheat the oven to 350°F. Lightly grease 4 individual casseroles, 16 oz capacity.

2. In a medium saucepan, heat 1 tbsp oil over medium heat. Add the yellow onions and sauté until translucent, 4 to 5 minutes. Add the garlic and sauté until fragrant, about 1 minute more. Add the tomato purée and oregano. Reduce the heat to low and simmer until good flavor develops, about 10 minutes. Season with salt and pepper and keep warm.

3. In a large sauté pan, heat the remaining oil over medium heat. Add the poblanos, jalapeños, and zucchini. Sauté until they are tender, 4 to 5 minutes. Add the mushrooms, green onions, and garlic. Sauté until the mushrooms are tender and the garlic is fragrant, 2 to 3 minutes. Stir in the corn, peas, tomatoes, and rice and heat through, about 1 minute. Keep warm.

4. Spoon some tomato sauce into the base of each casserole. Place a tortilla at the bottom and top with one-fourth of of the vegetable filling. Spoon some crème fraîche and more tomato sauce over the filling and top with another tortilla. Top with sauce and a generous sprinkling of cheese.

5. Bake, uncovered, until the cheese begins to melt and internal temperature reaches 165°F or more, 15 to 20 minutes. Serve hot.

**MAKES 4 SERVINGS**

# Stuffed Eggplant Parcels

*The filling for this eggplant can be complemented by other flavors and textures. Try other combinations of herbs, spices, grains, beans, and sauces to create a variety of different dishes. For example, fill the eggplant with the Mixed Grain Pilaf (page 180) and garnish with Roasted Red Pepper Marmalade (page 296) or Tapenade (page 14).*

1 medium eggplant, cut lengthwise into ¼-inch-thick planks

Olive oil, as needed

Salt and freshly ground black pepper, as needed

¾ cups cooked pinto beans (see chart, page 132)

½ recipe Simmered Mixed Grains (page 180)

½ tsp ground cumin, toasted

Pinch cayenne, plus more as needed

¼ cup grated Monterey Jack cheese

¼ cup grated pepper Jack cheese

½ jalapeño, seeded and minced

2 tbsp minced sun-dried tomatoes

2 tbsp chopped cilantro

GARNISH

Red Chile Salsa (page 308), as needed

1. Preheat the oven to 350°F.

2. Brush the eggplant lightly with oil and season well with salt and pepper. Transfer the eggplant to a baking sheet.

3. Roast the eggplant until it is tender and golden, 5 to 6 minutes. Remove from the oven but leave the oven on.

4. In a large bowl, combine the beans, grains, cumin, cayenne, cheeses, jalapeño, tomatoes, and cilantro. Season with salt and pepper. Divide filling among the eggplant slices and roll up the eggplant to encase the filling. (If desired, use toothpicks to keep the parcels closed.) Place the parcels seam side down on the baking sheet.

5. Bake the parcels until lightly browned and cooked through, 10 to 12 minutes.

6. Transfer to plates, garnish with salsa, and serve.

**MAKES 4 SERVINGS**

Stuffed Eggplant Parcels

# Chickpea Salad in Avocados

*Similar in taste, texture, and ease to tuna salad, this salad makes a great quick lunch.*

1½ cups cooked chickpeas
(see chart, page 131)

2 stalks celery, minced

¼ cup minced red bell pepper

1 bunch green onions, thinly sliced
(white and green parts)

⅓ cup mayonnaise, plus more as needed

2 tbsp fresh lemon juice, plus more as needed

2 tsp Dijon mustard

2 tbsp chopped flat-leaf parsley

Salt and freshly ground black
pepper, as needed

2 Hass avocados

Chopped chives, as needed

1. In a food processor, pulse the chickpeas a few times, until coarsely chopped. Transfer to a large bowl. Add the celery, red pepper, green onions, mayonnaise, lemon juice, mustard, and parsley. Season with salt and pepper. Mix well until combined, adding more mayonnaise if necessary. Cover and refrigerate at least 30 minutes.

2. Halve the avocados and remove and discard the pits. Squeeze a little bit of lemon juice over the avocados to prevent discoloration. Divide the chickpea salad among the avocado halves, mounding it with a spoon and pressing gently to ensure it stays in place. Sprinkle chives over the avocados and serve immediately.

**MAKES 4 SERVINGS**

# Chinese Stuffed Cabbage

*Cabbage is a great and easy vegetable to stuff—try stuffing it with some of the other fillings in this chapter.*

Salt, as needed

2 tbsp grapeseed or canola oil, plus more as needed for greasing

1 large head savoy cabbage

2 bunches green onions, minced (white and green parts)

½ cup minced red bell pepper

1 cup shiitake mushrooms, stemmed and thinly sliced

2 cloves garlic, minced

1 tbsp minced fresh ginger

1 cup brown rice

2 cups Vegetable Broth (page 287)

½ pound firm tofu, diced

3 tbsp toasted pine nuts, finely chopped

3 tbsp soy or tamari sauce

SOY-MUSHROOM SAUCE

¼ cup soy or tamari sauce

¼ cup rice vinegar

1 tbsp light brown sugar

2 cloves garlic, minced

1 tbsp minced fresh ginger

2 tsp Sriracha or other chili sauce

1½ cups Mushroom Broth (page 287)

1. Bring a large pot of salted water to a boil over high heat. Fill a large bowl with ice and water to make an ice water bath. Preheat the oven to 325°F. Lightly grease a large casserole.

2. Core the cabbage and carefully separate the leaves. Working in batches if necessary, add the leaves to the boiling water and cook until slightly soft and bright green, about 30 seconds to 1 minute. Remove the leaves with a skimmer and plunge into the ice water to stop the cooking and cool. Drain thoroughly. Set aside 12 large leaves and julienne the remaining cabbage.

3. Heat the oil in a medium ovenproof saucepan over medium heat. Add the green onions and sauté until translucent, 4 to 5 minutes. Stir in the red pepper, mushrooms, garlic, and ginger and cook until aromatic. Add the rice and toss to coat with the oil. Add the broth and julienned cabbage leaves. Reduce the heat to medium-low and bring to a simmer.

4. Cover the pot tightly and bake until the rice is tender and has absorbed all the liquid, 35 to 40 minutes.

5. Fluff the rice with a fork and transfer to a large bowl. Add the tofu, pine nuts, and soy sauce. Mix gently to combine.

6. Lay out the cabbage leaves on the work surface. Divide the rice mixture among the leaves, and roll each leaf burrito-style to completely encase the filling. Transfer the rolls to the casserole and set aside.

7. To make the sauce, in a medium saucepan combine the soy sauce, vinegar, sugar, garlic, ginger, Sriracha, and broth over medium heat. Bring to a simmer. Sauce should thicken slightly.

8. Pour half of the sauce over the cabbage rolls.

9. Cover the casserole loosely with aluminum foil and bake for 15 minutes or until the filling begins to heat through and the sauce is bubbling slightly. Uncover, spoon the remaining sauce over the cabbage and bake for 10 to 15 minutes more, until internal temperature is 165°F or more. Serve immediately.

**MAKES 6 SERVINGS, 12 ROLLS**

VARIATION: **Stuffed Cabbage with Tomato Sauce:** Replace the green onions with 1 medium yellow onion, minced, and replace the shiitakes with cremini mushrooms. Omit the ginger and soy sauce and add 1 tbsp chopped thyme, 2 tsp chopped rosemary, and 2 tsp chopped oregano. Replace the Soy-Mushroom Sauce with Tomato Sauce (page 303).

Grilled Corn and Black Bean Salsa on
Native American Frybread

# Grilled Corn and Black Bean Salsa on Native American Frybread

*Frybread is super simple to make and is the perfect vehicle for all sorts of toppings. It's great with just a bit of Salsa Roja (page 308), sour cream, and cilantro.*

**SALSA**

2 medium ears corn, husks on

½ cup diced red onion

1 clove garlic, minced

½ jalapeño, seeded and minced

1 cup seeded and diced tomatoes

1¼ cups cooked black beans (see chart, page 131)

2 tbsp fresh lime juice

1½ tsp ground cumin, toasted

2 tbsp chopped cilantro

Salt and freshly ground black pepper, as needed

**FRYBREAD**

2 cups all-purpose flour, plus more as needed for kneading and rolling

⅔ cup milk powder

2 tsp baking powder

½ tsp kosher salt

2 tbsp unsalted butter, soft

⅔ cup ice water

Grapeseed or canola oil, as needed for pan frying

**GARNISH**

Salsa Roja (page 308), as needed

1. Heat a grill or grill pan until hot.

2. Grill the corn, turning frequently, until the husks are charred and the kernels are tender, 6 to 8 minutes. Let cool slightly, then remove the husks and silk.

3. Cut the kernels from the cob into a large bowl. Add the onion, garlic, jalapeño, tomatoes, and beans. Toss to combine. Add the lime juice, cumin, and cilantro and toss to combine. Season well with salt and pepper. Set the salsa aside.

4. In a medium bowl, combine the flour, milk powder, baking powder, and salt. Make a well in the center and add the butter and ice water. Mix until the dough forms a shaggy mass.

5. Turn out the dough onto a lightly floured surface and knead until smooth, 1 to 2 minutes. The dough should be firm, not soft and sticky.

6. Divide into 8 pieces and round the pieces slightly. Cover with a damp paper towel and let sit for 10 minutes.

7. On the floured surface, roll out each piece of dough to a round shape about ½ inch thick. Using a sharp paring knife, score each dough round with two parallel slashes about ½ inch apart. Cover with a linen or muslin towel and let rest for 5 minutes.

8. While the dough is resting, in a large skillet, heat ½ inch oil over medium heat.

9. Working in batches if necessary, fry the bread without crowding the pan, turning once, until it is golden brown on both sides and slightly puffed, 5 to 7 minutes. Set the finished frybread on paper towels to drain slightly.

10. Serve the frybread while still warm, topped with the corn salsa and garnished with salsa roja.

**MAKES 4 SERVINGS, 2 BREADS EACH**

# Eggplant Paprikash

*Serve this flavorful Hungarian-inspired dish with egg noodles and lots of fresh parsley.*

2 medium eggplants, peeled and diced

1 tbsp kosher salt

2 tbsp olive oil

1 medium yellow onion, chopped

1 red bell pepper, chopped

4 garlic cloves, minced

¼ cup sweet Hungarian paprika

3 cups diced tomatoes

1 cup Vegetable Broth (page 287)

Salt and freshly ground black pepper, as needed

½ cup sour cream

GARNISH

2 tbsp chopped flat-leaf parsley

1. Place the eggplant in a colander and toss with the salt. Let the eggplant sit for 10 minutes to release excess moisture. Blot dry.

2. In a large sauté pan, heat the oil over medium heat. Cook the eggplant until tender, 8 to 10 minutes. Remove the eggplant from the pan and set aside.

3. Add the onion and cook until translucent, 4 to 6 minutes. Add the red peppers and cook until they begin to soften, about 5 minutes more. Add the garlic and paprika and sauté until fragrant, about 1 minute more. Add the eggplant, tomatoes, and broth. Season with salt and pepper. Bring to a simmer and cook until all the vegetables are completely tender, 15 to 20 minutes.

4. Stir in the sour cream and cook just until the sauce is heated through. Serve garnished with parsley.

**MAKES 4 SERVINGS**

# Matar Paneer

*Paneer, a farmer-style cheese predominantly found in India, is covered in a flavorful sauce in this dish. Add more vegetables and serve with rice to make it a more substantial meal.*

2 tbsp grape seed or canola oil

1 cup diced yellow onion

1 clove garlic, minced

1 tbsp minced fresh ginger

1 tbsp cumin seeds

1 tsp ground turmeric

1 tbsp garam masala

½ tsp ground coriander

2 Thai bird chiles, seeded and minced

1 cup chopped tomatoes

2½ cups green peas (fresh or thawed frozen)

10 ounces paneer, cubed

3 tbsp whole-milk plain Greek-style yogurt

Chopped cilantro, as needed

Salt and freshly ground black pepper, as needed

1. In a large sauté pan, heat the oil over medium heat. Add the onion and cook until translucent, 4 to 5 minutes. Add the garlic, ginger, cumin, turmeric, garam masala, coriander, and chiles and cook until aromatic, 1 to 2 minutes more. Add the tomatoes and cook until the mixture is heated through and the tomatoes begin to break down, 8 to 10 minutes.

2. Stir in the peas and paneer and cook to heat through. Stir in the yogurt and cilantro and season with salt and pepper. Serve warm.

**MAKES 4 SERVINGS**

# Grilled Vegetable Jambalaya

*This recipe may look complex, but the ingredient list is simply long due to all the herbs and spices added for flavor. Try it out—you won't be disappointed.*

2 tbsp olive oil, plus more as needed for brushing

2 cups diced yellow onions

1¼ cups diced green bell pepper

1⅔ cups diced celery

2 cloves garlic, minced

1 tbsp paprika

Pinch freshly ground black pepper

Pinch freshly ground white pepper

Pinch cayenne

1⅔ cups diced tomatoes

3½ cups Vegetable Broth (page 287)

1 bay leaf

1 tsp dried oregano

1 tsp chopped thyme

2 tbsp chopped basil

1 tsp Tabasco sauce

1 tsp Worcestershire sauce

Salt, as needed

1 medium zucchini, sliced into ½-inch-thick rounds

1 medium yellow squash, sliced into ½-inch-thick rounds

1 red bell pepper, quartered

1 medium red onion, sliced ½ inch thick

1 medium eggplant, peeled, sliced into ½-inch-thick rounds

BBQ Spice Rub (page 313), as needed

2 cups hot cooked brown rice (see chart, page 176)

GARNISH

1 bunch green onions, thinly sliced (white and green parts)

1. In a large pot, heat the olive oil over medium heat. Add the yellow onions, green pepper, celery, garlic, paprika, black pepper, white pepper, and cayenne. Cover the pot and sweat until the vegetables begin to soften, about 10 minutes.

2. Add the tomatoes, broth, bay leaf, oregano, thyme, basil, Tabasco, and Worcestershire. Season with salt. Bring the jambalaya to a simmer.

3. Meanwhile, preheat a grill or grill pan until hot. Lightly brush the zucchini, squash, red pepper, red onion, and eggplant with oil and sprinkle with the spice rub on both sides. Grill the vegetables, turning once, until they are tender. (The grilling time for each vegetable will be different. As each is done, transfer to a baking sheet.)

4. Remove the bay leaf from the jambalaya and stir in the rice. Scoop into large warm bowls and top with the grilled vegetables. Garnish with the green onions.

**MAKES 4 SERVINGS**

Grilled Vegetable Jambalaya

Mushroom Strudel

# Mushroom Strudel

*The filling for this strudel is quick and easy. Keep phyllo dough on hand to make this strudel, even on short notice.*

**FILLING**

3 tbsp unsalted butter

1 cup minced onions

3 cups mushrooms, quartered

2 tsp minced garlic

2 cups spinach, packed

2 tbsp chopped flat-leaf parsley

1 tbsp chopped rosemary

⅓ cup grated Parmesan cheese

Salt and freshly ground black pepper, as needed

**STRUDEL**

12 sheets phyllo dough, thawed overnight in the refrigerator

8 tablespoons (1 stick) unsalted butter, melted, plus more as needed

Unseasoned dry bread crumbs, as needed

1. To make the filling, in a large sauté pan melt the butter over medium heat. Add the onions and sauté until translucent, 4 to 5 minutes. Add the mushrooms and garlic and cook until the mushrooms are tender, 10 to 12 minutes more. Add the spinach, parsley, and rosemary and stir until the spinach is wilted. Remove the pan from the heat and let the mixture cool to room temperature.

2. While the filling is cooling, preheat the oven to 400°F.

3. Pour the filling into a colander or strainer and press to remove any excess liquid. Transfer to a large bowl. Add the cheese, season with salt and pepper, and toss to combine. Divide the filling into four equal portions.

4. Lay out the phyllo dough on the work surface and cover with plastic wrap and then a dampened kitchen towel. Only remove 1 sheet to work with at a time.

5. Brush a sheet of phyllo with melted butter and sprinkle with a thin, even layer of bread crumbs. Top with another sheet of phyllo and repeat until you have stacked three layers of dough.

6. Place 1 portion of the filling 2 inches away from the edge of the layered dough. Roll the edge up and over the filling, fold in the ends, and continue to roll the dough around the filling, burrito-style, ending with the seam at the bottom. Transfer the dough to a baking sheet, and score the dough with a paring knife twice to allow steam to escape. Brush the finished strudel with melted butter.

7. Repeat with remaining phyllo dough and filling.

8. Bake the strudels until golden brown, 15 to 20 minutes.

**MAKES 4 SERVINGS**

# Poblanos Rellenos

This dish is excellent served with Squash Salsa (page 310), and Mushrooms with Guajillo Chiles and Garlic (page 40). If you can't find queso Chihuahua, double the amount of Monterey Jack.

5 poblano chiles

1 tbsp olive oil

½ cup small-diced yellow onion

2 cloves garlic, minced

¾ cup cooked black beans
(see chart, page 131)

¾ cup cooked brown rice
(see chart, page 176)

½ cup grated Monterey Jack cheese

½ cup grated *queso Chihuahua*

1 tsp chopped marjoram

½ tsp dried epazote

1 tsp dried Mexican oregano

Salt and freshly ground black
pepper, as needed

Grapeseed or canola oil, as needed for frying

4 large eggs, separated

½ tsp cream of tartar

1 cup all-purpose flour

**GARNISH**

¼ cup cilantro leaves

¼ cup sour cream

1. Grill the poblanos over an open flame or broil, turning often, until the skin blackens and blisters, 4 to 6 minutes. Place the poblanos in a heavy-duty resealable plastic bag, seal, and let sit for 20 minutes.

2. Peel the skin off of the poblanos, but be careful not to damage the flesh. Make a slit down one side and remove the seeds. Set the poblanos aside.

3. In a small sauté pan, heat the olive oil over medium heat. Add the onion and garlic and sauté until the onion is translucent, 4 to 5 minutes. Transfer to a large bowl. Add the beans, rice, cheeses, marjoram, epazote, and oregano. Season with salt and pepper. Mix until well combined.

4. Use a spoon to carefully stuff the poblanos with the filling.

5. In a large sauté pan, heat about ½ inch oil over medium heat.

6. In a medium bowl, whisk the egg whites with cream of tartar to stiff peaks. Sprinkle ½ cup of flour over the whites. Using the whisk, gently fold the flour into the whites.

7. In a separate bowl, whisk the yolks until pale and thick. Gently fold the yolks into the whites.

8. Place the remaining flour in a shallow dish and season with salt and pepper.

9. Dust the stuffed poblanos in the flour, making sure they are completely coated. Then dip the dusted chiles into the egg batter.

10. Fry the poblanos in the preheated oil and cook until they are golden brown on both sides and cooked through, 10 to 12 minutes.

11. Serve hot, garnished with cilantro and a dollop of sour cream.

**MAKES 4 SERVINGS**

VARIATION: **Chiles Rellenos with Vegetable Chili:** No need to coat these stuffed chilies with egg batter and pan fry. Replace the bean and rice filling with the Vegetable Chili on page 65. Top the poblanos generously with grated Cheddar and chopped green onions. Bake in 350°F oven until thoroughly heated. Garnish with sour cream and chopped fresh cilantro.

# Quesadillas with Black Beans and Two Sauces

Using a mix of cheeses takes any quesadilla out of the ordinary. Try different fillings such as Black Bean Mash (page 25) or Squash Salsa (page 310).

8 Flour or Corn Tortillas (pages 271 and 273 or store-bought)

½ cup shredded pepper Jack cheese

½ cup shredded Cheddar cheese

1 recipe Frijoles à la Charra (page 141)

¼ cup fresh cilantro leaves

3 tbsp unsalted butter

**GARNISH**

Salsa Verde (page 309), as needed

Salsa Roja (page 308), as needed

1. Lay out 4 tortillas on the work surface. Combine the cheeses and sprinkle half on the tortillas. Spoon one-quarter of the beans into the center of each tortilla. Sprinkle with the remaining cheese and the cilantro leaves, and sandwich with another tortilla.

2. In a large sauté pan, melt the butter over medium heat. Working in batches if necessary, cook the quesadillas until they are golden brown on each side and the cheese is melted, 5 to 6 minutes per side. Keep warm while cooking the remaining quesadillas.

3. Cut in halves or quarters, if desired. Serve warm with the salsas.

**MAKES 4 SERVINGS**

VARIATION: **Quesadillas with Sautéed Peppers and Onions:** In place of the beans, sauté 1 cup thinly sliced onion and 1 cup thinly sliced bell peppers in 2 tbsp grapeseed or canola oil until completely tender, 4 to 5 minutes. Stir in 1 tsp cayenne before adding to the quesadillas.

# Ragada

*Ragada is an Indian-inspired dish of pan-fried potato cakes in a spicy chickpea sauce.*

## POTATO CAKES

2 pounds russet potatoes, peeled and quartered

Salt, as needed

½ tsp ground cumin, toasted

¼ tsp ground coriander, toasted

½ tsp ground turmeric

½ tsp garam masala, toasted

⅓ cup unseasoned fresh bread crumbs

Grapeseed or canola oil, as needed for frying

## RAGADA

2 tbsp grapeseed or canola oil

1 medium yellow onion, diced

1 clove garlic, minced

1 jalapeño, minced

2 tsp minced fresh ginger

1 tbsp red curry paste

1 tbsp garam masala

1 tsp ground turmeric

1 tsp ground cumin

Pinch cayenne

1 cup canned crushed tomatoes

2 cups Vegetable Broth (page 287)

2½ cups cooked chickpeas (see chart, page 131) or one 14-ounce can chickpeas, drained and rinsed

½ cup plain Greek-style yogurt

2 tbsp coarsely chopped cilantro

Salt, as needed

## GARNISH

½ cup minced red onion

½ cup coarsely chopped cilantro

1. To make the potato cakes, place the potatoes in a medium pot. Cover with water by 2 inches, season with salt, and bring to a boil. Cook until the potatoes are tender, 20 to 30 minutes.

2. Drain the potatoes very well and transfer them to a large bowl. Mash them with a fork or potato masher until mostly smooth.

3. Stir in the cumin, coriander, turmeric, and garam masala and season with salt. Add the bread crumbs and mix to combine. Form into 8 patties.

4. In a large sauté pan, heat about ¼ inch oil over medium heat. Working in batches if necessary, add the cakes and sauté until golden brown and crisp on the outside, 4 to 5 minutes per side. Remove from pan, drain briefly on paper towels, and keep warm.

5. To make the ragada, in a large sauté pan heat the oil over medium heat. Add the onion and sauté until translucent, 3 to 4 minutes. Add the garlic, jalapeño, and ginger, and sauté until fragrant, about 1 minute. Add the curry paste, garam masala, turmeric, cumin, and cayenne, and stir until the spices are slightly toasted, about 30 seconds. Add the tomatoes and broth and bring to a simmer. Cook until slightly reduced and thick, 8 to 10 minutes.

6. Stir in the chickpeas, yogurt, and cilantro and cook until heated through, about 5 minutes. Season with salt.

7. Place 2 potato cakes on each plate and cover with the chickpea sauce. Garnish with red onion and cilantro.

**MAKES 4 SERVINGS**

Ragada

# Red Bean and Rice–Stuffed Portobello Mushroom Caps

*A simple side dish like red beans and rice can make a delicious filling. Try using different beans, grains, and herbs to season a basic stuffing like this.*

4 large portobello mushroom caps, stems and gills removed

3 tbsp olive oil

Salt and freshly ground black pepper, as needed

½ cup diced yellow onion

½ cup diced red bell pepper

¼ cup diced celery

1 clove garlic, minced

½ cup grated Monterey Jack cheese

1 tbsp chopped oregano

1 cup cooked red beans (see chart, pages 131–32)

1 cup cooked brown rice (see chart, page 176)

¾ cup panko bread crumbs

2 tbsp unsalted butter, melted

1. Preheat the oven to 375°F. Place the mushrooms gill side up on a baking sheet, brush lightly with 2 tbsp of the oil, and season with salt and pepper. Set aside.

2. In a medium sauté pan, heat the remaining oil over medium heat. Add the onions, red pepper, and celery and cook until the vegetables begin to soften, 4 to 5 minutes. Add the garlic and cook until fragrant, about 1 minute more. Transfer to a medium bowl.

3. Add the cheese, oregano, beans, and rice, season with salt and pepper, and mix to combine. Spoon the filling onto the mushroom caps, pressing lightly to ensure it stays in place.

4. In a small bowl, combine the panko and butter. Sprinkle on top of the filling. Bake until the mushrooms are tender, 10 to 12 minutes. Serve immediately.

**MAKES 4 SERVINGS**

# Roasted Cauliflower with Rice, Beans, and Mustard Vinaigrette

*Roasting is a flavorful way to prepare cauliflower, and the mustard vinaigrette is the perfect complement.*

**ROASTED CAULIFLOWER**

3 cups cauliflower florets

2 tbsp olive oil

Salt and freshly ground black pepper, as needed

**MUSTARD VINAIGRETTE**

3 tbsp olive oil

3 tbsp white wine vinegar

1 tbsp Dijon mustard

Salt and freshly ground black pepper, as needed

**RICE AND BEANS**

1½ cups cooked navy beans (see chart, page 132)

3 cups cooked brown rice (see chart, page 176)

1 medium tomato, chopped

½ cup chopped red bell pepper

2 stalks celery, sliced ¼ inch thick

1 bunch green onions, minced (white and green parts)

2 tbsp chopped flat-leaf parsley

1. Preheat the oven to 425°F.

2. In a large bowl, toss the cauliflower to coat with the oil. Season with salt and pepper and toss again. Spread the cauliflower in an even layer on a baking sheet. Roast the cauliflower until tender and golden brown, 10 to 15 minutes. Remove from oven and cool to room temperature.

3. In a small bowl, whisk the oil, vinegar, and mustard to combine. Season with salt and pepper.

4. In a large bowl, combine the beans, rice, tomatoes, red peppers, celery, green onions, and parsley. Add the roasted cauliflower and the dressing and toss to combine.

**MAKES 4 SERVINGS**

# Roasted Autumn Vegetables with Blue Cheese Bread Pudding and Spinach Pesto

*Make sure all the vegetables are cut to roughly the same size. Any type of bread can be used, but baguette or ciabatta are suggested. Use an 8-inch square baking pan to make one large bread pudding instead of using individual ramekins.*

**ROASTED AUTUMN VEGETABLES**

2 cups peeled, chopped beets

1 medium parsnip, cored and chopped

½ medium bulb fennel, cored and chopped

1 small butternut squash (about 12 ounces), peeled, seeded, and chopped

¾ cup chopped carrots

½ pound mushrooms, quartered

1 cup chopped red onion

1 cup chopped celery

1 red bell pepper, chopped

2 tbsp extra-virgin olive oil

1 tbsp chopped thyme

1 tbsp chopped rosemary

Salt and freshly ground black pepper, as needed

**BLUE CHEESE BREAD PUDDING**

1 cup heavy cream

1 clove garlic, minced

1 medium shallot, minced

2 large eggs

4 cups cubed bread (see Note above)

1 cup crumbled blue cheese

2 tbsp chopped fresh sage

Salt and freshly ground black pepper, as needed

Nonstick cooking spray, as needed

**SPINACH PESTO**

¾ pound spinach

½ bunch fresh basil, leaves only, chopped

2 tbsp extra-virgin olive oil, plus more as needed

3 cloves Roasted Garlic (page 315)

4 green onions (white and green parts), chopped

¼ cup toasted pine nuts

Salt and freshly ground black pepper, as needed

1. To make the roasted vegetables, preheat the oven to 350°F.

2. In a large bowl, toss the beets, parsnip, fennel, squash, carrots, mushrooms, onion, celery, and red pepper with the oil to coat. Sprinkle with the thyme and rosemary, season with salt and pepper, and toss again. Spread the mixture into a roasting pan or baking sheet and roast until tender, about 1 hour. Remove from the oven and set aside to keep warm. Reduce the oven temperature to 275°F.

3. To make the bread pudding, in a medium saucepan heat the cream with the garlic and shallot over medium-high heat. Bring to a simmer and immediately remove from the heat.

4. Whisk the eggs in a medium bowl. Slowly stream in the cream mixture to form a custard, whisking constantly so as to not scramble the eggs.

5. Return the mixture to the pot and cook over low heat, stirring often, until thick enough to coat the back of a spoon. Remove from the heat and cool to room temperature.

6. Combine the bread and cheese in a large bowl. Pour the custard over the bread and cheese and toss gently to coat. Stir in the sage and season with salt and pepper. Let the mixture sit for 15 minutes to allow the bread to absorb the liquid.

7. Spray 4- to 8-ounce ramekins with nonstick cooking spray. Fill each to the top with the bread mixture and place in a larger baking pan. Fill the pan with enough hot water to come about halfway up the ramekins.

8. Bake until the puddings are evenly browned and set, about 35 minutes.

9. While the puddings are baking, make the spinach pesto. Combine the spinach and basil in a blender or food processor. With the machine running, slowly add the oil, processing until blended. Add the garlic, green onions, and pine nuts, processing until the mixture forms a thick paste. Add more oil if necessary to reach the desired consistency. Season with salt and pepper.

10. Serve the warm roasted vegetables topped with the pesto alongside each portion of the bread pudding.

**MAKES 4 SERVINGS**

Roasted Autumn Vegetables with Blue Cheese Bread Pudding and Spinach Pesto

# Sopes with Refried Beans and Spicy Avocado Salad

*If you're making the salad in advance, add a little extra lime juice and cover it directly with plastic wrap. This will prevent the avocado from oxidizing and turning brown.*

3 avocados, diced

1 medium red onion, minced

2 cloves garlic, minced

1 jalapeño, seeded and minced

1 medium tomato, diced

¼ cup diced radishes

¼ cup fresh lime juice

½ tsp cumin seeds, toasted and crushed

Pinch cayenne

Salt and freshly ground black pepper, as needed

½ recipe Sopes (page 262)

½ recipe Vegetarian Refried Beans (page 21), warm

1. In a large bowl, toss the avocados, onion, garlic, jalapeño, tomatoes, radishes, lime juice, cumin, and cayenne to combine. Season well with salt and pepper.

2. Spread each of the warm sopes with 2 to 3 tbsp hot refried beans and top with avocado salad. Serve immediately.

**MAKES 4 SERVINGS**

# Peppers Stuffed with Amaranth and Quinoa

Amaranth is a good source of protein and amino acids, making it an all-around healthy grain that's good in a variety of dishes. Try serving these stuffed peppers with the Tomato Sauce on page 303.

1 to 2 tablespoons unsalted butter

½ cup minced onion

½ cup finely chopped celery

¾ tsp kosher salt

¼ tsp freshly ground black pepper

3 cups Vegetable Broth (page 287)

1 tbsp chopped fresh flat-leaf parsley

1 tsp chopped sage

1 tsp chopped rosemary

1 tsp chopped fresh thyme

½ cup puffed amaranth

½ cup quinoa, rinsed thoroughly and drained

6 bell peppers (any color), tops, seeds, and membranes removed

¾ cup unseasoned bread crumbs

½ cup grated Parmesan cheese

1 tbsp olive oil

1. Preheat the oven to 350°F.

2. In large saucepan, melt the butter over medium-low heat. Add onion, celery, salt, and pepper. Sauté until onion is tender and golden, 4 to 5 minutes. Add the broth, parsley, sage, rosemary, and thyme. Bring to a boil. Stir in the amaranth and quinoa, and return mixture just to a boil. Remove the pot from heat, and cover for 5 minutes or until liquid is absorbed. Fluff with a fork. Taste and adjust seasoning with salt and pepper.

3. Scoop the stuffing into the peppers. Place on a baking sheet.

4. In a small bowl, toss the bread crumbs, cheese, and oil to combine. Top each pepper with the bread crumb mixture.

5. Bake for 15 to 20 minutes, or until the peppers are tender and the tops are lightly browned. Serve immediately.

**MAKES 6 SERVINGS**

Peppers Stuffed with Amaranth and Quinoa

# Butternut Squash, Rice, and Leek Tart

*A tasty tart that's great as an appetizer or snack or perfect with Marinated Tomato, Cucumber, and Watercress Salad with Candied Walnuts (page 108).*

One 2-pound butternut squash, halved lengthwise and seeded

Salt and freshly ground black pepper, as needed

3 tbsp unsalted butter

2¼ cups chopped leeks (white and light green parts)

1 cup cooked brown rice (see chart, page 176)

½ cup grated Pecorino Romano

½ cup grated Parmigiano-Reggiano

All-purpose flour, as needed for rolling

1 recipe Tart Dough (page 282)

Egg Wash (page 315), as needed

1. Preheat the oven to 350°F. Line a baking sheet with parchment paper.

2. Season the cut side of the squash with salt and pepper. Roast the squash in a baking pan, cut side up, until the flesh is tender and lightly browned, about 30 to 35 minutes. Remove from the oven and cool slightly. Scoop out the flesh into a large bowl and discard the skin.

3. In a large sauté pan, melt the butter over medium heat. Add the leeks and sauté until translucent, 3 to 4 minutes. Remove pan from the heat and add leeks to the squash with the rice and cheeses. Toss to combine.

4. On a floured surface, roll out the dough into a rectangle 10 by 12 inches and about ¼ inch thick. Transfer the dough to the baking sheet.

5. Spoon the filling onto the dough, leaving a ½-inch border around the outside. Fold the dough up over the filling, using your fingers to crimp the edges. Lightly brush the dough with egg wash.

6. Bake until the crust is golden and the filling is bubbling, 35 to 40 minutes. Let cool for at least 10 minutes before serving. Serve with a drizzle of garlic dressing, if desired.

**MAKES 6 TO 8 SERVINGS**

VARIATIONS: **Pumpkin, Onion, and Blue Cheese Tart:** Replace the squash with an equal amount of pumpkin. Replace the leeks with diced yellow onion and add 2 cloves garlic, minced, in Step 3. Replace the Pecorino Romano with crumbled blue cheese and reduce the Parmigiano-Reggiano to ¼ cup. Follow above instructions.

# Vegetable Loaf

*Grating vegetables is a great way to ensure they are similar in size. Vegetables such as carrots, zucchini, celery, potatoes, and onions grate relatively easily.*

½ cup stemmed and thinly sliced shiitake mushrooms

3 tbsp extra-virgin olive oil

1 small red onion, minced

2 cloves garlic, minced

1 jalapeño, minced

1 cup grated zucchini

2 cups corn kernels (fresh or thawed frozen)

1 cup canned diced tomatoes, plus additional juice as needed

Salt and freshly ground black pepper, as needed

Nonstick cooking spray, as needed

1 large egg, lightly beaten

¼ cup cornmeal, plus more as needed

½ cup brown rice, cooked (see chart, page 176)

1. In a large sauté pan, cook the mushrooms in 1 tbsp of the oil over medium heat until softened, 2 to 3 minutes. Remove from the pan and set aside.

2. In the same pan heat the remaining oil over medium heat. Add the onion and cook until nearly translucent, 3 to 4 minutes. Add the garlic and jalapeño and cook until fragrant, about 1 minute. Stir in the zucchini, corn, and tomatoes and heat through. Stir in the mushrooms. Season with salt and pepper. Remove from the heat, transfer to a large bowl, and cool to room temperature.

3. Preheat the oven to 350°F. Spray a standard loaf pan with nonstick spray.

4. Stir the egg, cornmeal, and rice into the vegetables. If the mixture seems too wet, add a little more cornmeal as needed. If the mixture seems too dry, add more tomato juice as needed.

5. Press the mixture into the loaf pan. Bake until cooked through and lightly browned on top, 20 to 25 minutes.

**MAKES 4 TO 6 SERVINGS**

Vegetable Summer Rolls

# Vegetable Summer Rolls

*Try adding marinated tofu or seitan to this roll. Summer rolls may be made up to 6 hours ahead, wrapped in dampened paper towels, and stored in a sealed plastic bag in the refrigerator. Bring the rolls to room temperature and cut before serving.*

2½ ounces thin rice noodles

2 tbsp rice vinegar

10 summer roll wrappers (rice-paper rounds)

5 leaves iceberg lettuce, halved

⅓ cup mint leaves

⅓ cup basil leaves

⅓ cup cilantro leaves

¾ cup shredded napa cabbage

½ cup shredded carrot

½ cup thinly sliced red bell pepper

¾ cup bean sprouts

Peanut Dipping Sauce (page 301), as needed

1. Cover the noodles with hot water and soak until tender, about 15 minutes. Drain the noodles and toss with the vinegar.

2. Fill a shallow dish with warm water.

3. Working with 1 sheet at a time, soak the rice paper rounds in the water until pliable, 30 to 45 seconds, then transfer to a plate lined with damp paper towels. Place 1 piece lettuce on the rice paper and top with mint, basil, cilantro, cabbage, carrot, red pepper, seasoned noodles, and bean sprouts in a narrow line.

4. Fold the edges of the rice paper inward, then working away from yourself, tightly roll the wrapper around the filling. Set on a plate seam side down. Repeat with the remaining rice papers and fillings.

5. Halve the rolls on the diagonal and serve with the peanut sauce.

**MAKES 10 ROLLS**

# Green Onion Tamales

*Tamales are fun to make and have endless filling possibilities. Fill them with other veggies or with a mixture of cheeses, or steam the dough plain and serve with the Red Chile Salsa on page 308.*

10 to 12 corn husks

1 bunch green onions

1 clove garlic, minced

1 jalapeño, seeded and minced

8 tbsp (1 stick) unsalted butter

4 cups masa harina

1 tsp baking powder

¾ tsp kosher salt

¼ tsp freshly ground black pepper

1 quart Vegetable Broth (page 287)

GARNISH

Salsa Verde (page 309), as needed

1. In a large bowl, rehydrate the corn husks in hot water until soft. Drain and set aside.

2. Heat a grill or grill pan until hot. Grill the green onions until tender, 2 to 3 minutes. Halve them lengthwise and transfer to a medium bowl. Toss with the garlic and jalapeño and set aside.

3. In the bowl of a stand mixer fitted with a paddle, beat the butter on medium-high speed until very light, about 1 minute. Add half of the masa harina and beat until well blended. Add the baking powder, salt, and pepper, and mix to combine. Continue mixing, adding the remaining masa harina alternately with the broth. The final dough will be the consistency of a thick batter.

4. Spread ⅓ to ½ cup of the dough onto the wide end of the corn husk. Place two pieces of green onion in the center. Fold each side of the husk over the mixture. Gently press down on the tamale and tuck the empty half underneath to keep the husk closed.

5. Place a steamer basket into the bottom of a 1½- to 2-gallon pot. Add about 2 inches of water to the pot, cover with a lid and bring to a simmer. Place the tamales into the steamer basket over the simmering water. Cover and steam until the dough is cooked through, 40 to 50 minutes. Dough should be set and no longer pasty. Serve with salsa verde.

**MAKES 10 TO 12 LARGE TAMALES**

VARIATIONS: **Mushroom Tamales:** Replace the green onions with 1½ cups sliced mushrooms. Sauté the mushrooms in 2 tbsp grapeseed or canola oil until tender, 6 to 8 minutes. Season the mushrooms with dried epazote or Mexican oregano to taste. Fill the tamales with the masa dough and mushrooms and add a sprinkle of grated *queso Chihuahua* or Monterey Jack cheese. **Black Bean Tamales:** Replace the green onions with 1¼ cups cooked black beans. Sprinkle with shredded cheese before wrapping, if desired.

Black Bean Tamales and Salsa Verde (page 309)

# Glamorgan-Style Vegetarian Sausage

*When forming these "sausages" into links, be certain the sausages are slender to ensure they will hold their form when being fried. This mixture can also be formed into patties.*

4 slices white or whole-wheat sandwich bread, diced

½ cup grated Cheddar cheese

½ cup diced mushrooms

1 tbsp chopped flat-leaf parsley

1 tsp Dijon mustard

2 tbsp Vegetable Broth (page 287) or water

1 tbsp minced chives

2 tsp fennel seeds

Salt and freshly ground black pepper, as needed

1. In a food processor or blender, chop the bread, cheese, and mushrooms together until the mixture is smooth.

2. Transfer to a large bowl, and fold in the parsley, mustard, broth, chives, and fennel seeds. Season with salt and pepper.

3. Place the mixture on a piece of plastic wrap, and use the plastic wrap to form it into thin logs resembling sausages, about 3 to 4 inches in length and about ¾ inch in diameter. Refrigerate the sausages until they are firm enough to hold their shape, 30 minutes to 1 hour.

4. The sausages can now be pan fried in a small amount of olive oil or brushed with olive oil and grilled. Serve hot.

**MAKES 4 SERVINGS**

Nothing complements a meal like fresh bread or baked goods. Included in this chapter are a variety of simple but versatile baked items that can be used in conjunction with other recipes and are also delicious on their own.

8

# BREADS AND BAKED GOODS

# BAKING INGREDIENTS

Baking can seem complex because, unlike cooking, ingredients need to be carefully measured to achieve the desired results. Understanding each ingredient's role can lead to successful products.

## FLOUR

There are a variety of flours available, but wheat flour is one of the more predominant types available. The three main varieties of flours commercially available are bread flour (a "hard" flour, high in protein), cake flour (a "soft" flour, low in protein), and all-purpose flour (a blend of the two). The level of protein helps determine the texture of the finished product; yeast-raised breads, for example, need a high level of protein to form their structure and crust. Other flours and meals are also commonly available, including whole-wheat flour and cornmeal.

## SWEETENERS

A variety of components can be used as sweeteners in baked goods, including granulated sugar, light or dark brown sugar, confectioners' sugar, maple syrup, molasses, and honey. Different sweeteners have different flavors, but all give baked goods moisture, color, and contribute to the texture.

## SALT

Salt is more than a seasoning—it is a flavor enhancer, even for sweet dishes. In small amounts, salt does not actually add an identifiable flavor to a dish. Instead, it balances other flavors and brings out the natural flavors of other ingredients. There are hundreds of varieties of salt available, but for baking, we suggest using table or kosher salt.

## BUTTER AND OILS

Fats provide many functions in baking. They make items tender, add flavor and richness, contribute leavening strength, add moisture, and affect final texture.

## EGGS

Eggs have many roles in baking. They contribute proteins that give stability, fat, and moisture. They contribute to the final texture of a baked good and also have leavening power.

## LEAVENERS

The proper leavening of a baked product is crucial to its final appearance, structure, and texture. There are three primary ways baked goods can be leavened: organic leaveners (such as yeast), physical leaveners (such as steam), and chemical leaveners (such as baking powder and baking soda). Eggs, particularly whipped eggs, can provide leavening by way of trapped air that expands when heated, such as in a meringue or by providing moisture that converts to steam when heated.

In the case of puff pastry, whole butter can provide leavening by way of steam. When the whole butter melts between the layers of dough, the fat and water content of the butter separate from each other; the water converts to steam and exerts force against the dough, causing it to rise.

## TOASTING NUTS OR SEEDS

Nuts and seeds can be toasted in a dry sauté pan over medium heat or in the oven. Depending on the type of nut or seed, its appearance may change drastically or only slightly. The best way to determine if the item is properly toasted is its fragrance: Toasted nuts and seeds will have a pronounced aroma and golden color. Nuts with high fat content will become the most aromatic and darken or scorch the fastest.

# MIXING METHODS

Another important baking concept to understand is the difference among mixing methods. These methods, along with proper measuring, use of ingredients, and correct baking procedures, are vital to creating a good product. There are four mixing methods used in this book: the straight dough method, the creaming method, the blending method, and the cut-in method.

## STRAIGHT DOUGH METHOD

The straight dough mixing method is the most basic method for making breads and other yeast-raised products.

### Straight Dough Method

1. Place the warm liquid into a bowl or the bowl of a stand mixer.

2. Add the remaining ingredients.

3. Mix the dough until it starts to "catch." If using a mixer, the dough should form a ball around the dough hook.

4. Continue to mix the dough or knead by hand until it is smooth and springy.

5. Transfer the dough to an oiled container. Let it rise.

6. Deflate the dough.

7. Transfer the dough to a floured work surface.

8. Shape the dough.

9. Let it rise again.

10. Bake according to recipe instructions.

STRAIGHT DOUGH METHOD: *The simplest way to make bread and other yeast-raised doughs is the straight dough method. Mix all the ingredients together in a stand mixer fitted with a dough hook.*

*The finished dough should be smooth and uniformly combined.*

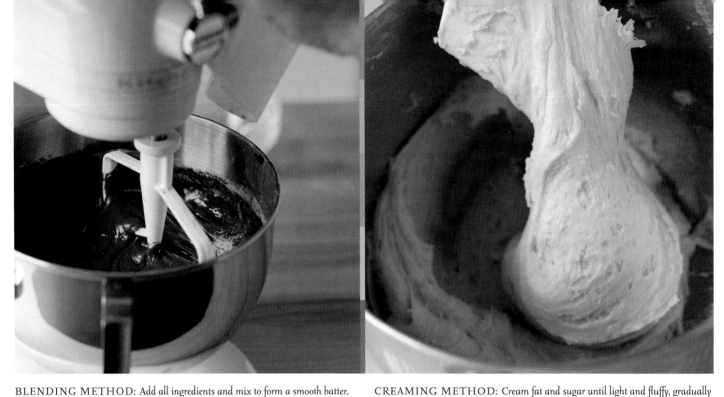

BLENDING METHOD: *Add all ingredients and mix to form a smooth batter.*

CREAMING METHOD: *Cream fat and sugar until light and fluffy, gradually add the eggs and any flavoring, then add the dry ingredients, mixing just to combine.*

## BLENDING METHOD

One of the most basic mixing methods, the blending method is commonly used for quick breads, muffins, and other baked goods.

### Blending Method

1. Sift the dry ingredients together.

2. Combine the liquid ingredients.

3. Add the dry ingredients to the liquid ingredients.

4. Mix until the batter is evenly combined.

5. Add any garnish or finishing ingredients.

6. Fill the prepared pans and bake according to recipe instructions.

7. Remove the item from the pans, cool to room temperature, and serve or store.

## CREAMING METHOD

The creaming method is very versatile and can be used to make cakes and cookies. In this book, it is used to make some types of quick breads and other baked goods.

### Creaming Method

1. Allow the butter to come to room temperature.

2. Sift the dry ingredients.

3. Cream the butter and sugar until the mixture is light and fluffy.

4. Add the eggs slowly and mix until the batter is smooth.

5. Add the dry ingredients and liquid ingredients alternately until fully incorporated.

6. Scoop the batter into prepared pans.

7. Bake according to recipe instructions.

8. Remove the item from the pans, cool to room temperature, and serve or store.

## CUT-IN METHOD

Also known as the *rub-in method*, this method is what gives biscuits, pie and tart dough, and puff pastry–style baked goods their flaky texture.

### Cut-In Method

1. Sift the dry ingredients.

2. Cut the shortening into the dry ingredients until the mixture resembles coarse meal. Shortening left in large pieces yields a very flaky dough. Finer-sized pieces of shortening yield a less flaky outcome.

3. Add the liquid ingredients and mix just until a shaggy mass forms.

4. Knead the dough very briefly to create a smooth texture.

5. Shape the dough as desired, place on prepared baking sheets, and bake according to recipe instructions.

6. Remove the items from the oven and serve or cool and store.

CUT-IN METHOD: *Rub the butter into the dry ingredients to form a mixture that resembles a coarse meal.*

## EVENLY DISTRIBUTING INGREDIENTS

In some baked goods (especially quick breads and muffins), garnishes are folded into the final dough or batter. Proper mixing will ensure that these ingredients are well incorporated but will not keep them so during baking. Tossing inclusions such as nuts, seeds, dried fruit, or chocolate in a small amount of flour before folding them into the dough or batter will ensure that the ingredients stay suspended in the finished baked item.

Cornbread (front) and Blue Cornbread (rear)

# Blue Cornbread

*A twist on classic cornbread, but be careful not to overbake—if it is baked too long, it will be tough.*

8 tablespoons (1 stick) unsalted butter, softened, plus more for the pan

1 cup blue cornmeal

1 cup all-purpose flour

2 tsp baking powder

½ tsp baking soda

1 large egg

¾ tsp kosher salt

1½ cups buttermilk

1. Preheat the oven to 425°F. Butter a 9-inch square baking pan.

2. In the bowl of a stand mixer fitted with a paddle, heat the butter to soften, add cornmeal, flour, baking powder, baking soda, egg, and salt on low until combined. Scrape down the sides of the bowl well. Add the buttermilk and mix just to combine. Do not overmix.

3. Pour the batter into the prepared pan and bake until a tester inserted into the center comes out clean, about 25 minutes. Remove from the oven and cool on a rack to warm or room temperature. Serve. This bread does not store well.

**MAKES 9 PIECES 3″ SQUARE**

VARIATION: **Cornbread:** Replace the blue cornmeal with white or yellow cornmeal.

# Corn Cakes

*These corn pancakes are great for breakfast with eggs, and they are also great with salsa and sautéed seitan for lunch or dinner.*

1¼ cups corn kernels (fresh or thawed frozen)

1 cup buttermilk

1 large egg

1 tbsp unsalted butter, melted

⅔ cup all-purpose flour

⅓ cup cornmeal

⅓ tsp baking powder

⅓ tsp baking soda

½ tsp sugar

Pinch salt

Pinch freshly ground black pepper

4 green onions (white and green parts), thinly sliced

Grapeseed or canola oil, as needed for cooking

1. In a food processor or blender, purée the corn and buttermilk until smooth.

2. Transfer the mixture to the bowl of a stand mixer fitted with a whisk. Add the egg and butter and whisk on medium speed to combine.

3. In a large bowl, mix the flour, cornmeal, baking powder, baking soda, sugar, salt, and pepper to combine. Slowly add the dry ingredients to the wet ingredients while whisking, mixing just until incorporated. Fold in the green onions.

4. Heat ⅛ inch oil in a heavy-bottomed nonstick omelette pan, and scoop or pour 3 ounces of batter into the pan. Cook until the cake is golden brown, 2 to 3 minutes per side. Keep cakes warm until all cakes are cooked. These cakes could also be made on an electric griddle.

**MAKES 4 SERVINGS**

# Angel Biscuits (Yeasted Buttermilk Biscuits)

*The key to light and flaky biscuits is cutting in the butter correctly. For more information, see page 255.*

1 tsp active dry yeast

1 tbsp warm water (100°F)

¼ cup all-purpose flour, plus more as needed for rolling

1½ tsp baking powder

½ tsp baking soda

1 tsp sugar

2 tsp kosher salt

8 tablespoons (1 stick) cold unsalted butter, sliced

1 cup buttermilk

Grapeseed or canola oil, as needed for greasing

Melted unsalted butter, as needed

1. In a small bowl, dissolve the yeast in the water and let stand for 5 minutes.

2. Sift the flour, baking powder, baking soda, sugar, and salt together into the bowl of a stand mixer. Fit the mixer with a paddle. Add the butter a little at a time, mixing on low speed until it has a similar consistency to cornmeal.

3. Stir the buttermilk into the yeast mixture. Slowly add this to the dry ingredients. Mix on medium speed just to combine, about 2 minutes.

4. Lightly grease a baking sheet with oil. On a floured surface, gently roll the dough to about 1 inch thick. Using a 3-inch round cookie cutter, cut the dough into circles, and place them on the baking sheet about ½ inch apart. Gather and re-roll the scraps.

5. Brush the biscuit tops with melted butter and let rest in a warm place about 20 minutes. Meanwhile, preheat the oven to 425°F.

6. Bake the biscuits until golden brown, 10 to 15 minutes. Rotate the pan halfway through baking to ensure even baking.

7. Remove from the oven and brush the biscuits again with melted butter. Let cool slightly before serving.

**MAKES 12 BISCUITS**

# Herb-Tomato Gougères

*Gougères are a simple, crisp pastry, small cheese-filled rounds made from pâte à choux. The cheese can also be cubed and pushed into the dough after it's been piped, before baking.*

1 cup water

5⅓ tablespoons (⅔ stick) unsalted butter

½ tsp sugar

½ tsp kosher salt

1 cup bread flour

3 large eggs

Pinch freshly ground black pepper

¾ cup grated Gruyère

¼ cup minced sun-dried tomatoes

1 tbsp chopped basil

1½ tsp chopped thyme

Egg Wash (page 315), as needed

1. Preheat the oven to 350°F. Line a baking sheet with parchment paper.

2. In a medium pot, bring the water, butter, sugar, and salt to boil over medium heat, stirring constantly.

3. Remove from the heat, add the flour all at once, and stir vigorously to combine. Return the pan to medium heat and cook, stirring, until the mixture pulls away from the sides of the pan, approximately 3 minutes.

4. Transfer the mixture to a bowl. Stir for a few moments to cool. Add the eggs one at time, beating until smooth after each addition. Stir in the pepper, cheese, tomatoes, basil, and thyme.

5. Transfer the batter to a pastry bag fitted with a medium round tip. Pipe small domes approximately 1 inch in diameter and spaced 1 inch apart, onto the prepared baking sheet.

6. Using a pastry brush, brush each gougère lightly with egg wash.

7. Bake until the gougères are puffed and golden brown, 30 to 35 minutes. Best served warm.

**MAKES ABOUT 36 GOUGÈRES**

# Arepas

Arepas are flat patties made from very fine precooked corn meal. They can be grilled, fried, or sautéed, and they are as versatile as a tortilla. A classic way to serve arepas is filled with melted cheese: Shred 1 cup cheese, cut a pocket in the cooled arepas, fill with the cheese, and warm in the oven until the cheese melts.

3 cups Masarepa or other precooked arepa flour

3 cups warm water

1 tbsp kosher salt

Grapeseed or canola oil, as needed for frying

1. In the bowl of a stand mixer fitted with a paddle, combine the flour, water, and salt. Mix until a smooth dough forms, adding more water if needed.

2. Form the dough into 24 small balls, then use the palm of your hand to flatten the dough into disks about 1 inch thick and 2 inches across. If the disks are cracking, add more water to the dough.

3. Heat about 1 inch oil in a large, heavy-bottomed skillet. Working in batches if necessary, fry the arepas until they are golden and float to the surface of the oil, 3 to 4 minutes per side. Drain on paper towels. Alternately, the arepas can be cooked using only a spritz of oil on an electric griddle.

4. The arepas are now ready to be served. Or the arepas may be filled with cheese or cheese and beans and baked until the cheese is melted.

**MAKES ABOUT 24 AREPAS**

Sopes, page 262 (left) and Arepas (right)

# Sopes

*Sopes are small griddle-cooked disks made from masa harina. Pinch the edges of the dough once the sopes come off the griddle to make the signature "walls" of a sope.*

4 cups masa harina

1 tbsp kosher salt

1 tsp baking powder

3 cups warm water

Nonstick cooking spray

1. In the bowl of a stand mixer fitted with a paddle, combine the masa harina, salt, and baking powder.

2. Add the water and mix on medium speed just to combine. Raise the speed to high and mix until the dough is smooth, about 3 minutes.

3. Lightly spray a bowl with nonstick spray. Transfer the dough to the bowl, cover, and let rest for 30 minutes.

4. Divide the dough into 24 pieces. Use your hands to flatten the dough into disks slightly less than ¼ inch thick.

5. Heat a skillet over medium heat. Spray pan lightly with spray oil. Cook the pressed dough in the skillet until warmed through, turning the sope once. Remove the dough from the skillet, and using a clean dish towel, pinch the edges of the dough to form ¼-inch walls around the edges.

6. The sopes can be served immediately with your favorite salsa or pico de gallo, or allowed to cool and reheated in a 350°F oven topped with cheese or other filling of choice.

**MAKES ABOUT 24 SOPES**

# Pumpkin Bread

*This moist bread is great for an after-dinner treat topped with ice cream, or plain.*

⅓ cup grapeseed or canola oil, plus more for greasing

2 cups all-purpose flour

½ tsp baking powder

½ tsp baking soda

¾ tsp kosher salt

1 tbsp ground cinnamon

½ tsp ground ginger

½ tsp freshly grated nutmeg

1 cup canned pumpkin purée

1 cup light brown sugar

⅓ cup milk

1 large egg

2 tsp pure vanilla extract

1. Preheat the oven to 350°F. Lightly grease a 9-inch loaf pan.

2. In a large bowl, combine the flour, baking powder, baking soda, salt, cinnamon, ginger, and nutmeg. In another large bowl, beat the pumpkin, sugar, oil, milk, egg, and vanilla until smooth. Slowly add the flour mixture, stirring just to combine.

3. Pour the batter into the prepared pan. Bake until a tester inserted into the center of the loaf comes out clean, 45 minutes to 1 hour. Cool on a rack for 15 to 20 minutes before slicing.

**MAKES ONE 9-INCH LOAF**

# Streusel Topping

*This tasty streusel is hiding some healthy ingredients that make your muffins or favorite fruit crisp better for you as well as more delicious. Try replacing the walnuts with pecans, almonds, pumpkin seeds, sunflower seeds, or flax seeds.*

1 cup rolled oats

¾ cup wheat germ or flax meal

8 tablespoons (1 stick) unsalted butter, soft

½ cup light brown sugar

½ cup wheat or oat bran

½ cup chopped toasted walnuts

1½ tsp ground cinnamon

Pinch salt

1. In the bowl of a stand mixer fitted with a paddle, mix all ingredients to combine. The mixture should be well combined but crumbly. If the mixture is too soft after mixing, refrigerate it slightly to firm up before using. Crumble the streusel on muffin tops before baking.

2. Store in a covered container in the refrigerator until needed. Let it come back to room temperature before using.

**MAKES ABOUT 3 CUPS, ENOUGH TO GENEROUSLY COVER ONE 10″ PIE, 2 DOZEN MUFFINS, TWO 9″ SQUARE PANS OR ONE 9×13″ PAN**

# Banana Muffins

*The best way to use up overripe bananas is to make these muffins. If you have bananas that are too ripe, peel and freeze them in plastic bags until you're ready to make banana muffins or banana bread.*

⅔ cup grapeseed or canola oil, plus more as needed for greasing

1¼ cups sugar

4 bananas, mashed until smooth

2 large eggs

2½ cups all-purpose flour

1 tsp baking soda

1 tsp baking powder

½ tsp kosher salt

¼ cup milk

½ tsp pure vanilla extract

¾ cup walnuts, roughly chopped

1. Preheat the oven to 350°F. Lightly grease 16 muffin pan cups.

2. In a large bowl, combine the oil, sugar, and bananas. Beat until the mixture is smooth. Add the eggs, flour, baking soda, baking powder, salt, milk, and vanilla, stirring just until the ingredients are mixed. Gently fold in the walnuts.

3. Scoop the batter into the prepared pan; it should only go about three-quarters of the way up each cup. (Fill any unused cups with water to prevent discoloration.)

4. Bake until a tester inserted into the center of a muffin comes out clean, about 25 minutes. Cool for 10 minutes on a cooling rack.

**MAKES 16 MUFFINS**

Clockwise from front: Bran Muffins, Banana Muffins (page 263), and Potato-Chive Muffins (page 268)

# Bran Muffins

*Healthy, moist, and delicious—try these bran muffins with dried apples, dried apricots, dried currants, or dried cranberries, in place of the raisins.*

Grapeseed or canola oil or nonstick cooking spray, as needed for greasing

1¾ cups all-purpose flour

¼ cup whole-wheat flour

2¼ tsp baking powder

½ tsp baking soda

1 tsp kosher salt

1½ tsp ground cinnamon

1½ tsp ground ginger

8 tablespoons (1 stick) unsalted butter, soft

⅔ cup dark brown sugar, packed

2 large eggs

1 tbsp pure vanilla extract

2 tbsp molasses

¼ cup sour cream

¾ cup buttermilk

1⅓ cups wheat bran

¾ cup raisins (optional)

1. Preheat the oven to 350°F. Lightly grease a muffin pan.

2. In a large bowl, mix the flours, baking powder, baking soda, salt, cinnamon, and ginger until combined.

3. In the bowl of a stand mixer fitted with a paddle, cream the butter and sugar together on medium speed until light and fluffy, 2 to 3 minutes.

4. Add the eggs one at a time, scraping the bowl well after each addition.

5. Add the vanilla, molasses, and sour cream and mix until smooth and well blended.

6. Reduce the speed to low and alternately add the buttermilk and the flour mixture, mixing just until combined.

7. Fold in the bran and raisins, if using. Scoop the batter into the prepared muffin pan, dividing it evenly.

8. Bake until a tester inserted into a muffin comes out clean, about 25 minutes. Cool for 10 minutes on a cooling rack.

**MAKES 12 MUFFINS**

VARIATION: **Orange Bran Muffins:** Add the grated zest of 1 orange with the vanilla extract and replace ¼ cup of the buttermilk with orange juice.

# English Muffins

To make these, you'll need to use a pre-ferment that sits overnight. In the morning, you can mix the dough and form the English muffins—just in time for breakfast or brunch!

**PRE-FERMENT**

¾ cup cold water

1⅓ cups bread flour

¼ tsp active dry yeast

**DOUGH**

1½ cups warm water

2 tbsp unsalted butter, soft

4¼ cups bread flour, plus more as needed for kneading

1 tbsp active dry yeast

1 tbsp kosher salt

2 tsp sugar

Canola oil, as needed for the bowl

1. In a large bowl, mix together the ingredients for the pre-ferment until completely combined. (This mixture will be lumpy and very wet, not smooth like a finished dough.) Cover the bowl with plastic wrap and refrigerate overnight.

2. In the bowl of a stand mixer fitted with a dough hook, combine the pre-ferment and the warm water, mixing on low speed for 1 minute.

3. In a small bowl, rub the butter and flour together until the mixture resembles sand. Add the yeast and mix to combine. Add this mixture into the pre-ferment on low speed to combine. Add the salt and sugar. Mix on medium speed for 4 minutes, until a smooth dough forms. Mix for 2 minutes more on high speed to further develop the gluten.

4. Transfer the dough to a lightly oiled bowl and cover with plastic wrap. Let the dough rest 30 to 45 minutes or until nearly doubled in size.

5. Turn out the dough onto a lightly floured surface. Press the dough by hand to about 1½ to 2 inches thick and fold into thirds. Cover with plastic wrap and rest 15 minutes more.

6. Roll the dough out to a rectangle no thicker than ½ inch. Use a pizza cutter to cut the dough into squares approximately 2½ to 3 inches wide. Cover dough with plastic wrap. Let the muffins proof about 30 minutes more or until nearly doubled in size.

7. While the muffins are proofing, preheat the oven to 475°F. Line a baking sheet with parchment paper.

8. Heat a dry nonstick sauté pan or cast-iron skillet or griddle over medium-low heat. Working in batches if necessary, cook the muffins until they are nicely browned on each side, about 5 minutes per side. During this step the muffins will rise considerably.

9. Transfer the muffins to the baking sheet. Bake until they have risen to about 1½ to 2 inches and are baked through, 9 to 11 minutes.

**MAKES 12 TO 15 MUFFINS**

English Muffins

# Potato-Chive Muffins

These muffins are an excellent way to use leftover mashed potatoes and are super easy to make. If you want to make these muffins with fresh potatoes, cook and drain 3 russet potatoes and mash them with 2 tbsp unsalted butter and ¼ cup heavy cream.

Grapeseed or canola oil or nonstick cooking spray, as needed for greasing

1¾ cups all-purpose flour

2 tsp baking powder

¾ tsp kosher salt

1 cup mashed potatoes

¾ cup whole milk

1 large egg

4 tbsp (½ stick) unsalted butter, melted, plus more as needed for brushing

3 tbsp chopped chives

1. Preheat the oven to 350°F. Lightly grease a muffin pan.

2. In a medium bowl, combine the flour, baking powder, and salt. In a large bowl, mix the mashed potatoes, milk, egg, butter, and chives until smooth.

3. Slowly add the flour mixture to the potato mixture, mixing just until combined.

4. Scoop the batter into the prepared muffin pan, dividing it evenly. Brush the muffin tops with melted butter.

5. Bake until a tester inserted into the center of a muffin comes out clean, 15 to 20 minutes. Cool for 10 minutes on a cooling rack.

**MAKES 12 MUFFINS**

# Extra-Virgin Olive Oil Financiers

*Financiers are small French cakes made with almond flour. This version is flavored with good-quality extra-virgin olive oil and only slightly sweet—perfect to serve with the Roasted Beet "Tartare" with Goat Cheese and Extra-Virgin Olive Oil Financiers on page 15.*

Grapeseed or canola oil or nonstick cooking spray, as needed for greasing

½ cup all-purpose flour

¾ cup almond flour

1 cup confectioners' sugar

¼ tsp kosher salt

¾ cup extra-virgin olive oil

2 large egg whites

1. Preheat the oven to 350°F. Lightly grease a mini muffin pan.

2. In a large bowl, sift together the flours, sugar, and salt. Make a well in the center. Add the olive oil in three additions, whisking continuously to combine, until all of the olive oil has been added, making a smooth batter.

3. In a separate bowl, whisk the egg whites to soft peak. Gently fold the egg whites into the batter ⅓ at a time.

4. Portion about 2 tbsp of the batter into each indentation of the prepared pan. Bake until golden brown, 15 to 20 minutes. The financiers can be served warm or at room temperature.

**MAKES ABOUT 24 FINANCIERS**

# Palmiers with Pesto and Parmesan

*Palmiers are made from flaky puff pastry. This recipe is for the basic blitz method of puff pastry, which is simpler and less time consuming than classic puff pastry. For a sweet treat, leave out the cheese and pesto and sprinkle the palmiers with cinnamon sugar before baking.*

2 cups all-purpose flour, plus more as needed for rolling

1 tsp kosher salt

½ pound (2 sticks) cold unsalted butter, cubed ½ inch

½ cup plus 1 tbsp ice water

1 cup Pesto (page 297)

½ cup grated Parmesan

1. In a large bowl, combine the flour and salt. Add the butter and toss to coat. Make a well in the center. Add the water, and using your hands, mix the dough until it forms a loose, shaggy mass.

2. On a floured surface, roll the dough into a rectangle about ½ inch thick. Fold the left and right quarters into the center so they meet like an open book. Fold the left half over the right to form a closed book. Transfer the dough to a parchment paper—lined baking sheet, cover loosely with plastic wrap, and rest in the refrigerator for at least 30 minutes.

3. Repeat Step 2 a total of three times, resting the dough for at least 30 minutes between repetitions.

4. When you are ready to bake, preheat the oven to 400°F. Line a baking sheet with clean parchment paper.

5. Roll out the pastry on a floured surface to a 10-inch square. Spread the pesto across the surface of the dough and sprinkle with the cheese. Roll the left and right sides in toward the center until they meet. At this point the dough will look like a scroll. Roll the left roll once more so that it lies on top of the right roll.

6. Slice the pastry into ¼-inch-thick slices and place cut side down on the baking sheet. At this point the slices will resemble 2 spirals side by side, attached at the bottom edge. Bake until evenly golden brown, about 10 minutes. Move carefully to a wire rack to cool slightly. It may be served hot, cold, or at room temperature.

**MAKES 24 PALMIERS**

VARIATION: **Palmiers with Tapenade:** Replace the pesto with Tapenade (page 14).

# Flour Tortillas

*These tortillas are made with butter much like the cut-in method (page 255) but are even easier because you can use a food processor.*

2 cups all-purpose flour, plus more as needed for rolling

5⅓ tbsp (⅔ stick or 16 tsp) cold unsalted butter, cubed

1 tsp kosher salt

½ cup hot water, plus more as needed

1. In a food processor or large bowl, combine the flour and butter until the mixture has the texture of coarse meal. Transfer the mixture from the processor to a large bowl.

2. Stir in the salt and water just until the mixture forms a smooth dough. Cover the bowl with plastic wrap and let the dough rest for 15 to 20 minutes at room temperature.

3. On a lightly floured surface, divide the dough into 12 equal pieces, approximately 1¾ to 2 ounces each. Roll the portioned dough into tight balls, cover with plastic wrap, and rest for another 20 minutes.

4. Press each dough ball into a disk. On a lightly floured surface, using a rolling pin, roll each dough disk to about ⅛ inch thick and 6 inches across. Stack the tortillas between pieces of parchment paper as they are rolled.

5. Heat a griddle or cast-iron skillet over medium heat. Working in batches if necessary, cook the tortillas until they are lightly browned on each side, 2 to 3 minutes per side. The tortillas may bubble or puff up slightly. This is a good thing. As the tortillas are cooked, stack them one on top of the other and keep wrapped in a clean towel in a warm oven. Serve immediately or cool down, wrap tightly in plastic wrap, and freeze for another time. The cooked tortillas may also be cut crossways into 6 wedges and deep-fried for delicious homemade flour tortilla chips.

**MAKES ABOUT 12 TORTILLAS**

Flour Tortillas, page 271 (bottom)
and Corn Tortillas (top)

# Corn Tortillas

*Making your own tortillas makes all the difference in the world when it comes to superior flavor and texture. Make a big batch in advance and freeze them until you need them.*

2½ cups masa harina

1½ tsp kosher salt

2 cups hot water, plus more as needed

Nonstick spray, as needed

1. In a large bowl, combine the masa harina, salt, and water and mix until it forms a smooth dough. The dough should be tacky but not stick to your skin. To test for the correct moisture content of the dough, roll a small chunk of dough into a tight ball. Press the ball between your hands to flatten it. If the edges remain smooth, you have added enough water. If the edges crack, you will need to add more water to the dough and check it again. Cover with plastic wrap and let rest at room temperature for 30 minutes.

2. Divide the dough into 12 equal pieces and roll the dough portions into smooth balls. Place the dough balls on a sheet pan and cover with plastic wrap while forming the tortillas.

3. Cut several pieces of plastic wrap approximately 8 inches square. Use the palm of your hands to flatten each dough ball into a disk. Place one disk in the middle of a plastic sheet and lay another piece of plastic over it. Using a tortilla press or the bottom of an 8-inch sauté pan, press the dough into a circular shape about ⅛ inch thick and 6 to 7 inches across. Repeat this process until all tortillas have been pressed. Keep the pressed tortillas between sheets of plastic until ready to cook them.

4. Heat a griddle or cast-iron skillet over medium heat. Working in batches if necessary, gently peel the plastic sheet off each side of the tortilla and cook the tortillas until each side has browned slightly, 1 to 2 minutes per side. The tortillas may puff up slightly. This is a good thing. As the tortillas are cooked, stack them one on top of the other and keep wrapped in a clean towel in a warm oven. Serve immediately or cool down, wrap tightly in plastic wrap, and freeze for another time. The cooked tortillas may also be cut crosswise into 6 wedges and deep-fried for delicious homemade corn tortilla chips!

**MAKES ABOUT 12 TORTILLAS**

# Pita Bread

*Pita bread can be used for such a variety of things: sandwiches, salads, as a "pizza" base. Keep some fresh baked on hand, or some dough in the freezer.*

¼ ounce dry yeast

1 tsp sugar

2½ cups warm water (100°F)

1 lb bread flour

1 lb whole-wheat flour

1½ tbsp kosher salt

2 tbsp olive oil, plus more as needed for greasing

All-purpose flour or corn meal, as needed for rolling and holding

1. In the bowl of a stand mixer fitted with a paddle, combine the yeast, sugar, and warm water and mix well on low speed.

2. Switch to the dough hook. Combine the flours, add the flours, salt, and oil, and mix well on low.

3. Knead the dough on medium-low until it is quite elastic, 3 to 4 minutes. Place in a very large oiled bowl, cover with plastic wrap, and allow to proof at room temperature until doubled in size.

4. Line 2 baking sheets with parchment paper. Lightly deflate the dough. Divide the dough into 12 to 14 pieces approximately 4 ounces each, and round each piece into a ball. Place 6 balls on each baking sheet, well separated. Cover with plastic wrap. Proof the dough at room temperature until the balls are half again as big, approximately 15 to 20 minutes.

5. Lightly flour a work surface. Line a baking sheet with parchment paper and dust the paper generously with flour or cornmeal. Roll out each ball to about 7 inches in diameter. Store the rolled breads on the parchment paper, covering each layer of bread with another sheet of paper and flouring that sheet before placing the next layer of breads. Allow the breads to rest another 20 minutes.

6. The pitas can be cooked by a variety of methods. To bake, preheat the oven to 550°F. Place the breads on several parchment-lined baking sheets dusted with flour or cornmeal and bake until puffed but not browned, 4 to 8 minutes.

7. Alternatively, heat a grill or griddle to medium-high heat. Cook the breads until bubbly and beginning to puff on the first side, 3 to 4 minutes, then turn over and cook until fully puffed but not brown, about 3 to 4 minutes.

8. Wrap the finished breads in a napkin to keep warm for serving. Extra breads may be cooled, stacked with parchment paper between them, and stored in a resealable bag in the freezer.

**MAKES ABOUT TWELVE TO FOURTEEN 4-OUNCE PITAS**

# Pizza Dough

*Keeping pizza dough on hand in the freezer makes homemade pizza a quick treat for dinner.*

6 cups bread flour

1 tbsp active dry yeast

1 tbsp kosher salt

1½ tsp sugar

2 tbsp olive oil, plus more as needed for brushing

2 cups warm water, 100°F

Nonstick cooking spray, as needed for greasing

All-purpose flour, as needed for rolling

Cornmeal, as needed for baking

1. In the bowl of a stand mixer fitted with a dough hook, combine the flour, yeast, salt, sugar, oil, and 2 cups warm water. Mix on medium speed until it forms a smooth dough, about 4 minutes. Increase the speed to high and mix for 3 minutes more.

2. Transfer the dough to a lightly greased bowl, cover with plastic wrap, and rest at room temperature until doubled in volume, about 30 minutes.

3. On a lightly floured surface, divide the dough into 2 equal pieces. The dough can now be frozen or used.

4. To freeze, oil the outside of the dough and place it in a resealable plastic freezer bag. Remove the dough from freezer the day before you want to use it and thaw in the refrigerator.

5. To use the dough, preheat the oven to 450°F and sprinkle 1 or 2 baking sheets with cornmeal. Roll out a piece of dough to a 12-inch circle, about ½ inch thick. Transfer the dough circle to a baking sheet. Top with desired toppings, brush the edge with olive oil, and bake until the pizza has risen and is golden brown around the edges, 14 to 16 minutes.

**MAKES ENOUGH DOUGH FOR TWO 12-INCH PIZZAS**

# Pissaladière

*Pissaladière is a yeast-raised tart, most commonly topped with onions and olives. Serve a slice or two alongside a salad for a wholesome meal.*

½ tsp active dry yeast

1½ cups all-purpose flour, plus more as needed for rolling

1 large egg

1 tbsp plus 2 tsp extra-virgin olive oil, plus more as needed for greasing

¼ cup warm water, or more as needed

3 medium yellow onions, thinly sliced

1 cup chopped tomatoes

3 cloves garlic, minced

Salt and freshly ground black pepper, as needed

1 cup halved pitted Kalamata olives

1. In the bowl of a stand mixer fitted with a dough hook, combine the yeast and flour.

2. Add the egg, 2 tsp of the oil, and ¼ cup water. Mix on low speed until the dough forms a ball and pulls away from the sides of the bowl, about 5 minutes. Put the dough into a greased bowl, cover with plastic wrap, and let rest at room temperature until doubled in volume, 30 to 40 minutes.

3. While the dough is proofing, preheat the oven to 400°F. Line a baking sheet with parchment paper.

4. In a large sauté pan, heat the remaining oil over medium heat. Add the onions, reduce heat to low, and slowly cook the onions until very tender, 8 to 10 minutes.

5. Increase the heat to high, add tomatoes and garlic, and continue to cook until all of the liquid has evaporated, 5 to 10 minutes more. Season with salt and pepper and cool to room temperature.

6. On a floured surface, roll the dough to a circle about 8 inches in diameter. Place on the baking sheet. Top the dough with the onion mixture and olives. Allow to rest 10 minutes more before baking.

7. Bake until the crust is golden brown and the topping is bubbly, 25 to 30 minutes.

8. Let cool slightly and cut into wedges. Serve warm or at room temperature.

**MAKES ONE 8-INCH TART, APPROXIMATELY 4 SERVINGS OR 8 APPETIZER PORTIONS**

Pissaladière

# Paratha

Paratha is a whole-wheat Indian flatbread. It is often stuffed with potatoes, paneer, herbs, or spices. Add them before beginning to fold the bread, and the filling will get folded into the thin layers.

1⅓ cups water

3¼ cups whole-wheat flour

1 cup bread flour

1 tbsp kosher salt

Grapeseed or canola oil or nonstick cooking spray, as needed for oiling the bowl

All-purpose flour, as needed for rolling

8 tablespoons (1 stick) unsalted butter, melted, plus more as needed

1. In the bowl of a stand mixer fitted with a dough hook, combine 1⅓ cups water, the whole-wheat and bread flours, and salt on low speed until the mixture forms a smooth dough, about 6 minutes.

2. Transfer the dough to a lightly oiled bowl, cover with plastic wrap, and let rest at room temperature for 30 minutes.

3. On a lightly floured surface, divide the dough into 15 equal pieces. Use the palm of your hand to lightly flatten each piece into a disk. Using a rolling pin, roll each piece of dough into a circle about 5 inches across. Brush the dough generously with butter. Working from the sides, fold the circle into thirds to form a long rectangle. Brush with butter, and starting at the top of the rectangle fold into thirds again. You will end up with a square.

4. Heat a large skillet over medium heat.

5. Working in batches, roll out each piece of dough again to about 6 inches in diameter. Brush both sides with butter, and cook until each side is brown, 3 to 5 minutes per side. Serve immediately while hot.

**MAKES ABOUT 15 BREADS**

VARIATION: **Stuffed Paratha:** Before folding the dough, sprinkle each circle with 1 tbsp crumbled paneer and 1 tsp coarsely chopped cilantro. Continue as directed.

# Roti

*Roti is a flaky flatbread from India and Southeast Asia. It is often used as a wrap or served with stews. Finish it with a sprinkling of coarse salt while it's still warm, if desired.*

1½ cups all-purpose flour, plus more as needed for rolling

1 tsp kosher salt

1½ tsp baking powder

4 tbsp (½ stick) cold unsalted butter, cubed

¾ cup water, or more as needed

Unsalted butter, melted, as needed

1. In a food processor, mix the flour, salt, baking powder, and cold butter until it forms a coarse meal. Transfer to a large bowl.

2. Add ¾ cup water and mix just until the mixture forms a smooth dough, about 5 minutes. (Add more water 1 tbsp at a time if needed. Dough should be tacky but not sticky.) Cover with plastic wrap and let rest at room temperature for 15 to 20 minutes.

3. On a lightly floured surface, divide the dough into 8 equal pieces, and form each piece into a tight ball. Roll each ball of dough into a 6-inch circle. Brush the dough lightly with melted butter.

4. Roll the dough into a tight cylinder shape (like a cigar), then twist the cylinder into a snail-like coil. Cover with a damp towel, and let the dough rest for 10 to 15 minutes more.

5. Roll out each coil to a 6-inch circle. Brush again with melted butter.

6. Heat a large skillet over medium heat. Working in batches, cook the roti until golden brown and crisp on both sides, 2 to 3 minutes per side.

**MAKES ABOUT 8 BREADS**

Roti (front), Paratha (middle), and Naan, page 280 (rear)

# Naan

An Indian flatbread traditionally cooked in a tandoori oven, this recipe uses a very hot skillet for similarly delicious results.

3½ cups all-purpose flour, plus more as needed for rolling

1½ tsp active dry yeast

1 tsp sugar

2 tsp kosher salt

1 cup warm water

⅓ cup plain yogurt

Grapeseed or canola oil or nonstick cooking spray, as needed for oiling the bowl

Unsalted butter, melted, as needed for cooking

Kosher salt, as needed

1. Sift the flour, yeast, sugar, and salt together into the bowl of a stand mixer. In a small bowl, combine 1 cup warm water and the yogurt.

2. Place the bowl on the mixer, fit with a dough hook, and add the yogurt mixture. Mix on low speed until completely combined.

3. Increase the speed to high and mix about 8 minutes to develop the gluten. Transfer the dough to a lightly oiled bowl. Cover with plastic wrap and let rest for 30 minutes or until the dough has doubled in size.

4. Divide the dough into 8 equal pieces. Form each piece into a smooth ball. Allow to rest 10 minutes. On a lightly floured surface, roll out each piece to a circle about ¼ inch thick.

5. Heat a large cast-iron skillet over medium heat. Working in batches, brush the naan with melted butter and sprinkle with salt. Cook in the skillet until the naan is golden brown and puffed on both sides, 3 to 5 minutes per side. Serve immediately.

**MAKES 8 FLATBREADS**

VARIATIONS: **Garlic Naan:** Mince 2 cloves garlic and sprinkle on top of the naan with the salt. **Onion Naan:** Dice enough yellow onion to make ½ cup, and sprinkle on top of the naan with the salt. **Cilantro Naan:** Coarsely chop enough cilantro to make ¼ cup and sprinkle on top of the naan with the salt.

# Scones

*Garnishes for these scones can be anything: dried fruit such as raisins, cherries, or cranberries, grated citrus zest, candied ginger, nuts, chocolate, cheese, herbs, or even vegetables.*

3 cups all-purpose flour

1 tsp kosher salt

1½ tbsp baking powder

3 tbsp plus 1 tsp sugar

12 tbsp (1½ sticks) cold unsalted butter, cubed

1 large egg

1 large egg yolk

¾ cup plus 2 tbsp heavy cream

**GARNISH (OPTIONAL)**

1 cup dried fruit, chopped nuts, small-diced vegetable, or chopped chocolate *or* 2 to 3 tbsp grated citrus zest *or* ¼ cup chopped fresh herb *or* 1 to 1½ cups grated cheese

**EGG WASH**

1 large egg

1 large egg yolk

2 tsp water

Pinch salt

1. Line a baking sheet with parchment paper.

2. In a large bowl, whisk the flour, salt, baking powder, and sugar together to combine.

3. Add the butter, toss to combine, then cut in the butter until it is distributed in small pieces about the size of a large pea (¼ to ½ inch).

4. If adding a garnish, gently fold it into the flour mixture. In a medium bowl, whisk together the egg, egg yolk, and cream. Add to the flour mixture and mix just until a dough forms.

5. Divide the dough into three equal size pieces. Transfer the dough pieces to the baking sheet. Lightly flour your hands and pat each dough piece into an 8 inch disk approximately 1 to 1½ inch thick. Cover with plastic wrap and chill until firm, 15 to 20 minutes.

6. While the dough is chilling, preheat the oven to 400°F. In a small bowl, whisk together the egg wash. Add more water as needed to achieve a thin, brushable consistency.

7. Using a floured knife, cut each disk into 8 wedges. Separate the wedges and position so there is a space of at least 1 inch between the wedges. Lightly brush the scones with the egg wash. Bake until golden, 12 to 15 minutes. Allow to cool briefly, and serve warm.

**MAKES ABOUT 24 SCONES**

# Tart Dough

*This dough is excellent for sweet or savory applications.*

1 cup all-purpose flour, plus
more as needed for rolling

6 tbsp (¾ stick) cold unsalted butter, cubed

2 tablespoons shortening

¼ tsp kosher salt

3 tbsp ice water, plus more as needed

1. Place the flour, butter, shortening, and salt in a large bowl. Cut the butter and shortening into the flour until the pieces are the size of large peas.

2. Add the water and blend just until the dough starts to form moist clumps, adding a bit more water if necessary.

3. Form into a disk, wrap in plastic, and chill at least 30 minutes before rolling.

**MAKES ONE 10-INCH TART**

There are a number of staple items every cook should have on hand. Identify those that are most important to you, which you use most frequently. The moment the last bit of any of these items is used, put it on your list to replace immediately. This will help you keep a variety of finished dishes within easy reach.

9

# PANTRY

# BROTH

Probably the most-used ingredient in this book, a good, basic broth is vital to any kitchen. A good broth can be used to build flavor in soups, stews, grain dishes, and in many other applications. Unlike broths and stocks made from chicken, beef, or veal, vegetable broths need much less simmering time and can be made quickly and much more easily. Coarsely chop the vegetables and cover them with water in a large pot. The simmering time will depend on ingredients used, but an hour is a good basic guideline. Try different combinations, or use a lot of one ingredient to really highlight its flavor (garlic, mushrooms, and onions, for example, make delicious broths). For more ideas, see the chart below.

# HOW TO MAKE IT YOUR OWN: BROTHS AND STOCKS

By traditional culinary standards, a broth is made using water, meat, bones, and vegetables, and a stock is made using water, bones, and vegetables. In the case of vegetarian cooking standards, a stock or a broth would be made using vegetables only. How these broths and stocks will vary is based on types of vegetables chosen for primary flavoring and the method in which they are combined and cooked.

## BROTHS AND STOCKS

| BROTH/STOCK | INGREDIENTS | APPLICATION/USES | COOKING METHOD |
|---|---|---|---|
| **VEGETABLE BROTH** | 70% aromatic vegetables, 30% mushroom stems, tomato, cabbage leaf, garlic, potato, and herbs | This neutral stock can be used for almost anything. | Simmer. |
| **MUSHROOM BROTH** | 70% assorted mushrooms and mushroom trim (use some dried mushrooms for added depth of flavor), 30% leeks, celery, parsnips, tomato, potato, garlic, herbs such as thyme | Mushroom broth has a delicious, meaty flavor great for a variety of purposes, including soups, sauces, and braises. | Sweat or roast the vegetables first for optimal flavor, then simmer. |
| **RED PEPPER STOCK** | 50–60% raw or roasted red peppers, 40–50% mirepoix vegetables, tomato, garlic, leek, herbs | Great for soup, chili, or sauce. For a spicy version, try using Anaheim or poblano chiles. | Roast, sweat or simmer. |
| **CORN STOCK** | 60–70% fresh corn, including the cobs, 30–40% onions, celery, parsnips, leeks or green onions | Corn chowder, polenta, tamales. | Simmer; consider roasting or grilling corn before making the stock. |
| **DRIED CHILE STOCK** | 15–20% dried chiles such as dried ancho or New Mexico red chiles (toasted until aromatic), 80–85% combination of red bell peppers, onion, tomato, and garlic | Spicy South American or Mexican soups. | Roast or toast all vegetables first, then simmer. Consider puréeing this stock before straining for ultimate flavor and color. |
| **ONION BROTH** | 70–80% assorted onions (Spanish, yellow, red, Vidalia, leek, etc.), 20–30% parsnips, garlic, celery, herbs, and dried mushrooms | Onion soup, bread pudding, polenta, immunity-building broths. | Sweat or caramelize the vegetables first, then simmer. |
| **ROASTED GARLIC STOCK** | 25% roasted garlic, 45% onions, 15% celery, 15% parsnips and herbs | Adds delicious flavor to soups, sauces, pasta, legumes, or grains. | Roast all vegetables first, then simmer. |

A broth usually has a bolder, richer, or stronger flavor. Stock requires 4 to 5 pounds vegetables per gallon of water. Broth requires 6 to 8 pounds vegetables per gallon of water.

Vegetables of all sorts can be used for broths, but usually not the cruciferous varieties, such as broccoli, Brussels sprouts, and cabbage (used very sparingly). The flavor can be swayed just by changing the ratio of ingredients. For instance, if you want to make a mushroom stock you would use 50 to 70 percent mushrooms and mushroom stems and 30 to 50 percent aromatics (carrots, celery, and various types of onion) and supporting flavors such as herbs and garlic. The use of seaweed will add an "ocean-like" flavor perfect for a vegetarian Manhattan chowder! A small amount of starchy potato or some seaweed high in agar agar can be added during the cooking process to add body or viscosity to the stock or broth.

# VINAIGRETTES AND DRESSINGS

Vinaigrettes are extremely useful, especially in the vegetarian kitchen. They can be used not only to dress salads, but also as dipping sauces, glazes, or marinades for other foods. Keep a selection of vinaigrettes on hand, as they have vastly different flavor profiles and come in handy for creating variety in your dishes. Keep in mind that all of the ingredients used will affect the flavor of the final vinaigrette: Try different oils (such as walnut, peanut, or sesame), different vinegars (raspberry, balsamic, or apple cider), and even different finishing components (herbs, spices, or fruit juice). For other ideas, see the chart on page 000.

In a classic vinaigrette, the ingredients are emulsified, usually with the aid of a binding agent such as egg yolk, prepared mustard, garlic, or vegetable purées. The basic vinaigrettes here are easier and faster to produce, because they are temporary emulsions and will need to be stirred or whisked prior to use. A great way to make this type of vinaigrette is to place all the ingredients into a glass jar fitted with a lid. Shake the ingredients to combine, use as much as you need, then store the vinaigrette in the refrigerator for the next use.

# SALSAS AND SAUCES

Typically made from uncooked fruits or vegetables, salsas are a quick and easy way to boost flavors in finished dishes. Play with different ingredients and textures to achieve different results. Fruits such as mangoes, tomatoes, and pineapple and vegetables such as peppers, corn, and onions all make great additions to salsas. Coarsely chopping or dicing vegetables and fruits will lead to a chunky, thicker salsa, whereas blending or puréeing the ingredients will lead to a smooth salsa with a thinner consistency.

## FLAVORING OILS AND VINEGARS

Oils and vinegars can be infused with a variety of flavors, including spices, herbs, onions, garlic, fresh or dried fruit, or fresh or dried vegetables. Heat the oil or vinegar over very low heat with desired flavoring, just until it becomes fragrant. Remove from the heat, cover, and let the mixture steep until cooled to room temperature. Then, depending on the desired texture and flavor, the flavoring ingredient can be strained out of the liquid, the mixture can be puréed until smooth, or the liquid can be stored with the flavoring to continue infusing. Store the finished oil or vinegar in clean bottles or containers. It is best to store infused oils and vinegars in the refrigerator, particularly if made with fresh, raw ingredients. When infused with cooked or dehydrated ingredients, infused oils and vinegars can safely be stored at room temperature. Oil infused with raw garlic should never be stored at room temperature or for prolonged periods of time even under refrigeration, as this combination can create botulism. Most other infused oils and vinegars can be stored for extended periods of time.

While salsas are simple and can include a wide range of ingredients, there are a variety of other sauces that are also excellent to keep in the kitchen. For example, a barbecue sauce simmered for a long time to develop wonderful, rich layers of flavor is ideal for pumping up sandwiches, salads, or vegetables. Other ideas include compotes, yogurt sauces, marmalades, and purée or coulis sauces. Oftentimes sauces that you commonly pair with one dish can go well with a variety of others—so get creative! Remember that a cook's personal creativity with ingredients is the key to making deliciously interesting food.

# CONDIMENTS

While many condiments can be purchased premade from your favorite grocery or gourmet store, making some condiments at home allows you to control and manipulate the flavors to your own liking. Some commonly used condiments include: mustard, ketchup, chutneys, hot sauce, and relishes.

## PURÉES

Puréeing foods is a wonderful way to introduce smooth textures into a finished dish or product. Puréed fruits and vegetables can be used to make a coulis, and puréed beans and legumes are a great way to thicken soups, sauces, or stews. Depending on the ingredients and how long they are processed, purées can be thick or thin, smooth or coarse. Thicker purées can also be used as a binder or even as a side dish (think cauliflower, potatoes, or beans).

## STORING AND PRESERVING

In an effort to enjoy the bounty of each season, try different methods of storing and preserving your favorite foods. Freeze fruits or vegetables in a thin, even layer on a baking sheet. Once the product is solidly frozen, it can be transferred to heavy-duty resealable plastic bags or other storage containers and used as needed. Dehydrating is also a great idea for fruits and vegetables, and the end product can be stored either frozen or at room temperature. Also consider preserving—making jams or jellies, canning fruits and vegetables, and pickling are fun, relatively simple, and a great way to enjoy spring and summer's products all year long. Refrigerator jams and pickles are even easier: They don't need to be processed or sealed; just remember they can't be stored at room temperature!

# Vegetable Broth

*Replacing water with stock or broth in recipes such as soups or rice dishes adds tons of flavor and nutrients.*

4 cloves garlic, crushed

2 cups Spanish onions, cut into eighths

½ cup carrot, very coarsely chopped

2 ounces green cabbage,
very coarsely chopped

4 stalks celery, very coarsely chopped

½ cup parsnips, very coarsely chopped

2 tbsp vegetable oil

1 bay leaf

6 black peppercorns

2 sprigs thyme

¼ bunch fresh flat-leaf
parsley stems, washed

1 cup mushroom stems, washed

1 gallon water

1. Preheat the oven to 350°F.

2. In a roasting pan, toss the garlic, onions, carrots, cabbage, celery, and parsnips with the oil. Spread in a single layer and roast until the vegetables are wilted but not brown, 10 to 15 minutes.

3. Transfer the vegetables to a large pot. Add the bay leaf, peppercorns, thyme, parsley, mushroom stems, and 1 gallon of water. Bring to a boil over high heat, lower the heat to medium, and simmer for 1 hour, skimming often.

4. Strain through a fine-mesh sieve or several layers of cheesecloth into a storage container, and cool to 45°F in a cold-water bath. Store in a sealed container in the refrigerator for up to 5 days or freeze up to 3 months.

**MAKES 1 GALLON**

VARIATIONS: **Mushroom Broth:** Omit the cabbage and parsnips and add 1 sliced fresh mushrooms and 2 ounces dried mushrooms. **Garlic Broth:** Add 3 heads of garlic cut in half, raw, to the vegetables before roasting. **Tomato Broth:** Add 4 cups chopped fresh tomatoes to the vegetables before roasting.

# Almond-Fig Vinaigrette

*Try sprinkling the finished salad with toasted almonds.*

1 cup almond oil

½ cup chopped, stemmed dried figs

¼ cup balsamic vinegar

2 tbsp red wine vinegar

¼ cup red wine, such as Zinfandel or Merlot

1 tbsp minced shallots

1 cup olive oil

Salt and freshly ground black
pepper, as needed

Juice of 1 lemon

Tabasco sauce, as needed

1. In a food processor, combine the almond oil and figs. Purée until smooth. Transfer to a medium bowl.

2. Whisk in the vinegars, wine, and shallots. Gradually whisk in the olive oil. Season with salt and pepper. Add the lemon juice and Tabasco.

**MAKES ABOUT 3 CUPS**

Clockwise from back, Apple Cider Vinaigrette, Chipotle-Sherry Vinaigrette (page 291), Almond-Fig Vinaigrette (page 287), Champagne Vinaigrette (page 290), and Roasted Tomato Vinaigrette (page 292)

# Apple Cider Vinaigrette

*Tarragon is a great complement for apples. Try puréeing this vinaigrette for a smoother texture.*

1 cup apple cider

½ cup apple cider vinegar

½ Granny Smith apple, peeled and shredded

1½ cups canola or grapeseed oil

1 tbsp chopped tarragon

1½ tsp maple syrup

Salt and freshly ground black pepper, as needed

1. In a medium pot, bring the cider to a simmer, and cook until the cider has reduced to about ½ cup. Transfer to a medium bowl.

2. Stir in the vinegar and shredded apple. Gradually whisk in the oil. Stir in the tarragon and maple syrup. Season with salt and pepper.

**MAKES ABOUT 3 CUPS**

# Shallot-Tarragon Vinaigrette

*Other fresh herbs would also go well in this vinaigrette. Dried herbs would work in a pinch too, but only use half as much as called for in the recipe.*

2 medium shallots, minced

¼ cup apple cider vinegar

¼ tsp Tabasco sauce

1 tbsp Dijon mustard

1 tsp sugar

2 tbsp chopped flat-leaf parsley

1 tbsp chopped tarragon

¾ cup extra-virgin olive oil

Salt and freshly ground black pepper, as needed

In a medium bowl, combine all ingredients, whisking well to combine. Season with salt and pepper. Serve immediately or refrigerate in a covered container for later use.

**MAKES ABOUT 1½ CUPS**

# Champagne Vinaigrette

*This basic vinaigrette is great with other light, subtle herbs, too—try marjoram, savory, thyme, or oregano.*

1 cup champagne vinegar

1 tbsp minced garlic

2 tbsp chopped fresh flat-leaf parsley

2 cups extra-virgin olive oil

Salt and freshly ground black pepper, as needed

In a medium bowl, whisk all ingredients together to combine. Season with salt and pepper.

**MAKES ABOUT 3 CUPS**

# Guava-Curry Vinaigrette

*Guava paste is available in international, specialty, and gourmet markets. If you can't find it, substitute guava jelly or boil ½ cup guava juice down to 2 to 3 tbsp and use it instead.*

2 to 3 tbsp guava paste, more if you prefer a sweeter dressing

½ cup red wine vinegar

1 tbsp curry powder, toasted

Juice of 2 limes

1½ cups olive oil

1 Scotch bonnet chile, seeded, minced

1 tbsp coarsely chopped cilantro

Salt and freshly ground black pepper, as needed

1. In a blender or food processor, combine the guava paste, vinegar, and curry powder. Transfer to a medium bowl.

2. Add the lime juice, oil, minced chile, and cilantro, and whisk to combine. Season with salt and pepper.

**MAKES 2 CUPS**

# Chipotle-Sherry Vinaigrette

*This sweet and spicy vinaigrette is also great as a dipping sauce.*

½ cup sherry vinegar

Juice of 1 lime

3 chipotles in adobo sauce, minced

1 medium shallot, minced

1 clove garlic, minced

1½ cups extra-virgin olive oil

¼ cup chopped herbs, such as cilantro, chives, epazote or parsley

1 tbsp light brown sugar

Salt and freshly ground black pepper, as needed

In a medium bowl, stir together the vinegar, lime juice, chipotles, shallots, and garlic. Whisk in the oil gradually. Gently fold in the herbs and brown sugar. Season with salt and pepper.

**MAKES ABOUT 3 CUPS**

VARIATION: **Sherry Vinaigrette:** Omit the lime juice and chipotles. Whisk 2 tbsp Dijon mustard and 1 tbsp honey with the vinegar and shallots, and add 1 tbsp each chopped thyme, oregano, and parsley.

# Virginia Peanut Dressing

*Finish a salad tossed in this dressing with chopped toasted peanuts or even sliced bananas.*

1 tbsp minced garlic

1½ tbsp chopped tarragon

1 tbsp minced chives

1 tbsp chopped flat-leaf parsley

¼ cup light brown sugar, packed

¾ cup malt vinegar

1 cup peanut oil

½ cup canola oil

½ cup peanut butter, smooth or crunchy

1 tsp Tabasco sauce or to taste

1 tsp Worcestershire sauce

Salt and freshly ground black pepper, as needed

In a medium bowl, whisk together all the ingredients until well combined. Season with salt and pepper. If using immediately, keep at room temperature, as room temperature dressing will mix easier with the greens. Store leftover dressing in the refrigerator in a covered container. Bring to room temperature and remix before using.

**MAKES 3 CUPS**

# Tahini-Soy Dressing

*This dressing is great on green salads and makes an exceptionally good noodle salad as well.*

3 tbsp tamari

¼ cup sherry vinegar

2 tsp minced fresh ginger

1 medium shallot, minced

2 tsp light brown sugar

2 tbsp tahini

1 jalapeño, seeded and minced

½ cup vegetable oil

2 tbsp toasted sesame oil

Juice of 2 limes

Salt, as needed

In a small bowl, whisk all ingredients until they are fully combined. Chill until needed.

**MAKES ABOUT 1½ CUPS**

# Roasted Tomato Vinaigrette

*Try roasting the tomatoes on the grill or over an open flame for a smokier flavor.*

5 plum (Roma) tomatoes, whole

3 garlic cloves, coarsely chopped

2 canned chipotle, diced

¾ tsp smoked paprika, toasted

1 cup extra-virgin olive oil

⅓ cup sherry vinegar

2 tsp chopped thyme

1 tbsp chopped basil

Juice of 1 lime

Tabasco sauce, as needed

Salt and freshly ground black pepper, as needed

1. Preheat the oven to 400°F.

2. Place the tomatoes on a baking sheet and roast until the skin is slightly blackened and blistered and the flesh is softened, 12 to 15 minutes.

3. Transfer the tomatoes to a food processor or blender. Add the garlic and chipotles and purée until the mixture is totally smooth.

4. Transfer to a medium bowl. Whisk in the paprika, oil, vinegar, thyme, basil, and lime juice until well combined. Season with Tabasco, salt, and pepper.

**MAKES ABOUT 2 CUPS**

NOTE: Smoked paprika is also known as pimentón. It can typically be found in Spanish or Latin grocery stores. Pimentón comes in dulce (sweet), piquante (hot), or agridulce (bittersweet).

# Creamy Garlic Dressing

*If this dressing begins to break after adding the mayonnaise or remaining olive oil, whisk in warm water 1 tsp at time until it's smooth again.*

¾ cup extra-virgin olive oil

⅔ cup thinly sliced garlic

¼ cup white wine vinegar

⅓ cup mayonnaise

Salt and freshly ground black pepper, as needed

1. In a small saucepan, heat half of the oil over low heat. Add the garlic and cook until the garlic starts to become golden, about 5 minutes. Remove from the heat and cool down quickly to prevent over browning the garlic.

2. Transfer to a food processor or blender and purée until smooth.

3. Transfer to a medium bowl and whisk in the vinegar. Let cool to room temperature.

4. Add the mayonnaise, whisking until blended to a creamy consistency. Slowly whisk in the remaining oil. Season with salt and pepper.

**MAKES ABOUT 2 CUPS**

# Creamy Avocado Ranch Dressing

*Avocado is rich and creamy and gives this dressing a flavorful—and healthy—twist.*

2 cloves garlic, minced

½ cup buttermilk

2 tsp fresh lime juice

½ cup crème fraîche

½ cup mayonnaise

1 avocado, diced

¼ tsp cayenne

1 tbsp chopped chives

1 tbsp chopped flat-leaf parsley

1 tbsp chopped basil

1 tbsp extra-virgin olive oil

Salt and freshly ground black pepper, as needed

In a blender or food processor, purée the garlic, buttermilk, and lime juice until smooth. Add the crème fraîche and mayonnaise and blend until fully combined. Add the avocado, cayenne, chives, parsley, basil, and olive oil. Blend until fully combined and smooth. Season with salt and pepper. Chill before using.

**MAKES ABOUT 2 CUPS**

# Apple-Pepper Compote

*This compote shows how sweet red bell peppers can be. It's great on sandwiches or Crostini (page 15).*

3 cups Golden Delicious apples, peeled and diced

1 cup red bell pepper, peeled and minced

½ cup diced red onion

¼ cup sugar

¼ cup apple cider vinegar

½ cup apple cider

Pinch freshly grated nutmeg

Pinch ground allspice

Pinch ground cinnamon

Pinch ground ginger

Salt, as needed

1. In a medium saucepan, combine the apples, red pepper, onion, sugar, vinegar, and cider and simmer over medium heat until most of the moisture is evaporated. The compote will be thick and the fruit will be soft.

2. Remove from the heat and stir in the nutmeg, allspice, cinnamon, and ginger. Season with salt. Serve at room temperature or store in a glass jar with tight-fitting lid until needed.

**MAKES ABOUT 2 CUPS**

# Barbecue Sauce

*This sauce is best when left to gently simmer until it's thick and flavorful—the longer, the better.*

¼ cup vegetable oil

1 cup thinly sliced yellow onions

3 cloves garlic, coarsely chopped

4 plum (Roma) tomatoes, chopped

1 tbsp Dijon mustard

2 tbsp chili powder, toasted

1 tbsp ground cumin, toasted

1 tbsp ground coriander, toasted

1 tsp dried oregano

1 canned chipotle, diced

⅓ cup apple cider vinegar

1 tbsp molasses

1⅓ cups ketchup

Salt, as needed

1. In a large saucepan, heat the vegetable oil over low heat. Sauté the onion until golden, 4 to 5 minutes. Add the garlic, cover, and sweat until fragrant, about 1 minute.

2. Add the remaining ingredients and bring to a simmer over medium heat. Simmer until it has reduced slightly and has developed good flavor, 20 to 25 minutes or longer.

3. Transfer to a food processor or blender and process until it forms a smooth sauce. Store in the refrigerator in an airtight container until needed, or reheat and use immediately.

**MAKES ABOUT 2½ CUPS**

Barbecue Sauce, (left), Apple-Pepper Compote
(right), and Ketchup, page 311 (rear)

# Cranberry-Orange Compote

*This compote is delicious on the Bulgur Cereal with Dried Apricots, Prunes, and Lemon Zest (page 189) or oatmeal. It will last for several weeks in the refrigerator.*

1 cinnamon stick

6 cloves

¼ tsp freshly grated nutmeg

2 allspice berries

3 juniper berries

4½ cups fresh cranberries

½ cup triple sec or Grand Marnier

½ cup sugar

6 oranges, peeled and cut into suprêmes (see page 321), juice reserved

¾ cup fresh orange juice, reserved from cutting the suprêmes

1 cup dried cranberries

Salt, as needed

1. Cut a square of cheesecloth and place the cinnamon, cloves, nutmeg, allspice, and juniper in the center. Tie into a sachet with kitchen twine. To release the flavors fast and for extra strong flavor, lightly crush the sachet before using.

2. In a medium saucepan, combine the fresh cranberries, triple sec, sugar, and orange juice. Add the sachet and bring to a boil.

3. Reduce heat to low and simmer until the cranberries begin to burst and the sauce has thickened slightly, 15 to 20 minutes.

Be careful that the liquids don't completely evaporate. This could cause scorching.

4. Remove pan from the heat, remove and discard the sachet, and stir in the orange segments and dried cranberries. Season with a pinch of salt.

5. Transfer the compote to a storage container, cover, and refrigerate until needed.

**MAKES ABOUT 4 CUPS**

# Onion Marmalade

*This savory marmalade is an ideal sandwich spread or condiment.*

4 cups thinly sliced red onions

1 cup sugar

½ cup red wine vinegar

½ cup red wine

Salt and freshly ground black pepper, as needed

Combine all ingredients in a medium saucepan over medium heat and bring to a boil. Reduce the heat to low and simmer until the onions are tender and the marma-lade has a syrupy consistency, 15 to 25 minutes. Season with salt and pepper.

**MAKES ABOUT 2 CUPS**

VARIATION: **Roasted Red Pepper Marmalade:** Replace 3 cups of the onions with peeled, diced roasted red peppers. Replace the red wine vin-egar with balsamic vinegar and the red wine with white wine.

# Pesto

*A drizzle of olive oil will prevent pesto from turning brown in storage or while sitting out on an appetizer.*

3 cups basil leaves, packed loosely

4 cloves garlic, or more for extra garlicky pesto

¼ cup toasted pine nuts

½ cup extra-virgin olive oil

½ cup Parmesan cheese

Salt and freshly ground black pepper, as needed

1. In a food processor or blender, process the basil, garlic, and pine nuts to a coarse paste.

2. With the machine running, slowly add the olive oil in a thin stream and process to form a smooth paste. Add the cheese and pulse the processor a few times just to incorporate. Season with salt and pepper.

**MAKES ABOUT 2 CUPS**

# Z'hug

*Z'hug is a spicy, relish-style condiment originally from Yemen. Serve it with anything you want to add a little kick to.*

1 pound jalapeños, roasted and peeled

4 cloves garlic

1 cup cilantro leaves, moderately packed

½ cup fresh flat-leaf parsley leaves, moderately packed

½ cup mint leaves

1 tsp ground cardamom

1 tsp cumin seeds, toasted

½ cup olive oil

3 tbsp fresh lemon juice

Salt and freshly ground black pepper, as needed

In a food processor or blender, pulse the jalapeños, garlic, cilantro, parsley, mint, cardamom, and cumin until finely chopped. With the machine running, slowly add the olive oil and purée until smooth.

Transfer to a bowl and stir in the lemon juice. Season with salt and pepper. Cover and refrigerate until needed.

**MAKES ABOUT 1 CUP**

# Red Onion Preserve

*This preserve is delicious on crackers with a soft, mild cheese (such as fresh goat cheese).*

2 tbsp grapeseed or canola oil

5 medium red onions, thinly sliced

6 tbsp sugar

6 tbsp red wine vinegar

1 cup red wine

Salt and freshly ground black pepper, as needed

1. Combine the oil and onions in a medium saucepan. Place over medium heat and cook just to wilt and soften the onions, about 30 minutes.

2. Stir in the sugar, vinegar, and wine. Cook, stirring occasionally, until all the liquid has evaporated and the preserve is thick.

3. Season with salt and pepper. Chill before using.

**MAKES ABOUT 2 CUPS**

# Birch Beer Cranberry Sauce

*Birch beer gives this sauce both sweetness and bitterness that make it great on vegetables or proteins.*

2 cups birch beer

1 cup cranberry juice

2 tbsp unsalted butter

Salt, as needed

1. In a medium saucepan, bring the birch beer to a simmer over medium heat. Cook until it is reduced to ¾ cup.

2. Add the cranberry juice and whisk in the butter. Season with salt. Serve the sauce warm or store until needed and reheat.

**MAKES ABOUT 2 CUPS**

# Mole Coloradito Oaxaqueño (Oaxacan Red Mole)

*This sauce is the real deal. It takes time and patience, but it is worth it. Mole makes an excellent sauce for enchiladas, Sopes (page 262), or Black Bean Tamales (page 248). It is also ideal for use with alternative proteins.*

3 ancho chiles, quickly rinsed and dried

2 guajillo chiles, quickly rinsed and dried

2 tbsp raisins

2 plum (Roma) tomatoes, quartered

2 cloves garlic, unpeeled

1 quart Vegetable Broth (page 287)

4 tbsp vegetable oil

1 Corn Tortilla (page 273 or store-bought), coarsely torn

4 black peppercorns

1-inch piece of Mexican cinnamon

1 clove

6 almonds, blanched

¼ cup sesame seeds

¾ tsp dried Mexican oregano

¼ tsp dried marjoram

1 small white onion, diced

2 tbsp finely chopped Mexican chocolate, optional

Pinch sugar

Salt and freshly ground black pepper, as needed.

1. In a dry cast-iron skillet, toast the chiles on both sides over high heat until aromatic but color has not changed, 1 to 2 minutes. Remove and discard the stems and seeds. Place the chiles in a medium bowl, and add the raisins. Cover with hot water and rehydrate for 15 to 20 minutes.

2. While the chiles and raisins are soaking, char the tomatoes and garlic in a skillet over high heat until blistered and skin is blackened, 8 to 10 minutes. Peel the garlic.

3. Drain the chiles and raisins and discard the soaking water. Transfer the chiles and raisins to a blender and process to a smooth purée using a small amount of broth. Remove the purée and reserve. In the same blender pitcher, purée tomatoes and garlic with a small amount of broth. Remove the purée and reserve.

4. Heat 2 tbsp of the oil in a small sauté pan over medium heat, add the tortilla pieces and onion, and sauté 2 minutes. Add the peppercorns, cinnamon, clove, almonds, sesame seeds, oregano, and marjoram, and sauté until aromatic. Remove from the heat and place into the blender pitcher. Process to a smooth paste using a small amount of broth. Reserve. You now have 3 separate purées.

5. In a 1-gallon sauce pot, heat the remaining oil to the smoke point. Add the chile-raisin purée all at once to fry the purée. It will splatter some, but stir constantly as the purée cooks and thickens, approximately 5 minutes. Lower the heat to medium, add the tomato-garlic purée, and simmer 5 minutes. Add the spice purée. Continue cooking for an additional 5 minutes to develop the flavors.

6. Add any remaining broth and the optional finely chopped chocolate. Simmer until the sauce has reduced to a thick, smooth consistency, approximately 30 minutes. Stir in the sugar and season with salt and pepper. If sauce is not smooth, purée once more with an immersion blender.

7. Serve immediately or cool and pour into a glass jar with a tight-fitting lid. Store in the refrigerator for up to 5 days, or freeze for future use.

**MAKES ABOUT 3 TO 4 CUPS**

NOTE: This sauce tastes even better if you make it a day or two before you plan to use it.

# Mushroom Gravy

*This gravy is a rich and flavorful classic.. Try it with the Tofu-Seitan Cutlets (page 167).*

4 tbsp (½ stick) unsalted butter

2 tbsp all-purpose flour

1 cup cremini mushrooms, minced

2 cloves garlic, minced

1 tbsp chopped flat-leaf parsley

2 tsp chopped thyme

2 tsp chopped rosemary

1½ cups dry white wine

5 cups Mushroom Broth (page 284)

Salt and freshly ground black pepper, as needed

Heavy cream, as needed (optional)

1. In a small bowl, mix 2 tbsp of the butter with the flour until it forms a smooth paste. Set aside.

2. Melt the remaining butter in a medium saucepan over medium heat. Add the mushrooms and garlic and sauté until they are tender, 4 to 5 minutes. Stir in the parsley, thyme, and rosemary. Add the wine and bring to a simmer. Cook until the wine has been almost entirely reduced and the mixture is almost dry.

3. Add the broth and bring to a simmer. Cook until the liquid has reduced to approximately 3 cups, 15 to 20 minutes. Whisk in the butter-flour paste. Bring to a boil and cook, whisking constantly, until the gravy has thickened, 6 to 8 minutes. Season well with salt and pepper. Serve immediately.

4. For added richness, finish this sauce with a few tablespoons of heavy cream.

**MAKES ABOUT 3 CUPS**

# Peanut Dipping Sauce

*This sauce is a yummy Thai-style sauce that is as versatile as it is delicious. Try it as a dipping sauce for warm blanched vegetables or tossed with rice noodles.*

2 tsp peanut oil

2 tsp red curry paste

¼ tsp ground turmeric

¼ cup peanut butter

¼ cup coconut milk

¼ cup Vegetable Broth (page 287)

3 tbsp fresh lime juice

1 tbsp sweet Thai chili sauce

GARNISH

3 tbsp toasted and coarsely chopped peanuts

1. Heat the oil in a medium sauté pan over medium heat. Add the curry and turmeric until it bubbles slightly, about 1 minute. Add the peanut butter, coconut milk, broth, lime juice, and chili sauce and reduce the heat to low. Cook, stirring constantly, for 3 minutes. When the liquid begins to bubble, remove it from the heat and continue to stir for 1 minute. Serve immediately, garnished with chopped peanuts.

2. If not using the sauce right away, do not garnish. Cover and refrigerate it. Properly stored, it will keep 2 to 3 days. When needed, heat it in a saucepan over low heat just until warm. Garnish with the peanuts when serving.

MAKES 1 CUP

# Stewed Black Bean and Ancho Chile Sauce

*This sauce is an excellent complement to the Black Bean Crêpes on page 26, but it would also be delicious tossed with soba noodles.*

2 tbsp olive oil

1 cup diced yellow onion

2 cloves garlic, thinly sliced

¾ cup cooked black beans (see chart, page 131)

¼ pound smoked tofu, small dice

1 ancho chile, toasted, seeded, sliced into ⅛ inch strips (julienne)

¼ cup thinly sliced sun-dried tomatoes

1 cup mushroom broth

Salt and freshly ground black pepper, as needed

In a medium saucepan, heat the oil over medium heat. Add the onions, cover, and sweat until translucent, 4 to 5 minutes. Add the garlic and sauté until fragrant, about 1 minute. Add the beans, tofu, chile, tomatoes, and broth. Simmer until the mixture has good flavor and has thickened, 7 to 10 minutes. Season with salt and pepper. Serve warm or store in the refrigerator in an airtight container. Reheat over low heat to avoid scorching.

**MAKES ABOUT 2½ CUPS**

# Sweet Chili Sauce

*This sauce is sweet, sour, and spicy all at once. Great as a dipping sauce, on top of noodles or stir fries, or even on sandwiches!*

⅓ cup Vegetable Broth (page 287)

⅓ cup sugar

½ cup rice vinegar

3 cloves garlic, minced

1 tsp red chili paste

Pinch red pepper flakes

Salt, as needed

1. In a small saucepan, bring the broth, sugar, vinegar, and garlic to a simmer over medium heat. Stir to dissolve the sugar.

2. Remove from the heat and stir in the chili paste and pepper flakes. Season with salt. Chill before using.

**MAKES ABOUT 1 CUP**

# Mushroom Sauce

*This brothy mushroom sauce is great tossed with pasta, served with vegetables, or with tofu or seitan. Try using different types of mushrooms or a medley of mushrooms for added depth of flavor.*

1 tbsp olive oil

1 medium shallot, minced

2 cloves garlic, minced

2 cups thinly sliced cremini mushrooms

2 cups Vegetable Broth (page 287)

1 tbsp chopped flat-leaf parsley

2 tsp chopped thyme

Salt and freshly ground black pepper, as needed

2 tbsp butter (optional)

1. In a medium saucepan, heat the oil over medium heat. Add the shallot and garlic and sauté until soft, about 5 minutes. Add the mushrooms and cook until they are tender, about 2 minutes more. Add the broth, parsley, and thyme and bring to a boil. Reduce the heat to low and simmer until the liquid has reduced by about half, about 15 minutes. Serve the sauce as is, or purée until smooth.

2. For added body, swirl 2 tablespoons of butter into the finished sauce.

**MAKES ABOUT 2 CUPS**

# Tomato Sauce

*This is a very basic tomato sauce. Feel free to add other vegetables, add wine after the vegetables have cooked, or add other herbs to finish the sauce.*

3 tbsp olive oil

2 medium yellow onions, diced

8 cloves garlic, minced

5½ cups chopped, fresh plum (Roma) or heirloom tomatoes, peeled, seeded

1 tbsp chopped basil

Salt and freshly ground black pepper, as needed

1. Heat the oil in a large saucepan over medium-high heat. Add the onions and sauté until translucent, 4 to 6 minutes. Add the garlic and sauté until fragrant, about 1 minute more. Add the tomatoes and bring the sauce to a boil. Reduce the heat to medium low and simmer until sauce is desired thickness, approximately 20 to 25 minutes.

2. Stir in the basil and simmer for 5 minutes more. Season with salt and pepper.

**MAKES ABOUT 3½ CUPS**

# Yellow Mole

*This sauce is delicious with many dishes, especially the Black Bean and Quinoa–Stuffed Zucchini on page 219.*

1 tbsp extra-virgin olive oil

½ cup sliced yellow onion

2 tsp sliced garlic

1 large yellow bell pepper, chopped

1 cup top removed, cored, chopped fennel bulb

1 small stick Mexican cinnamon

Pinch ground allspice

Large pinch dried epazote

1½ tsp sugar

½ cup water

1 tomatillo, quartered

2 tbsp fresh lime juice

Salt and freshly ground black pepper, as needed

1. In a heavy-bottomed medium saucepan, heat the oil over medium heat. Add the onions and garlic, cover, and sweat until the onions are translucent, about 5 minutes.

2. Stir in the yellow pepper, fennel, cinnamon, allspice, epazote, sugar, and ½ cup water. Cover and simmer for 15 minutes or until the yellow peppers are extremely soft.

3. Remove the cinnamon stick. Transfer cooked vegetables to a blender and add the tomatillo. Purée until very smooth. Strain through a large-holed strainer to remove any skin and seeds that may not be completely puréed. The finished sauce should be velvety smooth.

4. Stir in the lime juice and season with salt and pepper. Serve immediately, while still hot.

**MAKES ABOUT 2 CUPS**

# Ruby Red Grapefruit Salsa

*If you're making this salsa ahead of time, combine all ingredients except the fruit. Add the grapefruit and oranges just before you're ready to serve. When you cut the fruit, be sure to cut it over a bowl to collect the juices.*

2 tbsp minced red onion

2 tbsp extra-virgin olive oil

1½ tbsp chopped cilantro

1 tbsp seeded and minced Scotch bonnet chile

1 tbsp chopped flat-leaf parsley

4 ruby grapefruits, peeled and cut into suprêmes (see page 321), juice reserved

2 oranges, peeled and cut into suprêmes (see page 321), juice reserved

Fresh orange juice, as needed to make ½ cup juice, including the reserved juices

Salt and freshly ground black pepper, as needed

Rinse the onion in a fine-mesh strainer under cold running water (to make it milder) and drain thoroughly. In a medium bowl, whisk together the oil, cilantro, onion, chile, parsley, and juices. Add the grapefruit and orange segments and gently toss to coat. Season with salt and pepper. Serve immediately.

**MAKES ABOUT 2 TO 3 CUPS**

# Pico de Gallo

*The amount of cilantro in this recipe may be increased to as much as ¾ cup to suit individual taste.*

6 large plum (Roma) tomatoes, seeded and diced ½ inch (about 2½ cups)

1 cup white onion, diced ¼ inch

2 serrano chiles, seeded and minced

Juice of 1 lime

¼ cup chopped cilantro

Salt and freshly ground black pepper, as needed

In a medium bowl, toss together all the ingredients to combine. Season with salt and pepper. Refrigerate for at least 15 minutes before serving to allow the flavors to meld.

**MAKES ABOUT 3 CUPS**

# Green Mango Salsa

*This salsa can also be made with green papayas.*

2 to 3 unripe mangoes, peeled, shredded

1 large carrot, peeled, shredded

Juice of 1 lime

1 tbsp chopped cilantro

1 tsp minced fresh ginger

1 clove garlic, minced

1 tbsp red wine vinegar

2 tsp molasses

Salt and freshly ground black pepper, as needed

Shred the mangoes on the coarse side of a box grater, into a medium bowl. Discard the pits. Shred the carrot into the same bowl and toss the two together. Add the lime juice, cilantro, ginger, garlic, vinegar, and molasses and toss to combine. Season with salt and pepper and toss again. Serve chilled.

**MAKES 3 TO 4 CUPS**

# Pineapple-Jícama Salsa

*This fresh salsa is a great addition to the Seitan Fajitas on page 164, giving them a light, tropical flavor.*

¼ cup olive oil

Juice of 4 limes

¼ cup chopped cilantro

1 large jícama, approximately 4-inch diameter, peeled and cut in fine julienne

½ medium pineapple, peeled, cored, and diced small

1 cup minced red onions

1 red bell pepper, diced small

2 serrano chiles, seeded, minced

Salt and freshly ground black pepper, as needed

In a large bowl, whisk the oil, lime juice, and cilantro to combine. Gently fold in the jícama, pineapple, onion, red peppers, and chiles. Season with salt and pepper. Cover and chill until needed.

**MAKES ABOUT 3 TO 4 CUPS**

FACING PAGE, *clockwise from top: Green Mango Salsa, Salsa Verde (page 309), Ruby Red Grapefruit Salsa (page 305), Pico de Gallo (page 305), Squash Salsa (page 310), and Red Chile Salsa (page 308)*

# Red Chile Salsa

*Any dried red chile can be used for this recipe (we suggest 3 ancho and 3 guajillo), but if the chiles are especially large, only use 3 or 4.*

6 large dried red chiles, stems and seeds removed

4 cups hot water

1 plum (Roma) tomato, roasted

¼ cup chopped yellow onion, roasted

2 cloves Roasted Garlic (page 315)

2 tsp dried Mexican oregano

Salt and freshly ground black pepper, as needed

1. Preheat the oven to 350°F.

2. Place the chiles on a baking sheet and toast until aromatic but not browned, 3 to 4 minutes. Transfer the chiles to a bowl and cover with 2 cups hot water. Soak until soft, at least 15 minutes. Discard the soaking liquid. Transfer the chiles and 2 cups clean hot water to a food processor or blender and pulse until smooth. Add the tomato, onion, and garlic and purée until smooth.

3. Transfer the mixture to a small saucepan. Bring to a simmer over medium heat. Cook, stirring occasionally, until the salsa is thick, 10 to 15 minutes.

4. Remove from the heat and stir in the oregano. Season with salt and pepper. Serve immediately or cool and store until needed.

**MAKES ABOUT 1½ CUPS**

# Salsa Roja

*Rehydrating chiles makes them easier to incorporate into a salsa or sauce.*

6 guajillo chiles

3 arbol chiles

1 cup hot water

3 cloves garlic, unpeeled

1 tsp vegetable oil

2 tbsp minced white onion

2 cups peeled and diced tomatoes

1 canned chipotle, seeded

1½ tsp light brown sugar

Salt, as needed

1. Heat a dry cast-iron skillet over medium-high heat. Toast the guajillos and arbols on both sides just until fragrant. Remove the stems and seeds. Place the chiles in a bowl and soak in 1 cup hot water until soft, about 20 minutes.

2. Place the garlic in the same skillet over medium heat and cook, turning frequently, until soft and blackened in spots, about 15 minutes. Cool. Peel off and discard the skin.

3. In a small sauté pan, heat the oil over medium heat. Add the onion and sauté until lightly browned. Remove from the heat.

4. Drain the chiles and discard the soaking liquid. Combine the chiles, the garlic, tomato, onions, chipotle, and sugar in a blender. Purée until very smooth. Adjust the texture with more water as necessary. Season with salt.

**MAKES ABOUT 2 CUPS**

# Salsa Verde

*Try making this salsa with raw rather than roasted ingredients or with the addition of 2 diced avocados folded in.*

¾ pound tomatillos, halved

1 serrano chile, stemmed

2 cups diced yellow onions

2 cloves garlic, peeled

2 tbsp vegetable oil

Salt and freshly ground black pepper, as needed

½ cup Vegetable Broth (page 287)

3 tbsp chopped cilantro

1. Preheat the oven to 350°F.

2. In a large bowl, toss the tomatillos, chile, onion, and garlic with 1 tbsp of the oil to coat. Season with salt and pepper. Pour the mixture onto a baking sheet in an even layer. Roast until softened and lightly browned, about 10 to 15 minutes. (Don't let the vegetables get too dark.) Cool to room temperature.

3. In a food processor or blender, purée the tomatillo mixture, adding water as needed to yield a thick, semismooth sauce.

4. In a medium saucepan, heat the remaining oil over medium heat. Add the puréed mixture, and stir constantly until the mixture is heated through, 2 to 3 minutes.

5. Add the broth and bring to a boil. Reduce heat to low and simmer until the salsa is thick enough to coat the back of a spoon, about 10 minutes. Add the cilantro. Chill until needed.

**MAKES ABOUT 2 CUPS**

# Squash Salsa

*This is a chunky salsa made with a variety of vegetables. Use it as a condiment or a side dish with Red Bean and Rice–Stuffed Portobello Mushroom Caps (page 238).*

⅔ cup diced small carrots

1½ cups quartered lengthwise, seeded, and diced small yellow squash

1½ cups quartered lengthwise, seeded, and diced small zucchini

1 cup seeded and diced small plum (Roma) tomatoes

⅓ cup seeded and diced small tomatillos

½ cup red onion, diced small

1 canned chipotle, minced

¾ tsp chopped marjoram

3 tbsp cilantro chiffonade

1½ tbsp extra-virgin olive oil

1 tbsp rice vinegar

¼ tsp sugar

Freshly ground black pepper, as needed

1. Bring a large pot of lightly salted water to a boil over high heat. Fill a large bowl with ice and water to make an ice water bath.

2. Add the carrots to the boiling water and cook until barely tender, 2 minutes. Scoop out with a sieve and plunge the carrots into the ice water to stop the cooking and cool. Drain thoroughly and transfer to another large bowl.

3. Bring the water back to a boil. Add the yellow squash and cook until barely tender, 30 seconds. Scoop out with a sieve and plunge the squash into the ice water to stop the cooking and cool. Drain thoroughly and add to the carrots.

4. Bring the water back to a boil again. Add the zucchini and cook until barely tender, 30 seconds. Scoop out with a sieve and plunge the zucchini into the ice water to stop the cooking and cool. Drain thoroughly and add to the carrots and squash.

5. Add the tomatoes, tomatillos, red onion, chipotle, marjoram, cilantro, oil, vinegar, and sugar to blanched drained vegetables and toss to combine. Season with salt and pepper. Serve immediately.

**MAKES ABOUT 4 CUPS**

NOTE: This Salsa is very hot. To reduce the heat adjust the amount of chipotle chile.

# Sweet Potato Coulis

*A delicious and nutritious sauce that's beautifully colorful and simple to make.*

2 medium sweet potatoes, peeled and cubed

Salt, as needed

¼ cup Vegetable Broth (page 287), plus more as needed

2 tsp curry powder, toasted

Pinch cayenne, toasted

Freshly ground black pepper, as needed

1. Place the sweet potatoes in a medium pot and cover by at least 1 inch with cold salted water. Bring to a boil and cook until the potatoes are tender, 15 to 20 minutes.

2. Drain the potatoes and transfer them to a food processor or blender. Purée the potatoes while gradually adding the broth and process until the mixture forms a smooth, thick sauce.

3. Stir in the curry powder and cayenne and season with salt and pepper. Refrigerate until needed. Reheat over low heat prior to using.

**MAKES ABOUT 2 CUPS**

# Ketchup

*Canned tomatoes (whole tomatoes that have been coarsely chopped, or crushed tomatoes) can also be used.*

1 tbsp olive oil

½ cup diced yellow onion

3 cloves garlic, minced

2 tbsp chopped thyme

2 cups coarsely chopped tomatoes

3 tbsp sugar

3 tbsp apple cider vinegar

1 tbsp tomato paste

1 bay leaf

¼ tsp dry mustard

Pinch cayenne

Pinch ground allspice

Salt, as needed

1. In a medium saucepan, heat the oil over medium heat. Add the onion and garlic, cover, and sweat until the onions are translucent, 3 to 4 minutes.

2. Add the remaining ingredients and bring to a boil. Reduce the heat to low and simmer, stirring occasionally to keep the ketchup from scorching, until it is slightly thickened, 35 to 45 minutes.

3. Remove and discard bay leaf. In a food processor or blender, purée the ketchup until smooth, adding up to ½ cup water as needed to bring the mixture to the correct consistency.

4. Cool the ketchup to room temperature and store in the refrigerator until needed.

**MAKES ABOUT 2 CUPS**

# Blackberry Ketchup

*This sweet, but savory, condiment is a great accompaniment for grilled vegetarian dishes.*

4½ cups blackberries

1 cup red wine vinegar

1 cup water

1½ cups brown sugar, packed

Pinch ground cloves

½ tsp ground ginger

½ tsp ground cinnamon

½ tsp cayenne

½ tsp fresh salt

3 tbsp unsalted butter

1. Stir together the blackberries, vinegar, 1 cup water, sugar, cloves, ginger, cinnamon, cayenne, and salt in a large saucepan over medium heat. Bring to a boil. Reduce the heat to low and simmer for 30 minutes or until it thickens slightly.

2. Transfer to a food mill fitted with a fine screen and purée until smooth. This will also remove the seeds. Whisk in the butter.

3. Cool to room temperature before storing in the refrigerator or using.

**MAKES ABOUT 3 CUPS**

# Gremolata

*This fragrant sauce can be used as a condiment or sauce, or it can even be rubbed onto vegetables or proteins before cooking.*

2 cups chopped fresh flat-leaf parsley

¼ cup grated lemon zest

3 cloves garlic, minced

¾ cup olive oil

Salt and freshly ground black pepper, as needed

In a small bowl, combine the parsley, zest, and garlic. Stir in the oil, mixing to combine. Season with salt and pepper.

**MAKES ABOUT 2 CUPS**

# Ancho-Cumin Crust

*This is a good, flavorful crust that's ideal on vegetables, tofu, or seitan.*

5 ancho chiles

3 tbsp cumin seeds

3 tbsp coriander seeds

2 tbsp black peppercorns

2 tbsp dried thyme

2 tbsp dried oregano

½ cup kosher salt

2 tbsp dry mustard

1 tbsp onion powder

1 tbsp garlic powder

1. Preheat the oven to 350°F.

2. Remove the stems and seeds from the anchos and coarsely chop them. Combine the chiles, cumin, coriander, and peppercorns on a rimmed baking sheet and toast until fragrant, about 5 minutes. Transfer from the baking sheet to a plate and cool to room temperature.

3. In a spice grinder, combine the roasted spices with the thyme, oregano, salt, mustard, onion powder, and garlic powder and grind to a medium fine texture. Store in an airtight container in a cool, dry place and use as needed.

**MAKES ABOUT 2 CUPS**

# BBQ Spice Rub

*This rub is especially great on grilled vegetables, such as in the Grilled Vegetable Jambalaya on page 230.*

1 cup kosher salt

2 tsp cayenne

2 tsp freshly ground black pepper

1 tsp freshly ground white pepper

½ cup paprika

1 tbsp onion powder

1 tbsp garlic powder

Combine all the ingredients and mix well. Store in an airtight container in a cool, dry place.

**MAKES ABOUT 1 CUP**

# Curry Marinade

This marinade is ideal for tofu, seitan, or tempeh. Try substituting your favorite curry paste for the curry powder for more intense flavor.

2 tbsp soy or tamari sauce

1 tbsp honey

2 tbsp curry powder, toasted

1 tbsp ground turmeric

4 cloves garlic, minced

1 tsp ground coriander

½ tsp ground cumin

⅓ cup unsweetened coconut milk

⅓ cup peanut oil

In a medium bowl, whisk together all the ingredients. Refrigerate if not using immediately.

**MAKES ABOUT 1 CUP**

# Jamaican Jerk Marinade

This marinade is ideal for a number of items such as portabello mushrooms, tofu, seitan, or fruits such as peaches or pineapple. Pour the marinade into a shallow container, add the item, and let it marinate, refrigerated, for at least 4 hours and up to overnight.

¼ cup ground allspice

1 tbsp ground cinnamon

1 tsp ground cloves

2 tsp freshly grated nutmeg

5 green onions (white and green parts), thinly sliced

2 cups diced yellow onion

2 tbsp minced fresh ginger

1 tbsp chopped thyme

2 jalapeños, seeded and minced

¼ cup dark rum

½ cup soy or tamari sauce

½ cup vegetable oil

Combine all the ingredients in a blender or food processor and purée until very smooth. Refrigerate until needed.

**MAKES ABOUT 2 CUPS**

# Garlic Croutons

*Try making croutons with other breads as well—rye, sourdough, pita, and whole wheat are just a few suggestions.*

1 baguette, diced

3 cloves garlic, minced

½ cup extra-virgin olive oil

Salt and freshly ground black pepper, as needed

1. Preheat the oven to 325°F.

2. Place the bread in a large bowl. In a small bowl, combine the garlic and oil. Pour over the bread and toss to combine. Season with salt and pepper. Transfer to a baking sheet and spread in an even layer. Bake until the croutons are lightly browned and crisp, about 10 minutes.

MAKES ABOUT 3 CUPS

# Roasted Garlic

*This flavorful ingredient can be used in soups, sauces, purées, vinaigrettes, or as a spread on sandwiches.*

1 head garlic, unpeeled

Olive oil, as needed

1. Preheat the oven to 350°F.

2. Slice the top off the garlic head to expose the cloves. Rub the head with oil and place it cut side down in a small baking pan. Roast until soft, 30 to 45 minutes.

3. As needed, remove the outer papery layers, separate into cloves, and squeeze out the roasted garlic.

MAKES 1 HEAD

# EGG WASH

When egg wash is called for, whisk 1 large egg with 2 tablespoons milk or water. Keep this proportion when making more as needed.

# APPENDIX

## WEIGHT CONVERSION TABLES

To calculate weight, use following equations:

1 oz = 28.35 grams

1 pound = 453.59 grams

Round to the nearest gram or to two decimal places for kilograms.

## U.S. TO METRIC WEIGHT MEASURES

| U.S. UNIT | METRIC EQUIVALENT | U.S. UNIT | METRIC EQUIVALENT | U.S. UNIT | METRIC EQUIVALENT |
|---|---|---|---|---|---|
| ¼ oz | 7 g | 11 oz | 312 g | 4 lb | 1.81 kg |
| ½ oz | 14 g | 12 oz (¾ lb) | 340 g | 4¼ lb | 1.93 kg |
| ¾ oz | 21 g | 13 oz | 369 g | 4½ lb | 2.04 kg |
| 1 oz | 28 g | 14 oz | 397 g | 4¾ lb | 2.16 kg |
| 1½ oz | 43 g | 15 oz | 425 g | 5 lb | 2.27 kg |
| 1¾ oz | 50 g | 16 oz (1 lb) | 454 g | 6 lb | 2.72 kg |
| 2 oz | 57 g | 1 lb 4 oz (1¼ lb) | 567 g | 7 lb | 3.18 kg |
| 2½ oz | 71 g | 1 lb 8 oz (1½ lb) | 680 g | 8 lb | 3.63 kg |
| 3 oz | 85 g | 1 lb 12 oz (1¾ lb) | 794 g | 9 lb | 4.08 kg |
| 3½ oz | 99 g | 2 lb | 907 g | 10 lb | 4.54 kg |
| 4 oz (¼ lb) | 113 g | 2¼ lb | 1.02 kg | 11 lb | 4.99 kg |
| 5 oz | 142 g | 2½ lb | 1.13 kg | 12 lb | 5.44 kg |
| 6 oz | 170 g | 2¾ lb | 1.25 kg | 13 lb | 5.90 kg |
| 7 oz | 198 g | 3 lb | 1.36 kg | 14 lb | 6.35 kg |
| 8 oz (½ lb) | 227 g | 3¼ lb | 1.47 kg | 15 lb | 6.80 kg |
| 9 oz | 255 g | 3½ lb | 1.59 kg | 20 lb | 9.07 kg |
| 10 oz | 284 g | 3¾ lb | 1.70 kg | 25 lb | 11.34 kg |

# VOLUME CONVERSION TABLES

1 tbsp = 15 milliliters

1 cup (8 fl oz) = 240 milliliters

## U.S. TO METRIC VOLUME MEASURES

| FLUID OUNCES | TEASPOONS/ TABLESPOONS | CUPS/PINTS | QUARTS/GALLONS | METRIC EQUIVALENT |
|---|---|---|---|---|
| | ¼ tsp | | | 1 mL |
| | ½ tsp | | | 2 mL |
| | ¾ tsp | | | 3 mL |
| | 1 tsp | | | 5 mL |
| ½ fl oz | 1 tbsp | | | 15 mL |
| 1 fl oz | 2 tbsp | | | 30 mL |
| 1½ fl oz | 3 tbsp | | | 45 mL |
| 2 fl oz | 4 tbsp | ¼ cup | | 60 mL |
| 2⅔ fl oz | 5 tbsp plus 1 tsp | ⅓ cup | | 80 mL |
| 3 fl oz | 6 tbsp | | | 90 mL |
| 4 fl oz | 8 tbsp | ½ cup | | 120 mL |
| 5 fl oz | 10 tbsp | ½ cup plus 2 tbsp | | 150 mL |
| 5⅓ fl oz | 10 tbsp plus 2 tsp | ⅔ cup | | 160 mL |
| 6 fl oz | 12 tbsp | ¾ cup | | 180 mL |
| 7 fl oz | 14 tbsp | ¾ cup plus 2 tbsp | | 210 mL |
| 8 fl oz | 16 tbsp | 1 cup ½ pint | ¼ quart | 240 mL |
| 9 fl oz | 18 tbsp | 1 cup plus 2 tbsp | | 270 mL |
| 10 fl oz | 20 tbsp | 1¼ cups | | 300 mL |
| 11 fl oz | 22 tbsp | 1¼ cups plus 2 tbsp | | 330 mL |

# U.S. TO METRIC VOLUME MEASURES, cont.

| FLUID OUNCES | TEASPOONS/ TABLESPOONS | CUPS/PINTS | QUARTS/GALLONS | METRIC EQUIVALENT |
|---|---|---|---|---|
| 12 fl oz | 24 tbsp | 1½ cups ¾ pint | | 360 mL |
| 13 fl oz | 26 tbsp | 1½ cups plus 2 tbsp | | 390 mL |
| 14 fl oz | 28 tbsp | 1¾ cups | | 420 mL |
| 15 fl oz | 30 tbsp | 1¾ cups plus 2 tbsp | | 450 mL |
| 16 fl oz | 32 tbsp | 2 cups 1 pint | ½ quart | 480 mL |
| 20 fl oz | | 2½ cups | | 600 mL |
| 22 fl oz | | 2¾ cups | | 660 mL |
| 24 fl oz | | 3 cups 1½ pints | ¾ quart | 720 mL |
| 28 fl oz | | 3½ cups | | 840 mL |
| 32 fl oz | | 4 cups 2 pints | 1 quart ¼ gallon | 960 mL* |
| 40 fl oz | | 5 cups | 1¼ quarts | 1.20 L |
| 48 fl oz | | 6 cups 3 pints | 1½ quarts | 1.44 L |
| 64 fl oz | | 8 cups 4 pints | 2 quarts ½ gallon | 1.92 L** |
| 96 fl oz | | 12 cups 6 pints | 3 quarts ¾ gallon | 2.88 L |
| 128 fl oz | | 16 cups 8 pints | 4 quarts 1 gallon | 3.84 L |
| 160 fl oz | | | 5 quarts 1¼ gallons | 4.80 L |
| 192 fl oz | | | 6 quarts 1½ gallons | 5.76 L |
| 224 fl oz | | | 7 quarts 1¾ gallons | 6.72 L |
| 256 fl oz | | | 8 quarts 2 gallons | 7.68 L |
| 288 fl oz | | | 9 quarts 2¼ gallons | 8.64 L |
| 320 fl oz | | | 10 quarts 2½ gallons | 9.60 L |

| FLUID OUNCES | TEASPOONS/ TABLESPOONS | CUPS/PINTS | QUARTS/GALLONS | METRIC EQUIVALENT |
|---|---|---|---|---|
| | | | 11 quarts 2¾ gallons | 10.56 L |
| | | | 12 quarts 3 gallons | 11.52 L |
| | | | 4 gallons | 15.36 L |
| | | | 5 gallons | 19.20 L |
| | | | 6 gallons | 23.04 L |

*32 fl oz/1 quart may be rounded to 1 L
**64 fl oz/2 quarts may be rounded to 2 L

# TEMPERATURE CONVERSION TABLES

To convert from Fahrenheit to Celsius:

$$(°F - 32) \times \tfrac{5}{9} = °C$$

## FAHRENHEIT TO CELSIUS, WITH MAJOR POINTS

| °F | °C | TEMPERATURE POINT | °F | °C | TEMPERATURE POINT | °F | °C | TEMPERATURE POINT |
|---|---|---|---|---|---|---|---|---|
| 32 | 0 | Freezing | 230 | 110 | Thread | 325 | 165 | |
| 40 | 4 | | 234 | 112 | Soft ball | 330 | 166 | |
| 45 | 7 | | 238 | 114 | | 335 | 168 | |
| 100 | 38 | | 240 | 115 | | 340 | 171 | |
| 105 | 41 | | 244 | 118 | Firm ball | 350 | 175 | Dark caramel |
| 110 | 43 | | 248 | 120 | | 375 | 190 | |
| 115 | 46 | | 250 | 121 | Hard ball | 400 | 205 | |
| 125 | 52 | | 260 | 125 | | 425 | 220 | |
| 150 | 65 | | 270 | 132 | Soft crack | 450 | 230 | |
| 175 | 80 | | 275 | 135 | | 475 | 245 | |
| 200 | 95 | | 290 | 143 | | 500 | 260 | |
| 212 | 100 | Boiling | 300 | 150 | Hard crack | 575 | 275 | |
| 220 | 105 | | 310 | 155 | | 600 | 315 | |
| 225 | 107 | | 320 | 160 | Light caramel | | | |

# GLOSSARY

**AMARANTH** A grain, very similar to quinoa, which is a complete protein.

**BATON/BATONNET** Items cut into pieces ¼ inch by ¼ inch by 1 to 2 inches. French for "stick" or "small stick."

**BLANCH** To cook an item briefly in boiling water or hot fat before finishing or storing it. Blanching preserves the color, lessens strong flavors, and helps remove the peels of some fruits and vegetables.

**CAPONATA** A baked Sicilian dish typically made of cooked vegetables; a cooked vegetable salad.

**CARAMELIZE** To cook a vegetable, such as an onion, over low to medium heat, until it becomes brown in color but not burnt. This yields a very sweet flavor, as well as rich color.

**CHIFFONADE** Leafy vegetables or herbs cut into fine shreds; often used as a garnish.

**CONVECTION OVEN** An oven that circulates hot air around the food by the use of fans, thus cooking the food quickly and evenly.

**COUSCOUS** Pellets of semolina or cracked wheat usually cooked by steaming, traditionally in a couscoussière. Also, the stew in which this grain is traditionally served.

**CREAMING** To blend fats and sugar together to incorporate air.

**CRÊPE** A thin pancake made with egg batter, used in sweet and savory preparations.

**CURRY** A mixture of spices, used primarily in Indian cuisine. May include turmeric, coriander, cumin, cayenne or other chiles, cardamom, cinnamon, clove, fennel, fenugreek, ginger, and garlic. Also, a stew-like dish seasoned with curry.

**DEGLAZE** To use a liquid, such as wine, water, juice, or stock, to dissolve food particles and/or caramelized drippings left in a pan after roasting or sautéing. The resulting mix then becomes the base for the accompanying sauce.

**DOCK** To cut or puncture dough before cooking to allow steam to escape and control the expansion of the dough and/or to create a decorative effect.

**EGG WASH** A mixture of beaten eggs (whole eggs, yolks, or whites) and a liquid, usually milk or water, used to coat baked goods to give them a sheen.

**EMPANADA** A stuffed bread or pastry of Spanish, Latin American, or Portuguese origin, usually stuffed with a savory filling.

**FINANCIERS** A small, sponge-like cookie with a very delicate almond flavor and texture.

**FINE DICE** Items cut into pieces 1/16 inch by 1/16 inch by 1/16 inch.

**FOOD MILL** A strainer with a crank-operated curved blade. It is used to purée soft foods while straining out seeds, skins, etc.

**GRATIN** A cheese or crumble topping that has been browned in the oven or under a broiler.

**GRITS** A corn-based food common in the southern United States, consisting of coarsely ground whole corn kernels.

**HOMINY** Corn that has been milled or treated with a lye solution to remove the bran and germ. Ground hominy is known as grits.

**JULIENNE** Items cut into thin strips ⅛ inch by ⅛ inch by 1 to 2 inches.

**KASHA** Buckwheat groats that have been hulled and crushed and roasted; usually prepared by boiling.

**LARGE DICE** Items cut into pieces ¾ inch by ¾ inch by ¾ inch.

**MASA HARINA** A specialty corn meal used in Latin American cuisine for making corn tortillas, sopes, gorditas, etc.

**MEDIUM DICE** Items cut into pieces ½ inch by ½ inch by ½ inch.

**MEMBRANE** Also referred to as "ribs" in peppers; usually the lighter or white structure that the seeds are attached to; contains a lot of the heat in chiles.

**MILLET** A small, round, glutenless grain that may be boiled or ground into flour.

**MINCE** To chop into very small pieces.

**NAPPÉ** To coat with sauce. Also the consistency of a sauce that will coat the back of a spoon.

**PICO DE GALLO** An uncooked fresh salsa, usually consisting of tomatoes, onions, cilantro, garlic, and lime juice.

**PLUCHES** Whole herb leaves connected to a small bit of stem; often used as a garnish. Also called sprigs.

**POLENTA** Cornmeal mush cooked in simmering liquid until the grains soften and the liquid absorbs. Polenta can be eaten hot or cold, firm or soft.

**PURÉE** To process food by mashing, straining, or chopping it very fine in order to make it a smooth paste. Also, the product produced using this technique.

**REDUCE** To decrease the volume of a liquid by simmering or boiling; used to provide a thicker consistency and/or concentrated flavors.

**RISOTTO** Rice that is sautéed briefly in butter with onions and possibly other aromatics, then combined with stock added in several additions and stirred constantly, producing a creamy texture with grains that are still al dente. Also, the type of rice cooked using this technique.

**ROAST** A dry-heat cooking method in which the item is cooked in an oven or on a spit over a fire.

**RONDEAU** A shallow, wide, straight-sided pot with two loop handles, often used for braising, similar to a Dutch oven.

**SACHET D'ÉPICES** Literally, "bag of spices." Aromatic ingredients, encased in cheesecloth, which are used to flavor stocks and other liquids; a standard sachet contains parsley stems, cracked peppercorns, dried thyme, and a bay leaf.

**SAUTÉ** To cook quickly in a small amount of fat in a pan on the range top.

**SAUTÉ PAN** A shallow skillet with sloping sides and a single long handle; used for sautéing.

**SEITAN** Wheat gluten made by washing wheat flour in order to dissolve away all of the starch, leaving just the insoluble gluten, which is high in protein and iron. This definition is for vital wheat gluten. Seitan is actually a preparation made with vital wheat gluten.

**SIMMER** To maintain a temperature of a liquid just below boiling. Also, to cook in simmering liquid. The temperature range for simmering is 185°F to 200°F.

**SMALL DICE** Items cut into pieces ¼ inch by ¼ inch by ¼ inch.

**STEW** A cooking method nearly identical to braising, but generally involving smaller items and hence a shorter cooking time. Also a dish prepared by using the stewing method.

**SUPRÊME** The section of a citrus fruit, sliced so as to separate the flesh from the membrane of the fruit. Cut over a bowl to catch the juices and squeeze any remaining juice from the membranes.

**SWEAT** To cook an item, usually a vegetable, in a covered pan in a small amount of fat until it softens and releases moisture but does not brown.

**TAHINI** A paste made of sesame seeds (usually toasted).

**TAPENADE** A mixture of olives, capers, garlic, herbs, and olive oil that has been finely chopped in a food processor; often spread on toast or crackers.

**TEMPEH** A soy product made from whole soybeans that have been slightly fermented, giving it a completely different flavor and texture from tofu, as well as different nutritional characteristics.

**VITAL WHEAT GLUTEN** A food made from the gluten of wheat. It is made by washing wheat flour dough with water until all the starch dissolves, leaving insoluble gluten as an elastic mass, which is then cooked before being eaten.

**WHIP** To beat an item, such as egg whites or cream, with a whisk to incorporate air.

**ZEST** The thin, brightly colored outer part of citrus rind. It contains volatile oils, making it ideal for use as a flavoring.

# INDEX

Page numbers in *italics* indicate photographs or illustrations.